Lecture Notes in Computer Science 3323

Commenced Publication in 1973
Founding and Former Series Editors:
Gerhard Goos, Juris Hartmanis, and Jan van Leeuwen

Editorial Board

Grigoris Antoniou   Harold Boley (Eds.)

Rules and Rule Markup Languages for the Semantic Web

Third International Workshop, RuleML 2004
Hiroshima, Japan, November 8, 2004
Proceedings

Volume Editors

Grigoris Antoniou
University of Crete
Dept. of Computer Science, ICS-FORTH
P.O. Box 1385, 71110 Heraklion, Crete, Greece
E-mail: antoniou@ics.forth.gr

Harold Boley
e-Business National Research Council of Canada
Institute for Information Technology
Semantic Web Laboratory
46 Dineen Drive, Fredericton, NB, E3B 9W4, Canada
E-mail: harold.boley@nrc.gc.ca

Library of Congress Control Number: 2004114603

CR Subject Classification (1998): H.4, H.3, I.2, C.2, H.5, K.4, F.3

ISSN 0302-9743
ISBN 3-540-23842-5 Springer Berlin Heidelberg New York

Springer is a part of Springer Science+Business Media

springeronline.com

© Springer-Verlag Berlin Heidelberg 2004
Printed in Germany

Typesetting: Camera-ready by author, data conversion by PTP-Berlin, Protago-TeX-Production GmbH
Printed on acid-free paper   SPIN: 11349754   06/3142   5 4 3 2 1 0

Preface

The Semantic Web is a worldwide endeavor to advance the Web by enriching its content with semantic metainformation that can be processed by inference-enabled Web applications. Taxonomies and rules, along with their automated reasoning techniques, are the main components of Semantic Web ontologies.

Rule systems are considered to be a major area in the further development of the Semantic Web. On one hand, rules can specify declarative knowledge in ontology languages, expressing constraints or transformations, either in conjunction with, or as an alternative to, description logics. On the other hand, rules can specify behavioral knowledge, enforcing policies or reacting to events/changes.

Finally, rule markup languages such as RuleML allow us to publish rules on the Web, to process rules in general XML environments as well as special rule engines, to exchange rules between different applications and tools via XSLT translators, as well as to embed rules into other XML content and vice versa.

This workshop was dedicated to all aspects of rules and rule markup languages for the Semantic Web. RuleML 2004 was the third in a series of workshops that was initiated with the International Semantic Web Conference. The previous workshops were held on Sardinia, Italy (2002), and on Sanibel Island, USA (2003).

This year we had 25 submissions, of which 11 were accepted as regular papers and another five as short papers describing tools.

We are grateful to our two invited speakers, Mike Dean from BBN and Christine Golbreich from the University of Rennes. Our thanks also go to all submitters and reviewers without whom the workshop and these proceedings could not have succeeded.

September 2004

Grigoris Antoniou and Harold Boley
RuleML 2004 Program Chairs

Organization

Workshop Chairs

Grigoris Antoniou, Institute of Computer Science, FORTH, Greece
Harold Boley, NRC and University of New Brunswick, Canada

Steering Committee

Grigoris Antoniou, Institute of Computer Science, FORTH, Greece
Harold Boley, NRC and University of New Brunswick, Canada
Mike Dean, BBN Technologies/Verizon, USA
Andreas Eberhart, International University, Germany
Benjamin Grosof, MIT, USA
Steve Ross-Talbot, Enigmatec, UK
Michael Schroeder, TU Dresden, Germany
Bruce E. Spencer, NRC and University of New Brunswick, Canada
Said Tabet, Consultant, USA
Gerd Wagner, Technical University of Eindhoven, Netherlands

Program Committee

Grigoris Antoniou, Institute of Computer Science, FORTH, Greece
Nick Bassiliades, Aristotle University of Thessaloniki, Greece
Harold Boley, NRC and University of New Brunswick, Canada
Scott Buffett, NRC and University of New Brunswick, Canada
Carlos Damasio, New University of Lisbon, Portugal
Mike Dean, BBN Technologies/Verizon, USA
Andreas Eberhart, International University, Germany
Guido Governatori, University of Queensland, Australia
Ian Horrocks, University of Manchester, UK
Sandy Liu, NRC and University of New Brunswick, Canada
Jan Maluszynski, Linkoping University, Sweden
Massimo Marchiori, W3C, MIT, USA and University of Venice, Italy
Donald Nute, University of Georgia, USA
Michael Schroeder, TU Dresden, Germany
Michael Sintek, DFKI, Germany
Bruce Spencer, NRC and University of New Brunswick, Canada
Said Tabet, Consultant, USA
Dmitry Tsarkov, University of Manchester, UK
Gerd Wagner, Technical University of Eindhoven, Netherlands
Kewen Wang, Griffith University, Australia
Yuhong Yan, NRC and University of New Brunswick, Canada

Table of Contents

Semantic Web Rules: Covering the Use Cases

Mike Dean

BBN Technologies, Ann Arbor, Michigan, USA
mdean@bbn.com

Abstract. Rules represent the next step for the Semantic Web. A number of use cases for Semantic Web Rules have been formally and informally proposed, including ontology extension, ontology translation, data expansion, portable axiomatic semantics, matching, monitoring, and profile and process descriptions for Semantic Web Services. This talk will describe each of these use cases, provide examples, and assess the degree to which each is addressed by the Semantic Web Rule Language (SWRL) and other current alternatives.

1 Introduction

Following the development of the OWL Web Ontology Language [15], rules represent the next step for the Semantic Web. The Semantic Web Rule Language (SWRL) [11] has recently been acknowledged as a Member Submission by the World Wide Web Consortium (W3C), allowing it to be used as an input to a future Semantic Web Rules Working Group. Several groups [3] [18] are working on representations of first-order logic (FOL) for the Semantic Web. The FORUM Working Group [13] seeks to unify Web rule languages based on F-logic. Several existing Semantic Web tools such as cwm [1] and Jena 2 [12] include their own rule languages.

A number of use cases have been formally [7] and informally proposed for a Semantic Web rule language. The following sections describe each of these use cases, provide examples, and assess the degree to which each is addressed by SWRL and other current alternatives.

2 Ontology Extension

Because of its focus on decidability, there are a number of things that cannot be represented in OWL (Lite, DL, or Full). Many of these involve property chaining, e.g. the ability to express the uncle property as the composition of parent and brother. Another example is the inability to define an InternationalFlight as a Flight involving airports in different countries. These can easily be expressed in SWRL, which sacrifices decidability for expressiveness.

OWL is also limited in its ability to define classes based on datatype values. SWRL with builtins allows us to easily define a class Adult as a Person with age >=

G. Antoniou and H. Boley (Eds.): RuleML 2004, LNCS 3323, pp. 1–5, 2004.
© Springer-Verlag Berlin Heidelberg 2004

18, and even to compute age based on a Person's birthDate and some representation of the current date.

3   Ontology Translation

We expect that many different ontologies will be used on the Semantic Web. For example, an automotive ontology used by Ford may represent wheelbase in inches, while a similar ontology used by BMW might use centimeters. Structural differences may also occur. An application that needs to make use of data using multiple ontologies will need to translate some or all of the data into another ontology.

OWL provides some basic mapping primitives, including owl:sameClassAs and owl:samePropertyAs, and owl:sameAs. rdfs:subClassOf and rdfs:subPropertyOf can also be used to express relationships between classes in different ontologies. For more complex mappings, rules can provide a portable representation of mappings whether automatically or manually generated.

[6] relates some experience in using SWRL to translate between different ontologies.

The builtins for arithmetic conversions and other calculations added in SWRL 0.6 are a major step forward in supporting ontology translation, accommodating such functions as unit of measure conversion.

[6] also discusses a current limitation of SWRL is dealing with existentials. Data sets sometimes refer implicitly to individuals that are not explicitly named (e.g. the Company corresponding to a given Stock). In translating to another ontology that makes both individuals explicit, it is helpful to be able to refer to that implicit individual through the use of an existential, a free variable, or other means. In more generative applications (e.g. when creating a visualization for a given data set), one may prefer to think of this as creating a new instance. The Jena 2 rule language includes a makeInstance builtin, and cwm allows the use of bNode existentials in rule heads.

One ontology may represent an aggregation of another (e.g. reporting annual sales vs. quarterly sales). Straightforward aggregation (such as applying XQuery [2] sequence expressions over a collection of statements) is limited by the open world assumption of the Semantic Web, although one can explicitly enumerate the component values to be summed. A related example is defining a class of Pilots with more than a specified number of total flight hours. This doesn't require a closed world, but rather identifying a sufficient number of unique flights and summing their durations. It's currently beyond the capabilities of SWRL and most alternatives.

4   Data Expansion

Rules can be used to expand a compact data representation convenient for generation into an alternative representation more suitable for computation. An example is Subway Maps in OWL [5], which represents each subway Line using an ordered list of Stations. Rules are used to expand this compact representation into a representation where each Station is directly associated with one or more Lines and adjacent Stations.

Rules can similarly be used to specify conditions holding across entire data sets, e.g. dinner is served on all flights of a given airline that are over 2 hours long and depart between 1700 and 1900. The only major limitation here is the inability (due to concerns about non-monotonicity) to treat this as a default that can be over-ridden where necessary by specific instances.

5 Portable Axiomatic Semantics

The axiomatic semantics developed for DAML+OIL [9] provided a valuable resource for tool developers. Without an axiomatic semantics for OWL, developers of tools such as Jena 2 [12] and OWLJessKB [14] have had to develop their own sets of axioms based on the OWL Semantics and Abstract Syntax [16]. A Semantic Web rule language could potentially be used to express an axiomatic semantics for OWL in a machine processible form.

SWRL is limited for this purpose in that it does not allow variables in the predicate position. This would preclude, for example, an axiomatic definition of owl:TransitiveProperty.

On-going proposals for a FOL language would allow the definition of such axiomatic semantics.

6 Matching

Rules can be very effective in identifying matches between different data sets, such as reconciling credit card transactions, expense reports, and reimbursements in [4]. A key requirement here is being able to easily express that an individual has not already been matched, which touches on negation and open world assumptions. SWRL is limited in this regard.

Equivalence in the absence of a unique names assumption is a key issue for Semantic Web rules particularly relevant for matching. Two individuals may in fact be the same (e.g. duplicate credit card transactions). SWRL provides explicit atoms for sameAs and differentFrom, but one would like for this to be handled more automatically.

Matching also motivates the need for user-defined builtin functions. [6] cites the use of a great circle distance calculation as well as functions for parsing textual representations of latitude and longitude.

7 Monitoring

Rules can be very effectively used to watch for conditions in stream of data, alerting a user or triggering some automated response when specified conditions are met.

SWRL currently includes only non-side effecting builtins, which limits the range of response within the standard language. Actions might be performed using user-defined builtins or other mechanisms such as those under development by the reaction rules technical group within the RuleML Initiative [17].

8 Profile and Process Descriptions for Semantic Web Services

Perhaps the most demanding use case for Semantic Web rules has been in the area of Semantic Web Services. This is currently a very active topic of discussion in the Language Committee of the Semantic Web Services Initiative [19].

Simple uses of rules such as ensuring that the credit cards accepted by a service include one held by the client can be handled by SWRL. More complex examples involving non-monotonic defaults and negotiation go beyond SWRL.

Description of service process models to allow automated service composition has been a major motivation for the recent development of FOL RuleML [3].

9 Conclusions

The need for rules in the Semantic Web is well motivated. SWRL represents a significant first step, layered on top of the existing W3C Semantic Web Recommendations, but is currently insufficient to address the full range of use cases. Some have opposed SWRL because its computational complexity is not provably less than first order [8], but a growing number of implementers [6] [10] [20] have found it useful.

Ultimately, we may see several Semantic Web rule languages with different computational and usage characteristics in widespread use. Such proliferation comes at a cost in terms of interoperability and redundancy, and should be justified by real needs.

References

1. Berners-Lee, T., et al. cwm – a general purpose data processor for the semantic web. http://www.w3.org/2000/10/swap/doc/cwm
2. Boag, S., Chamberlin, D., Fernandez, M.F., Florescu, D., Robie, J., Simeon, J. XQuery 1.0: An XML Query Language. W3C Working Draft 23 July 2004. http://www.w3.org/TR/xquery/
3. Boley, H., Dean, M., Grosof, B., Sintek, M., Spencer, B., Tabet, S., Wagner, G. First-Order-Logic RuleML. http://www.ruleml.org/fol/
4. Dean, M. DAML Expense Reconciliation. http://www.daml.org/2001/06/expenses/
5. Dean, M. Subway Maps in OWL. http://www.daml.org/2003/05/subway/
6. Dean, M. Use of SWRL for Ontology Translation. WWW2004 Developer Day Rules on the Web Track. http://www.daml.org/2004/05/swrl-translation/Overview.html

7. Decker, S., Dean, M., McGuinness, D. Requirements and Use Cases for a Semantic Web Rule Language. http://www.isi.edu/~stefan/20030224/rulesusecases.html
8. Fensel, D. A rule language for the semantic web. SDK cluster meeting, Lausanne, 14 June 2004. http://www.wsmo.org/papers/presentations/SDK-cluster/lausanne/
9. Fikes, R., McGuinness, D.L. An Axiomatic Semantics for DAML+OIL. Stanford KSL Technical Report KSL-01-01. http://www.ksl.stanford.edu/people/dlm/daml-semantics/abstract-axiomatic-semantics.html
10. Golbreich, C. Reasoning with Ontologies and Rules Based on the Current Semantic Web Standards and Tools. Proc. Rules and Rule Markup Languages for the Semantic Web, Hiroshima, November 2004. http://2004.ruleml.org/
11. Horrocks, I., Patel-Schneider, P.F., Boley, H., Tabet, S., Grosof, B., Dean, M. SWRL: A Semantic Web Rule Language Combining OWL and RuleML. W3C Member Submission 21 May 2004. http://www.w3.org/Submission/2004/SUBM-SWRL-20040521/
12. Jena 2. http://www.hpl.hp.com/semweb/jena2.htm
13. Kifer, M., et al. FORUM Working Group and forum-flogic email archive. http://projects.semwebcentral.org/projects/forum/
14. Kopena, J. OWLJessKB: A Semantic Web Reasoning Tool. http://edge.cs.drexel.edu/assemblies/software/owljesskb/
15. McGuinness, D.L., van Harmelen, F. OWL Web Ontology Language Overview. W3C Recommendation 10 February 2004. http://www.w3.org/TR/2004/REC-owl-features-20040210/
16. Patel-Schneider, P.F., Hayes, P., Horrocks, I. OWL Web Ontology Language Semantics and Abstract Syntax. W3C Recommendation 10 February 2004. http://www.w3.org/TR/2004/REC-owl-semantics-20040210/
17. RuleML Initiative. http://www.ruleml.org/
18. SCL. http://cl.tamu.edu
19. Semantic Web Services Initiative. http://www.swsi.org/
20. Solanki, M., Cau, A., Zedan, H. Augmenting Semantic Web Service Description with Compositional Specification. Proc. Thirteenth International World Wide Web Conference, New York, May 2004.

Combining Rule and Ontology Reasoners
for the Semantic Web

Christine Golbreich

Laboratoire d'Informatique Médicale, Université Rennes 1
Av du Pr. Léon Bernard, 35043 Rennes, France
Christine.Golbreich@univ-rennes1.fr

Abstract. Using rules in conjunction with ontologies is a major challenge for the Semantic Web. We propose a pragmatic approach for reasoning with ontologies and rules, based on the Semantic Web standards and tools currently available. We first achieved an implementation of SWRL, the emerging OWL/RuleML-combining rule standard, using the Protégé OWL plugin. We then developed a Protégé plugin, SWRLJessTab, which enables to compute inferences with the Racer classifier and the Jess inference engine, in order to reason with rules and ontologies, both represented in OWL. A small example, including an OWL ontology and a SWRL rule base, shows that *all* the domain knowledge, i.e. the SWRL rule base *and* the OWL ontology, is required to obtain complete inferences. It illustrates that some reasoning support must be provided to interoperate between SWRL and OWL, not only syntactically and semantically, but also *inferentially*.

1   Introduction

The present challenge for the Web is to evolve towards a Semantic Web (SW) that can provide readable information for both human and machines, and an easier access to heterogeneous data distributed in multiple sites. Ontologies can be considered as playing a key part in the Semantic Web since they provide the vocabulary needed for semantic mark-up. But rules are also required for the Web, and most people now agree that a Web rule language is needed. According to the Semantic Web stack, rules are on the top of ontologies. But in many cases, ontologies alone (resp. rules) are not enough. Using rules *in conjunction* with ontologies is a major challenge for the Semantic Web.

A main motivation of this work is issued from our experience with ontologies in the biomedical domain. Indeed, it turned out that a Web rule language might be very helpful for biomedical ontologies in various situations [9]. For example (1) "standard-rules" are needed for chaining ontologies properties, such as the transfer of properties from parts to wholes, or the dependencies in the brain-cortex [2, 9], (2) "bridging-rules" for reasoning across several domains such as Genomics, Proteonomics, Pathology, when searching for correlations between diseases and the abnormality of a function of a protein coded by a human gene (3) "mapping rules" for mapping Web ontologies in data integration, e.g. for accessing patient data scattered in many

G. Antoniou and H. Boley (Eds.): RuleML 2004, LNCS 3323, pp. 6–22, 2004.
© Springer-Verlag Berlin Heidelberg 2004

Hospital Information Systems [12, 11], (4) "querying-rules" for expressing complex queries upon the Web in an ontology vocabulary [11], (5) "meta-rules" for facilitating ontology engineering (acquisition, validation, maintenance) [9, 4] etc.

There are presently two important trends of Semantic Web languages, corresponding respectively to description logic and rule paradigms: the Ontology Web languages OWL and the Rule Markup Language RuleML.

OWL, the Web Ontology Language [1], is the current W3C recommended standard for ontologies. OWL borrows its formal semantics from description logics (DL), a family of knowledge representation formalisms issued from frames and semantic networks. DL use an object oriented modeling paradigm, describing a domain in terms of individuals, concepts, roles. OWL is well suited for the "terminological" part of knowledge, and for representing "structured" knowledge by classes and properties, organized in taxonomies.

RuleML, the Rule Markup Language, is developed by the "Rule Markup Initiative", an international initiative for standardizing inference rules, forward and backward, on the basis of XML, so as to fulfill the various encountered needs of rules: diagnosis rules for engineering, business rules, marked up for e-Commerce, rules for intelligent agents, Web services, etc.

Description Logics and rules, thus OWL and RuleML, are *both* required for the Semantic Web [9]. Indeed, although some knowledge may be represented by either paradigm, and even though DL extensions are possible to overcome some expressiveness limitations, e.g. "role inclusion axioms" for expressing the transfer of properties along another property [17], it should be noted that (1) DL and rules expressiveness are generally different, (2) each paradigm better fits some particular type of knowledge and supports specific reasoning services. On one side, DL are really suited to the "terminological" part of a domain. Most of them, e.g. OWL DL, provide efficient means to reason on it, such as ontology checking, classification, and class recognition of instances. Such services are particularly essential in the biomedical domain where the ontologies are often *huge* (e.g. The Digital Anatomist Foundational Model contains approximately 70,000 concepts and over 110,000 terms; over 1.5 million relations from 168 relationships). But on the other side, rules are useful to represent the "deductive" part of the knowledge. For example, they allow to express the transfer of biomedical properties from parts to wholes, in a more natural way than in introducing inclusions axiom [17] or a specific "AnatomicalLocation" class dedicated to represent spatial anatomical locations in a *subsumption* hierarchy so as to get the desired inferences [11]. Besides, although OWL DL may be well suited to represent and reason with ontologies, and RuleML Datalog to express rules, some applications furthermore need a close integration of the two languages. Several medical examples [9] illustrate that an OWL sublanguage extended by a Web rule language is required.

The recent draft proposal [15] for a Semantic Web Rule Language SWRL[1] combining OWL DL and OWL Lite [1] with the Unary/Binary Datalog RuleML [2] sublanguages, is a first important step in that direction. At the moment, this proposal provides a syntactical and semantical specification of SWRL that extends OWL.

---

[1] http://www.daml.org/rules/proposal/

Obviously it is not enough; a step further is needed for interoperating between SWRL and OWL, not only syntactically and semantically, but also *inferentially*. In other words, a language for SWRL rules that can make use of the vocabulary of an OWL ontology, is not sufficient. A crucial point is to provide some support to reason in a consistent way with them, that is, a tool that exploits all the knowledge, both of the ontology and of the rule base, to get inferences. But the current draft proposal of the SWRL rule language extending OWL DL axioms so as to include Horn-like rules is not yet completely finished, and at that time no effective implemented reasoner enabling to interoperate between SWRL rules and OWL ontologies, is available. The difficulty is that OWL DL becomes undecidable when extended in this way, as rules can be used to simulate role value maps [18]. Thus, providing reasoning support for a SW rule language still raises theoretical and practical questions. For example, in the DLP approach, a combined logical formalism has been proposed [13], and a prototypical implementation of Description Horn Logic achieved based on a Datalog engine. But as noticed in [16] "DLP is less expressive than either the description logic or the rule language from which it is formed". How reasoning support might be provided for an OWL rules language is still an open issue, and several strategies are possible for it [16]. Some current initiatives, such as HOOLET[2], KAON EXT[3], ROWL[4] are discussed section 6.

The theoretical issue is outside the scope of this paper. Motivated by concrete needs for biomedical ontologies, we investigated a pragmatic approach for reasoning both with ontologies and rules, based on the current or emerging Semantic Web standards OWL, RuleML, and SWRL, and on the tools currently available, Protégé-OWL for editing, RACER and Jess engines for reasoning. Since at that time, the swrl.owl ontology given in the proposal could neither be loaded in Protégé with the OWL plugin[5], nor a fortiori inferentially processed, we first achieved a draft implementation of SWRL in Protégé-OWL. We then developed a prototypical plugin, SWRLJessTab, to bridge between Protégé OWL, RACER [14], and Jess [6] so as to allow reasoning with SWRL rules combined with OWL ontologies. A small example including an OWL ontology representing the usual family relationships, and a SWRL rule base representing their dependencies, has been prepared to illustrate that some reasoning support shall obviously be provided to interoperate between SWRL and OWL, not only syntactically and semantically, but also *inferentially*.

Section 2 briefly introduces the current SW standards, and section 3 the tools we use. Section 4 is devoted to our approach for reasoning with OWL ontologies combined with SWRL rules, based on the available tools. It describes the proposed implementation of SWRL in Protégé OWL and SWRLJessTab, a plugin achieved to bridge between Protégé OWL, RACER, and Jess. Section 5 presents the results of the inferences derived respectively (i) by RACER from the OWL ontology, (ii) next by Jess from the SWRL rules, and (iii) in combining both. Finally, we situate the work among other initiatives and discuss its limitations and perspectives in section 6.

---

[2] http://owl.man.ac.uk/hoolet/
[3] http://kaon.semanticweb.org/owl/.
[4] http://mycampus.sadehlab.cs.cmu.edu/public_pages/ROWL/ROWL.html
[5] http://protege.stanford.edu/plugins/owl/

2   SW Current or Emerging Standards

The Web Ontology Language OWL, is the current W3C recommended standard for ontologies. For rules, several languages and standards are proposed, among which SWRL, the RuleML-oriented extension of OWL.

2.1   OWL and RuleML

OWL[6], is a semantic markup language for publishing and sharing ontologies on the World Wide Web. OWL has been developed as a vocabulary extension of RDF (the Resource Description Framework) and is derived from the DAML+OIL Web Ontology Language. The OWL language provides three increasingly expressive sublanguages. OWL Lite is less expressive, OWL DL provides completeness and decidability[7], while OWL Full offers the maximal expressiveness and syntax freedom of RDF, but no computational guarantees. OWL DL semantics enables automatic deduction processes, in particular powerful automatic reasoning, such as ontology checking, classification, and instances retrieval, which are based on basic reasoning tasks including satisfiability, subsumption, instantiation. Powerful reasoning systems were developed for ontologies constrained by the restrictions required for OWL DL, such as RACER (§3).

For rules, several languages and standards have been proposed, corresponding to different needs and efforts. Some of the most popular are the RuleML Rule Markup Language[8] the Java Expert System Shell Jess [6] (§3), and now the emerging standard SWRL [15] (§2.2). The RuleML Initiative[8], initially created as a standards effort for delivering markup language for rules in XML, is more generally concerned with all issues for Rules and Rule Markup Languages for the Semantic Web. Started in 2000, a first public version of XML DTD's was released for several rule flavors in January 2001. Current work on the design of RuleML includes First-Order-Logic (FOL[9]) RuleML, Semantic Web Rule Language (SWRL[1]) RuleML, and OO RuleML[10]. There are now many participating institutions in the RuleML Initiative that are listed on the Website, and over a dozen prototype RuleML tools. Some of the most recent developments about languages, tools and applications for rules on the Web were presented at the Rules on the Web track[11] of the 2004 World Wide Web Conference, such as cwmr rules, a new N3 rules subset, Sweetrules[12], OO jDREW[13], the newest implementation of F-Logic/Flora 3 etc.

---

[6] http://www.w3.org/TR/owl-ref
[7] the OWL DL restrictions are the maximal subset of OWL Full against which current research can assure that a decidable reasoning procedure can exist for an OWL reasoner
[8] http://www.ruleml.org/
[9] http://www.ruleml.org/fol/
[10] http://www.ruleml.org/indoo/indoo.html
[11] cf. www2004-devday-report.pdf
[12] http://ebusiness.mit.edu/bgrosof/paps/home.html#SweetRules
[13] http://www.jdrew.org/jDREWebsite/jDREW.html

2.2 SWRL

The emerging standard for rules, SWRL[14] (Semantic Web Rule Language) based on a combination of OWL DL and OWL Lite sublanguages of OWL with the Unary/Binary Datalog RuleML sublanguages of the Rule Markup Language, has recently been proposed [15]. SWRL extends OWL axioms to include Horn-like rules.

2.2.1 Abstract Syntax

SWRL includes a high-level abstract syntax[15] for Horn-like rules, extending the abstract syntax of OWL and the already existing axioms e.g., subClassOf equivalentClass, disjointWith axioms, by rule axioms. This abstract syntax is specified by means of an extended BNF and is consistent with the OWL specification. A rule axiom consists of an antecedent (body) and a consequent (head), each of which consists of a possibly empty set of atoms:

```
rule ::= 'Implies(' [ URIreference ] { annotation } antecedent consequent ')'
         antecedent ::= 'Antecedent(' { atom } ')'
         consequent ::= 'Consequent(' { atom } ')'
```

Atoms are of the form C(x), P(x,y), sameAs(x,y) or differentFrom(x,y)[16], where C is an OWL description, P is an OWL property, and x, y are either variables, OWL individuals or OWL data values:

```
atom ::= description '(' i-object ')'
         | individualvaluedPropertyID '(' i-object i-object ')'
         | datavaluedPropertyID '(' i-object d-object ')'
         | sameAs '(' i-object i-object ')'
         | differentFrom '(' i-object i-object ')'
```

In the following, we use the "human more readable" syntax suggested in the proposal: antecedent $\Rightarrow$ consequent where antecedent and consequent are conjunctions of atoms written a1 $\wedge$ ... $\wedge$ an, variables are indicated by a question mark (e.g. ?x). For instance, a rule asserting that chaining the hasParent and hasSister properties implies the hasAunt property is written hasParent(?x, ?y) $\wedge$ hasSister(?y, ?z) $\Rightarrow$ hasAunt(?x, ?z). An XML syntax based on RuleML and an RDF concrete syntax based on the OWL RDF/XML exchange syntax are also given.

2.2.2 Model-Theoretic Semantics

The informal meaning of rules is the usual one "if [body] then [head]", i.e. if the antecedent holds, then the consequent must hold. An empty antecedent is considered as true, an empty consequent as false. A fact is a rule with an empty body. A non empty set of atoms composing antecedents and consequents is considered as a conjunction of its atoms. There is no restriction imposing that a consequent is atomic.

---

[14] http://www.daml.org/rules/proposal/

[15] http://www.daml.org/rules/proposal/abstract.html

[16] Version 0.5 of 19 November 2003, the last version now also includes built-in relations

The formal meaning of rules written in the above abstract syntax is provided by the classical model-theoretic semantics of Datalog Horn rules: "bindings, are defined as extensions of OWL interpretations that map variables to elements of the domain. A rule is satisfied by an interpretation iff every binding that satisfies the antecedent also satisfies the consequent. An interpretation satisfies an ontology iff it satisfies every axiom and fact in the ontology" (http://www.daml.org/2003/11/swrl/direct.html).

3   Some Current Tools for Ontologies and Rules

Our pragmatic approach is based on some currently available tools, which become more and more largely used for the Semantic Web. We use the Protégé OWL plugin for editing OWL ontologies and SWRL rules, RACER [14] for reasoning with OWL ontologies, the Jess inference engine [6] for reasoning with SWRL rules.

Protégé and its OWL Plugin. Protégé [22] is an open platform for ontology modeling and knowledge acquisition. It has a community of thousands of users. The Protégé OWL Plugin[5] is an extension of the Protégé ontology development environment. It is a large plugin with support for OW that can , edit OWL ontologies with custom-tailored graphical widgets, load and save OWL files in various formats.

RACER inference engine. The RACER[17] system [14] implements a highly optimized tableau calculus for the very expressive description logic *SHIQ*. This is the basic logic *ALC* augmented with qualifying number restrictions, role hierarchies, inverse and transitive roles. In addition to these basic features, RACER also provides facilities for algebraic reasoning. Based on the logical semantics of *SHIQ*, RACER can process basic inference reasoning including satisfiability, subsumption, instantiation, which are the basis of powerful automatic reasoning services, such as ontology checking, classification, and instances retrieval. RACER currently supports the Web ontology languages DAML+OIL, RDF and OWL. From about summer 2003, the Protégé OWL plugin is connected to RACER, thus benefits of its reasoning services based on DL. Concretely, RACER automatically translates OWL ontologies (classes, properties, axioms) into a T-Box and OWL individuals and properties assertions (facts) into an A-Box. When RACER loads OWL ontologies, it automatically classifies them, and identifies to which classes the individuals belong. RACER server offers two APIs used by the visualization tool RICE and the ontology editor Protégé.

Jess and JessTab. The Jess[18] Java Expert System Shell [6] is a popular rule system written in Java[TM]. Jess uses the Rete algorithm to process rules, a very efficient mechanism for solving the many-to-many matching problem. According to his author, it is one of the fastest rule engines available. The core Jess language is compatible with CLIPS, so many Jess scripts are valid CLIPS scripts and vice-versa. JessTab is a plugin for Protégé that allows using Jess and Protégé together. In particular, it extends

---

[17] http://www.cs.concordia.ca/~faculty/haarslev/racer/
[18] http://herzberg.ca.sandia.gov/jess/

Jess with additional functions that allow mapping Protégé knowledge bases to Jess facts (classes and individuals). It also provides primitives to manipulate Protégé classes and instances (e.g. instantiating and changing slot values).

4   Reasoning with SWRL Rules and OWL Ontologies

Until the version 105 of the Protege OWL Plugin (April 2004), it was not possible to load the OWL file swrl.owl of the proposal corresponding to the SWRL ontology. Therefore, we first achieved a prototypical implementation of SWRL in Protégé OWL (§4.1). Next, SWRLJessTab, a prototypical plugin was developped to bridge between Protégé OWL[19], RACER, and Jess [6] for reasoning with SWRL rules combined with OWL ontologies (§4.2).

4.1   SWRL Implementation in Protégé OWL

- The implementation of SWRL in OWL (**Fig. 1**) is close to the SWRL syntax and semantics specified in the proposal (Version 0.5 of 19 November 2003), although it exhibits some differences. In particular, 'body' is defined as a set of Atom (at that time rdf:List was problematic in Protégé OWL). Rules are represented as *instances* of the class **Imp** and their variables as *instances* of **Variable**. Like in the proposal, this ontology is OWL Full.

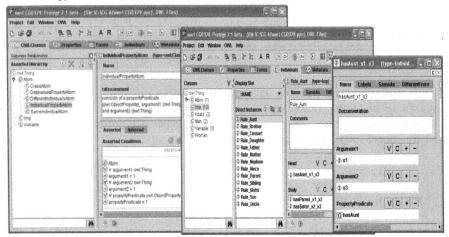

Fig. 1. The SWRL ontology in OWL Swrl.owl

The following classes have been defined, so that the resulting swrl.owl can be loaded in Protégé (Protégé 2.1, Owl Plugin 182):

- **Imp:** an implication (rule) consists of a rule head (consequent) and a rule body (antecedent) which consists of a set of Atom. Thus, restrictions on the properties **body** and **head** state that all values must be of type **Atom** (Table 1)
- **Atom:** the union of the subclasses ClassAtom, DatavaluedPropertyAtom, DifferentIndividualsAtom, IndividualPropertyAtom, and SameIndividualAtom
- **ClassAtom:** a ClassAtom has exactly one **ClassPredicate** whose value must be of type owl:Class and one **argument1** of type owl:Thing
- **IndividualPropertyAtom:** an IndividualPropertyAtom consists of a propertyPredicate which has exactly one value of type owl:ObjectProperty, an argument1 which has exactly one value of type owl:Thing, and argument2 with exactly one value of type owl:Thing
- **DatavaluedPropertyAtom:** a DatavaluedPropertyAtom consists of a property Predicate which has exactly one value of type owl:DatatypeProperty, an argument1 for which all values are of type owl:Thing, and an argument2 for which all values are of type Literal

Table 1. OWL ontology of SWRL Atoms

ClassAtom	C(x)	C OWL Class, x individual or variable
IndividualPropertyAtom	p(x, y)	p ObjectProperty, x and y individual or variable
DatavaluedProperyAtom	q(x, y)	q DatatypeProperty, x individual or variable, y literal or data value
SameIndividualAtom	sameAs(x, y)	x and y individual or variable
DifferentIndividualAtom	differentFrom(x, y)	x and y individual or variable

- **DifferentIndividualsAtom:** a DifferentIndividualsAtom consists of argument1 (owl:Thing) and argument2 (owl:Thing) whith different values
- **SameIndividualAtom:** a SameIndividualAtom consists of argument1 (owl:Thing) and argument2 (owl:Thing) having same values

4.2   SWRLJessTab

SWRLJessTab is a Protégé plugin intended to bridge between Protégé OWL, RACER and Jess, for reasoning with both OWL and SWRL. Using SWRLJessTab, it is possible to infer knowledge from an OWL ontology combined with a SWRL rule base, both represented in Protégé OWL. SWRLJessTab is based on several existing tools and widgets (§ 3), which have been extended. The Protégé OWL plugin is used for editing the ontologies. RACER for classifying them and identifying the individuals classes, JessTab [3] for integrating Jess and Protégé. Jess is used as a rule inference engine, Rice for visualizing the inferred results. Jess extensions allow interaction between SWRL and Jess: SWRL rules instances are mapped to Jess rules, and OWL individuals to Jess facts (Fig. 2).

For reasoning with OWL domain ontologies, we use the RACER classification and consistency checking services. Jess has been extended with a function to bridge RACER and Jess knowledge bases. This function uses JRacer, which provides a Java layer for accessing RACER server. The program enables to translate the roles assertions of a RACER knowledge base into Jess facts and reversely. Thus, when the Jess engine infers new facts from SWRL rules, these facts can be next sent to RACER, which then automatically re-classifies the corresponding individuals. The new classification of the individuals can be visualized with RICE in the pane displaying the instances of RACER A-Box or with the Inspect Final Relations tab of SWRLJessTab.

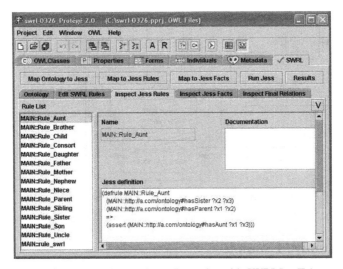

Fig. 2. Mapping Swrl rules to Jess rules with SWRLJessTab

For reasoning with the SWRL rules, we use the Jess inference engine. To bridge between Protégé, SWRL rules, and Jess, we use the Protégé plugin JessTab [5], allowing to integrate Protégé and Jess. We developed a function that maps Atoms of SWRL rules to Atoms of Jess rules: for each SWRL rule defined in Protégé, the set of Atoms of its antecedent is mapped to an IF-clause (LHS) and the set of Atoms of its consequent is into a THEN-clause (RHS).

The overall process assisted by SWRLJessTab, for reasoning with ontologies and rules, consists of the following steps (Fig. 3):

(1) The OWL ontology is loaded into RACER, which automatically classifies its classes and its individuals. The graph of relations among the individuals can be visualized with the "Showgraph" button of RICE.

(2) Concept and role instances of RACER Abox are translated into Jess facts, with the "Map to Jess Facts" button, and can be inspected with the "Inspect Jess Facts" tab.

(3) The SWRL rules stored in Protégé are converted into Jess Rules, using the "Map to Jess Rules" button and can be inspected with the "Inspect Jess Rules" tab

(4) Jess rule engine is launched by the "Run Jess" button. The new Jess facts inferred from the Jess rules can be inspected with the "Inspect Jess Facts" tab

(5) Jess facts are converted into RACER role assertions with the "Result" button, and can be inspected with the "Inspect Final Relation" tab. The resulting graph of relations between the Individuals can be visualized with RICE.

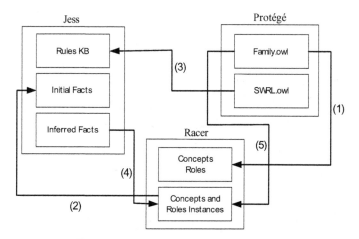

Fig. 3. Overall process with SWRLJessTab

5   The "Family" Example

A small example (Fig. 6) including an OWL ontology (§5.1) and SWRL rules (§5.2) has been prepared in order to exhibit the inferences derived respectively (i) in running RACER with the OWL ontology, (ii) next in running Jess with the SWRL rule base, and (iii) in combining the knowledge of the rule base with that of the ontology (§ 5.3).

5.1 Family.owl

The ontology family.owl is an OWL ontology describing the usual classes, e.g., Person, Man, Woman, Child, Daughter, Parent, Father, etc., and relationships, e.g., hasConsort, hasGender, hasChild etc. within a family. It has been edited with the Protégé OWL plugin. In the example, 10 Man and 10 Woman individuals have been defined, each individual having the relations depicted (Fig. 4). Initially, only the hasConsort, hasChild, hasGender properties were filled for men, and hasGender for women.

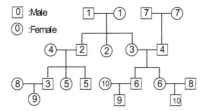

Fig. 4. The family ontology and the relations between its individuals

Each person has many relationships to other persons, such as father, mother, brother, sister, uncle, aunt etc. But, there are many dependencies between the relationships. Some ones can easily be represented in the ontology by OWL axioms, e.g., hasParent relation is the inverse of hasChild, Father is a subclass of Parent. But rules are required for other ones, in particular for chaining properties e.g. hasParent(?x, ?y) ∧ hasSister(?y ?z) ⇒ hasAunt(?x, ?z). In this example, 15 properties should be filled for each person, and the consistency between their values checked. But, using SWRL rules, it is enough to fill only three relationships for men (hasConsort, hasGender, hasChild) and one for women (hasConsort); the other relations are derived from the rules (Fig. 5).

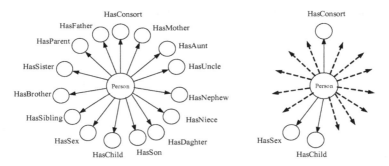

Fig. 5. Relationships for a person

5.2 SWRL Rules

A SWRL rule base (Fig. 6) including rules such as the Rule_Aunt rule: hasParent(?x1,?x2) ∧ hasSister(?x2,?x3) ⇒ hasAunt(?x1,?x3) has been built in Protégé for representing some dependencies between the properties. This SWRL rule base has been edited using the Protégé OWL plugin. Rules are represented as *instances* of the *Imp* class of the swrl.owl ontology (§ 4.1). For that, instances of the class *Variable* e.g. x1, x2, x3, are created for the atom variables ?x1,?x2,?x3. Next, instances of the classe *Atom*, respectively *ClassAtom*, *IndividualPropertyAtom* e.g., hasParent_x1_x2, etc. are edited. Then, instances of *Imp* e.g,. Rule_Aunt are created, specifying their *body* and *head* (**Fig. 1**).

OWL ontology

-1- Person := Man ∪ Woman

-2- Parent := Person ∩ hasChild   1   (a)

Child := Person ∩ hasParent   1   (b)

(hasChild) $^{-1}$ = hasParent   (c)

-3- Father := Parent ∩ Man   Mother := Parent ∩ Woman

-4- Son := Child ∩ Man   Daughter := Child ∩ Woman

-5- Brother := Sibling ∩ Man   Sister := Sibling ∩ Woman

-6- Nephew := Man ∩ (hasUncle ≥ 1 ∪ hasAunt ≥ 1)

-7- Relative := Child ∪ Parent ∪Aunt ∪ Nephew ∪ Niece ∪ Uncle ∪ Sibling

SWRL rules

Initial rule base

-8- hasParent(?x1,?x2) ∧ hasConsort (?x2,?x3) ⇒ hasParent(?x1,?x3)

-9- hasParent(?x1,?x2) ∧ hasSister(?x2,?x3) ⇒ hasAunt(?x1,?x3)

-10- hasParent(?x1,?x2)∧hasParent(?x3,?x2)∧differentFrom(?x1,?x3) ⇒ hasSibling(?x1,?x3)

-11- hasSibling (?x1,?x2) ∧ hasDaughter(?x2,?x3) ⇒ hasNiece(?x1,?x3)

Rules mirroring the ontology knowledge

MR1- hasSibling(?x1,?x2) ∧ Man(?x2) ⇒ hasBrother(?x1,?x2)

MR2- hasSibling(?x1,?x2) ∧Woman(?x2) ⇒ hasSister(?x1,?x2)

MR3- hasParent(?x1,?x2) ∧ Man(?x2) ⇒ hasFather(?x1,?x2)

Fig. 6. Extracts of the OWL ontology, the SWRL rule base and rules mirroring the ontology

5.3 Inferences with RACER and Jess

Initially there were 10 men M1,.., M10 with hasConsort, hasChild, hasGender relation assertions and 10 women F1,.., F10 with hasGender values (§5.1).

Table 2. RACER and Jess inferences

Class	Facts after RACER		After RACER and Jess	
			Initial SWRL rule base	
1. Person	M1->M10,F1->F10	[20]	M1->M10,F1->F10	[20]
2. Man	M1->M10	[10]	M1->M10	[10]
3. Woman	F1->F10	[10]	F1->F10	[10]
4. Parent	M1,M2,M3,M4,M6,M7,M8	[7]	M1,M2,M3,M4,M6,M7,M8, F1,F3,F4,F6,F7,F8,F10	[14]
5. Father	M1,M2,M3,M4,M6,M7,M8	[7]	M1,M2,M3,M4,M6,M7,M8	[7]
6. Mother			F1,F3,F4,F6,F7,F8,F10	[7]
7. Child	M2,M3,M4,M5,M6,M9,M10, F2,F3,F5,F6,F9	[12]	M2,M3,M4,M5,M6,M9,M10, F2,F3,F5,F6,F9	[12]
8. Son	M2,M3,M4,M5,M6,M9,M10	[7]	M2,M3,M4,M5,M6,M9,M10	[7]
9. Daughter	F2,F3,F5,F6,F9	[5]	F2,F3,F5,F6,F9	[5]
10. Sibling			M2,M3,M5,M6,F2,F3,F5,F6	[8]
11. Brother			M2,M3,M5,M6	[4]
12. Sister			F2,F3,F5,F6	[4]
13. Relative	M1->M10,F2,F3,F5,F6,F9	[15]	M1->M10,F1->F10	[20]
			Additional mapping rules	
14. Uncle			*M2,M5,M6*	*[3]*
15. Aunt			*F2,F3,F5,F6*	*[4]*
16. Nephew			*M3,M5,M6,M9,M10*	*[5]*
17. Niece			*F05,F06,F09*	*[3]*

Table 2 summarizes the inferences successively derived from these facts, after executing (i) RACER with family.owl, (ii) next, Jess with the swrl rules, (iii) then, in combining family.owl and SWRL rules.

(i) First, RACER engine has been run. From the family.owl definitions, a new hierarchy is inferred (Fig. 7), the classes Child, Parent, Sibling being moved. The 20 initially defined individuals are identified as belonging to the following classes (bold elements of column "Facts after RACER" in Table 2)

- Line 1: all the individuals are identified to be Person since they are men or women, from the OWL definition (-1- Fig. 6)
- Line 4: 7 men are identified as belonging to the class Parent since they have a child, (-2b-) and also to Father (Line 5) since they are Man (-3-)
- Line 7: 12 individuals are identified as belonging to Child since the hasChild relation is asserted to be the inverse of hasParent (-2c-)
- Line 8: among them 7 are Son (-4-) since they are Man
- Line 9: 5 are Daughter since they are Woman (-4-)
- Line 13: 15 individuals are identified as belonging to Relative since they are a Child, a Parent, or a Daughter, etc. (-7-)

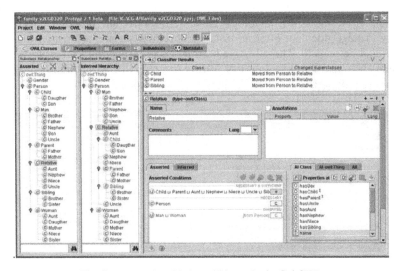

Fig. 7. Asserted and inferred hierarchy by RACER

(ii) Then, the Jess rule engine has been executed for reasoning with the SWRL rules (8-9-10-11 Fig. 6). The new facts derived from the SWRL rule base, are the following (bold elements of column "After RACER and Jess" in Table 2):

- Line 4: 7 additional individuals F1,F3,F4,F6,F7,F8,F10 are inferred as belonging to Parent, from the SWRL rule (-8- Fig. 6), hence they belong to Mother (Line 6)
- Line 10: 8 individuals to Sibling, from the SWRL rule (-10-)

- Line 11 - 12: 4 individuals to `Brother` and 4 to `Sister`, from the OWL definition (-5-)
- Line 13: 5 individuals `F1,F4,F7,F8,F10` added to `Relative` from the OWL definition (-7-).

(iii) Finally, after adding new SWRL rules for simulating the mapping of the ontology knowledge to Jess such as for example MR1 MR2 (Fig. 6), then new facts are derived (bold italic elements of column "`After RACER and Jess`" in Table 2):

- Line 14: 3 individuals are added to Uncle
- Line 15: 4 individuals to Aunt
- Line 16 - 17: 5 individuals to Nephew and 3 to Niece.

Indeed, for instance, chaining MR2 and rule (-9-) enables to infer new relations `hasAunt`, thus new `Nephew` individuals from the `Nephew` OWL definition (-6-). At the moment, the ontology is mapped to Jess in creating additional SWRL rules, but we are investigating using JessTab for automatically mapping OWL ontologies to Jess.

Based on the roles converted from the new inferred facts, RACER classifies the individuals from the OWL ontology class definitions and properties restrictions. Presently Protégé does not offer an instance checking service to identify the classes an individual belongs to. Therefore we used RICE to inspect the classes to which the individuals belong after executing RACER or Jess (Fig. 8). A function is provided to inspect these individuals classified by RACER from Protégé.

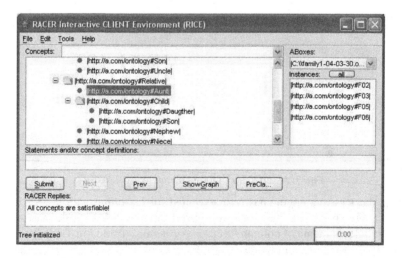

Fig. 8. RICE GUI displaying the individuals classified by RACER after Jess execution.

This example shows that *all* the domain knowledge i.e., knowledge from both the OWL domain ontology and the SWRL rules is required to derive complete inferences. Step (i) shows that the inferences are incomplete when executing RACER alone, and exhibits the needs of rules for representing properties dependencies. Step (ii) shows that in executing Jess after RACER, all facts are not yet derived. It illustrates that it does not make sense to perform inferences with SWRL rules without taking into account the OWL ontology knowledge. Step (iii) shows that extending the Jess knowledge base by rules simulating the mapping of the family ontology enables to get all the expected inferences.

6   Related Works and Discussion

Several alternative approaches aim at combining rules and description logics, including HOOLET[20], KAON EXT[21], ROWL[22].

HOOLET is an implementation of an OWL DL reasoner that uses a first order prover. The ontology is translated into a collection of axioms based on the OWL semantics, which are then given to a first order prover. HOOLET is implemented using the WonderWeb OWL API for parsing and processing OWL, and the Vampire prover for reasoning. The reasoner being based on a first order translation, the implementation has easily been extended to cover the SWRL extension of OWL, adding a parser for the RDF rule syntax and extending the translator for rules, based on the SWRL rules semantics. Only named classes can be used for the rules atoms. The authors do not claim that "Hoolet is, in any way an *effective* reasoner", and say that "such a naïve approach is highly unlikely to scale"[20].

KAON Extensions provide a prototypical implementation of Description Horn Logic based on a Datalog engine developed in the KAON project[23]. The underlying principle is quite similar to Hoolet: a given OWL DL ontology is translated into a corresponding logic program, which is then interpreted by the KAON datalog engine (instead of the FOL prover Vampire). But, the DLP restrictions are stronger than the HOOLET's named concepts one. According to [13], 'initial tests have been encouraging, but much more work needs to be done in order to determine if the benefits promised by the DLP-fusion approach are delivered by this implementation'.

ROWL enables users to specify rules in RDF/XML syntax using an ontology in OWL. Using XSLT stylesheets, the rules in RDF/XML are transformed into forward-chaining *defrules* in Jess.

Unlike our approach, HOOLET and KAON use a single inference engine for computations, based either on a FOL prover or a LP reasoner. Another difference with HOOLET and KAON EXT is that they do not bridge several existing tools and reasoners as we did, in particular, they are nor connected to Protégé OWL. ROWL maps OWL rules to Jess, like SWRLJessTab, but using XSLT stylesheets, instead of existing plugins.

---

[20] http://owl.man.ac.uk/hoolet/
[21] http://kaon.semanticweb.org/owl/.
[22] http://mycampus.sadehlab.cs.cmu.edu/public_pages/ROWL/ROWL.html
[23] http://kaon.semanticweb.org/

Providing reasoning support for a language extending OWL with Datalog RuleML sublanguages is still open. There are several possible strategies for it [16]. Depending on the form of restrictions on the rules and/or the DL, it would be possible to use a DL or LP reasoner like in the DLP approach, a FOL prover like HOOLET, or design an hybrid language from an OWL sublanguage extended by a Web rule language, with sound and complete algorithm like CARIN-ALN [8]. As far as we know, such a language is not yet available.

With SWRLJessTab, we are investigating a different approach, based on combining two existing DL and rule reasoners. We met some practical difficulties in implementing SWRLJessTab, partly because it is based on very recent languages and tools, which are still beta versions, not stable, or not completely documented. We are aware that the present widget has some limitations, which might be overcome in the next future. This work is still ongoing and we are developing a new version for improving it. The definition of head as a set of atoms can be replaced by a list, if wanted. We are introducing a loop calling RACER and JESS iteratively until an inconsistency is detected or no new fact is inferred. Another direction is now investigated, thanks to some recent changes in JessTab that makes it easier to replace the mapping from Protege to Jess. The OWL ontology will be translated to Jess, and then Jess will be used for reasoning with all the knowledge, including both the ontology and the rules.

A next perspective is to use SWRLJessTab for a large biomedical ontology, for example in anatomy or genomics. Another one concerns ontology engineering. As the 'family' ontology example illustrates, from only 3 initial properties, the SWRL rules enable to generate all the family relations, including 12 other properties. Thus, another motivating perspective is to use a SWRL base as a "conceptual" model of "meta-rules" for the construction of OWL ontologies and for their validation i.e., for checking their *semantic* consistency (which is stronger than their satisfiability). The method proposed, illustrated by the family example, is quite general and may be useful for many applications.

7   Conclusion

We presented an implementation of the SWRL emerging standard in Protégé OWL and a prototypical implementation of SWRLJessTab, a Protégé plugin intended to bridge between Protégé OWL, RACER and Jess. The main strength of the approach is that it provides not only reasoning support for SWRL, the RuleML-oriented extension of OWL, but also for reasoning with OWL ontologies *combined* with SWRL rules. Another original contribution is the inter-connection of several existing tools, in particular Protégé OWL with the RACER classifier, and the Jess rule inference engine, so as to join their advantages. Indeed on one hand, Protégé OWL becomes more and more largely used for Web ontologies, and DL reasoning services such as those of RACER are really precious for dealing with huge ontologies, such as for example the biomedical ones. On the other hand, Jess efficiency is a notable advantage for handling rules. Combining benefits of DL and rules in a friendly environment is an important challenge for the Semantic Web.

Acknowledgments. I thank Atsutoshi Imai for his participation in the design and development of the SWRLJessTab

References

1. Bechhofer, S., van Harmelen, F., Hendler, J., Horrocks, I. McGuinness, L. D., Patel-Schneider, P. F., Stein, L., A.: OWL Web Ontology Language Reference. W3C Working Draft (2003) http://www.w3.org/TR/owl-ref
2. Boley, H., Tabet, S., Wagner G., Design Rationale of RuleML: A Markup Language for Semantic Web Rules. International Semantic Web Working Symposium, 2001, Stanford, USA.
3. Dameron O., Burgun A., Morandi X., Gibaud B. Modelling dependencies between relations to insure consistency of a cerebral cortex anatomy knowledge base. Proceedings of Medical Informatics in Europe (2003)
4. Dameron O., Gibaud B., Musen M. Using semantic dependencies for consistency management of an ontology of brain-cortex anatomy, KR-MED 2004.
5. Eriksson, H.: Using JessTab to Integrate Protege and Jess. IEEE Intelligent Systems (2003), 18(2):43-50
6. Ernest J. Friedman-Hill: Jess 6.1 manual. Sandia National Laboratories (2003)
7. Gennari, J. Musen M., Fergerson R., Grosso W., Crubézy M., Eriksson H., Noy N., and Tu S.. The evolution of Protégé-2000: An environment for knowledge-based systems development. International Journal of Human-Computer Studies, 58(1):89–123, 2003.
8. Goasdoue, F., Lattes, V., Rousset, M.C. The Use Of Carin Language and Algorithms for Information Integration: The PICSEL System International Journal of Cooperative Information Systems, 9(4): 383-401, 2000.
9. Golbreich, C., Dameron O., Gibaud B., Burgun, A.: Web ontology language requirements w.r.t. expressiveness of taxonomy and axioms in medicine, International Semantic Web Conference (2003)
10. Golbreich C., Imai A., Combining SWRL rules and OWL ontologies with Protégé OWL Plugin, Jess, and RACER, 7th International Protégé Conference, Bethesda, 2004
11. Golbreich C., Mercier S., Construction of the dialysis and transplantation ontology: advantages, limits, and questions about Protege OWL, Workshop on Medical Applications of Protégé, 7th International Protégé Conference, Bethesda, 2004
12. Golbreich C., Burgun, Biomedical Information Integration, a hot issue, Poster at MEDINFO 2004, San Francisco, 2004.
13. Grosof B., Horrocks I., Volz R., and Decker S., Description Logic Programs: Combining Logic Programs with Description Logic In: Proc. 12th Intl. Conf. on the World Wide Web (WWW-2003), Budapest, Hungary, May 20-23, 2003.
14. Haarslev V., Möller R. : Description of the RACER System and its Applications. Description Logics 2001
15. Horrocks, I., Patel-Schneider, P., Harold, B., Tabet, S., Grosof, B., Dean, M.: SWRL: A Semantic Web Rule Language Combining OWL and RuleML. Version 0.5 Nov. 2003
16. Horrocks, I. and Patel-Schneider, P. F. A Proposal for an OWL Rules Language. In Proceedings International WWW Conference, New York, USA, 2004.
17. Horrocks, I., Sattler, U., Decidability of SHIQ with Complex Role Inclusion Axioms, IJCAI 03
18. Schmidt-Schauß Subsumption in KL-ONE is Undecidable. M. Schmidt-Schauß. Proc. of KR'89, pages 421-431, Morgan Kaufmann.

A System for Nonmonotonic Rules on the Web

G. Antoniou[1], A. Bikakis[1], and G. Wagner[2]

[1]Computer Science Department, University of Crete, Greece
Institute of Computer Science, FORTH, Greece
{ga,bikakis}@csd.uoc.gr
[2] Department of Technology Management
Eindhoven University of Technology, The Netherlands
G.Wagner@tm.tue.nl

Abstract. Defeasible reasoning is a rule-based approach for efficient reasoning with incomplete and inconsistent information. Such reasoning is, among others, useful for ontology integration, where conflicting information arises naturally; and for the modeling of business rules and policies, where rules with exceptions are often used. This paper describes these scenarios in more detail, and reports on the implementation of a system for defeasible reasoning on the Web. The system (a) is syntactically compatible with RuleML; (b) features strict and defeasible rules and priorities; (c) is based on a translation to logic programming with declarative semantics; and (d) is flexible and adaptable to different intuitions within defeasible reasoning.

1 Introduction

The development of the Semantic Web [9] proceeds in layers, each layer being on top of other layers. At present, the highest layer that has reached sufficient maturity is the ontology layer in the form of the description logic based languages of DAML+OIL [11] and OWL [13].

The next step in the development of the Semantic Web will be the logic and proof layers, and *rule systems* appear to lie in the mainstream of such activities. Moreover, rule systems can also be utilized in ontology languages. So, in general rule systems can play a twofold role in the Semantic Web initiative: (a) they can serve as extensions of, or alternatives to, description logic based ontology languages; and (b) they can be used to develop declarative systems on top of (using) ontologies. Reasons why rule systems are expected to play a key role in the further development of the Semantic Web include the following:

- Seen as subsets of predicate logic, monotonic rule systems (Horn logic) and description logics are orthogonal; thus they provide additional expressive power to ontology languages.
- Efficient reasoning support exists to support rule languages.
- Rules are well known in practice, and are reasonably well integrated in mainstream information technology.

G. Antoniou and H. Boley (Eds.): RuleML 2004, LNCS 3323, pp. 23–36, 2004.
© Springer-Verlag Berlin Heidelberg 2004

Possible interactions between description logics and monotonic rule systems were studied in [18]. Based on that work and on previous work on hybrid reasoning [20] it appears that the best one can do at present is to take the intersection of the expressive power of Horn logic and description logics; one way to view this intersection is the Horn-definable subset of OWL.

This paper is devoted to a different problem, namely *conflicts among rules*. Here we just mention the main sources of such conflicts, which are further expanded in section 2. At the ontology layer:

- Default inheritance within ontologies
- Ontology merging

And at the logic and reasoning layers:

- Rules with exceptions as a natural representation of business rules
- Reasoning with incomplete information

Defeasible reasoning is a simple rule-based approach to reasoning with incomplete and inconsistent information. It can represent facts, rules, and priorities among rules. This reasoning family comprises defeasible logics [24, 5] and Courteous Logic Programs [16]. The main advantage of this approach is the combination of two desirable features: enhanced representational capabilities allowing one to reason with incomplete and contradictory information, coupled with low computational complexity compared to mainstream nonmonotonic reasoning.

In this paper we report on the implementation of a defeasible reasoning system for reasoning on the Web. Its main characteristics are the following:

- Its user interface is compatible with RuleML [25], the main standardization effort for rules on the Semantic Web.
- It is based on Prolog. The core of the system consists of a translation of defeasible knowledge into Prolog. However, the implementation is declarative because it interprets the not operator using Well-Founded Semantics [14].
- The main focus was flexibility. Strict and defeasible rules and priorities are part of the interface and the implementation. Also, a number of variants were implemented (ambiguity blocking, ambiguity propagating, conflicting literals; see below for further details). This feature distinguishes this work from the parallel work reported in [27].

The paper is organized as follows. Section 2 describes the main motivations for conflicting rules on the Semantic Web. Section 3 describes the basic ideas of default reasoning, and sections 4 and 5 its translations into logic programs and XML files, respectively. Section 6 reports on the implemented system. Section 7 discusses related work, and section 8 concludes with a summary and some ideas for future work.

2   Motivation for Conflicting Rules on the Semantic Web

Reasoning with Incomplete Information: [3] describes a scenario where business rules have to deal with incomplete information: in the absence of certain information some assumptions have to be made which lead to conclusions not supported by classical predicate logic. In many applications on the Web such assumptions must be made because other players may not be able (e.g. due to communication problems) or willing (e.g. because of privacy or security concerns) to provide information. This is the classical case for the use of nonmonotonic knowledge representation and reasoning [23].

Rules with Exceptions: Rules with exceptions are a natural representation for policies and business rules [4]. And priority information is often implicitly or explicitly available to resolve conflicts among rules. Potential applications include security policies [8, 21], business rules [3], personalization, brokering, bargaining, and automated agent negotiations [15].

Default Inheritance in Ontologies: Default inheritance is a well-known feature of certain knowledge representation formalisms. Thus it may play a role in ontology languages, which currently do not support this feature. [19] presents some ideas for possible uses of default inheritance in ontologies.

A natural way of representing default inheritance is rules with exceptions, plus priority information. Thus, nonmonotonic rule systems can be utilized in ontology languages.

Ontology Merging: When ontologies from different authors and/or sources are merged, contradictions arise naturally. Predicate logic based formalisms, including all current Semantic Web languages, cannot cope with inconsistencies.

If rule-based ontology languages are used (e.g. DLP [18]) and if rules are interpreted as defeasible (that is, they may be prevented from being applied even if they can fire) then we arrive at nonmonotonic rule systems. A skeptical approach, as adopted by defeasible reasoning, is sensible because does not allow for contradictory conclusions to be drawn. Moreover, priorities may be used to resolve some conflicts among rules, based on knowledge about the reliability of sources or on user input). Thus, nonmonotonic rule systems can support ontology integration.

3   Defeasible Logics

3.1   Basic Characteristics

- Defeasible logics are rule-based, without disjunction
- Classical negation is used in the heads and bodies of rules, but negation-as-failure is not used in the object language (it can easily be simulated, if necessary [4])
- Rules may support conflicting conclusions
- The logics are skeptical in the sense that conflicting rules do not fire. Thus consistency is preserved
- Priorities on rules may be used to resolve some conflicts among rules
- The logics take a pragmatic view and have low computational complexity

3.2 Syntax

A *defeasible theory* D is a couple (R,>) where R a finite set of rules, and > a superiority relation on R. In expressing the proof theory we consider only propositional rules. Rules containing free variables are interpreted as the set of their variable-free instances.

There are two kinds of rules (fuller versions of defeasible logics include also defeaters): *Strict rules* are denoted by $A \rightarrow p$, and are interpreted in the classical sense: whenever the premises are indisputable then so is the conclusion. An example of a strict rule is "Professors are faculty members". Written formally: professor(X) $\rightarrow$ faculty(X). Inference from strict rules only is called *definite inference*. Strict rules are intended to define relationships that are definitional in nature, for example ontological knowledge.

Defeasible rules are denoted by $A \Rightarrow p$, and can be defeated by contrary evidence. An example of such a rule is faculty(X) $\Rightarrow$ tenured(X) which reads as follows: "Professors are typically tenured".

A *superiority relation* on R is an acyclic relation > on R (that is, the transitive closure of > is irreflexive). When $r_1 > r_2$, then r_1 is called *superior* to r_2, and r_2 *inferior* to r_1. This expresses that r_1 may override r_2. For example, given the defeasible rules

> r: professor(X) => tenured(X)
> r': visiting(X) => ¬tenured(X)

which contradict one another: no conclusive decision can be made about whether a visiting professor is tenured. But if we introduce a superiority relation > with r' > r, then we can indeed conclude that a particular visiting professor is not tenured.

A formal definition of the proof theory is found in [5]. A model theoretic semantics is found in [22].

3.3 Ambiguity Blocking and Ambiguity Propagation Behavior

A literal is *ambiguous* if there is a chain of reasoning that supports a conclusion that p is true, another that supports that ¬p is true, and the superiority relation does not resolve this conflict. We can illustrate the concept of ambiguity propagation through the following example.

> r_1: quaker(X) => pacifist(X)
> r_2: republican(X) => ¬pacifist(X)
> r_3: pacifist(X) => ¬hasGun(X)
> r_4: livesInChicago(X) => hasGun(X)
> quaker(a)
> republican(a)
> livesInChicago(a)
> $r_3 > r_4$

Here *pacifist(a)* is ambiguous. The question is whether this ambiguity should be propagated to the dependent literal *hasGun(a)*. In one defeasible logic variant it is detected that rule r_3 cannot fire, so rule r_4 is unopposed and gives the defeasible conclusion *hasGun(a)*. This behavior is called *ambiguity blocking*, since the ambiguity of *pacifist(a)* has been used to block r_3 and resulted in the unambiguous conclusion *hasGun(a)*.

On the other hand, in the ambiguity blocking variant, *pacifist(a)* is recognized to be nonprovable, thus rule r_3 is blocked, and rule r_4 fires and gives the conclusion *hasGun(a)*.

A preference for ambiguity blocking or ambiguity propagating behavior is one of the properties of nonmonotonic inheritance nets over which intuitions can clash [26]. Ambiguity propagation results in fewer conclusions being drawn, which might make it preferable when the cost of an incorrect conclusion is high. For these reasons an ambiguity propagating variant of DL is of interest.

3.4 Conflicting Literals

So far only conflicts among rules with complementary heads were deected and used. We considered all rules with head L as *supportive* of L, and all rules with head $\neg L$ as *conflicting*. However, in applications often literals are considered to be conflicting, and at most one of a certain set should be derived. For example, the risk an investor is willing to accept may be classified in one of the categories low, medium, and high. The way to solve this problem is to use constraint rules of the form

conflict :: low, medium
conflict :: low, high
conflict :: medium, high

Now if we try to derive the conclusion *high*, the conflicting rules are not just those with head $\neg high$, but also those with head *low* and *medium*. Similarly, if we are trying to prove $\neg high$, the supportive rules include those with head *low* or *medium*. In general, given a *conflict :: L, M*, we augment the defeasible theory by:

$r_i: q_1, q_2, \ldots, q_n \rightarrow \neg L$ for all rules $r_i: q_1, q_2, \ldots, q_n \rightarrow M$
$r_i: q_1, q_2, \ldots, q_n \rightarrow \neg M$ for all rules $r_i: q_1, q_2, \ldots, q_n \rightarrow L$
$r_i: q_1, q_2, \ldots, q_n \Rightarrow \neg L$ for all rules $r_i: q_1, q_2, \ldots, q_n \Rightarrow M$
$r_i: q_1, q_2, \ldots, q_n \rightarrow \neg L$ for all rules $r_i: q_1, q_2, \ldots, q_n \Rightarrow M$

The superiority relation among the rules of the defeasible theory is propagated to the "new" rules. For example, if the defeasible theory includes the following two rules and a superiority relation among them:

$r_1: q_1, q_2, \ldots, q_n \rightarrow L$
$r_2: p_1, p_2, \ldots, p_n \rightarrow M$
$r_1 > r_2$

we will augment the defeasible theory by :

$r_1': q_1, q_2, \ldots, q_n \rightarrow \neg M$
$r_2': p_1, p_2, \ldots, p_n \rightarrow \neg L$
$r_1 > r_2'$
$r_1' > r_2$

4 Translation into Logic Programs

The translation of a defeasible theory D into a logic program $P(D)$ has a certain goal: to show that

> p is defeasibly provable in $D \Leftrightarrow$
> p is included in the well-founded model of $P(D)$

In order to achieve this goal, we based our translation on the translation which makes use of control literals, presented in [7]. We have made some extensions to support superiority relations among rules, and to support both ambiguity blocking and ambiguity propagation behavior. The translation has two versions: the ambiguity blocking version and the ambiguity propagation version.

4.1 Translation of Ambiguity Blocking Behavior

Given a fact p we translate it into the program clause

> $a(p)$: $definitely(p)$.

Given a strict rule

> r: $q_1, q_2, ..., q_n \rightarrow p$

we translate it into the program clause

> $b(r)$: $definitely(p)$:- $definitely(q_1), definitely(q_2), ..., definitely(q_n)$.

Additionally, we introduce the clause

> $c(p)$: $defeasibly(p)$:- $definitely(p)$.

for every literal p. This last clause corresponds to the condition of the defeasible theory: a literal p is defeasibly provable if it is strictly (definitely) provable.

Given a defeasible rule

> r: $q_1, q_2, ..., q_n \Rightarrow p$

we translate it into the following set of clauses:

> $d_1(r)$: $defeasibly(p)$:- $defeasibly(q_1), defeasibly(q_2), ..., defeasibly(q_n)$,
> not^1 $definitely(\sim p), ok(r,p)$.
>
> $d_2(r)$: $ok(r,x)$:- $ok'(r,s_1), ..., ok'(r,s_m)$.

where $\{s_1, ..., s_m\}$ = {the set of defeasible rules with head: $\sim p$}

> $d_3(r,s_i)$: $ok'(r,s_i)$:- $blocked(s_i)$.   for all $s_i \in \{s_1, ..., s_m\}$
>
> $d_4(r,s_i)$: $ok'(r,s_i)$:- $defeated(s_i)$.   for all $s_i \in \{s_1, ..., s_m\}$

---

[1] Of course we will have to specify the semantics of *not*; we will be using well-founded semantics. For the implementation we use *tnot* of XSB Prolog. See section 6 for more details.

$d_5(r,q_i)$: blocked(r):- not defeasibly(q_i).   for all $i \in \{1,2,\ldots,n\}$

$d_6(r,s_i)$: defeated(r):- not blocked(s_i), sup(s_i,r).   for all $s_i \in \{s_1,\ldots,s_m\}$

Given a superiority relation

$r > s$

we translate it into the program clause

$e(r,s)$: sup(r,s).

- $d_1(r)$ says that to prove p defeasibly by applying r, we must prove all the antecedents of r, the negation of p should not be strictly (definitely) provable, and it must be ok to apply r.
- $d_2(r)$ says when it is ok to apply a rule r with head p: we must check that it is ok to apply r w.r.t. every rule with head $\sim p$.
- $d_3(r,s_i)$ says that it is ok to apply r w.r.t. s_i is blocked.
- $d_4(r,s_i)$ says that it is ok to apply r w.r.t. s_i is blocked.
- $d_5(r,q_i)$ specifies the only way a rule can be blocked: it must be impossible to prove one of its antecedents.
- $d_6(r,s_i)$ specifies the only way a rule r can be defeated: there must be at least one rule s with complementary head (conflicting rule), which is not blocked and is superior to r.

For a defeasible theory with ambiguity blocking behavior D we define $P(D)$ to be the union of all clauses $a(p)$, $b(r)$, $c(p)$, $d_1(r)$, $d_2(r)$, $d_3(r,s_i)$, $d_4(r,s_i)$, $d_5(r,q_i)$, $d_6(r,s_i)$, $e(r,s)$.

4.2 Translation of Ambiguity Propagation Behavior

We must make some changes to the procedure of the translation that we described above to support ambiguity propagation behavior. Our goal is to ensure that the ambiguity of a conclusion is propagated to its dependents. To achieve this we must define a new predicate: *supported*.

The program clauses $a(p)$, $b(r)$, $c(p)$ remain unchanged. In this version we add a new program clause $s(p)$:

$s(p)$: supported(p):- definitely(p).

for every literal p. This clause says that p is supported if it is strictly (definitely) provable.

The program clauses $d_1(r)$, $d_2(r)$, $d_4(r,s_i)$, $d_5(r,q_i)$, $d_6(r,s_i)$, $e(r,s)$ also remain the same. In order to support the ambiguity propagation behavior, we must change $d_3(r,s_i)$ and add two more program clauses for the defeasible rules. So, given a defeasible rule

r: $q_1,q_2,\ldots,q_n => p$

we translate it into the following set of clauses:

$d_1(r)$, $d_2(r)$,

$d_3{}'(r,s_i)$: ok'(r,s_i):- obstructed(s_i).   for all $s_i \in \{s_1,\ldots,s_m\}$

$d_4(r,s_i)$, $d_5(r,q_i)$, $d_6(r,s_i)$,

$d_7(r,q_i)$: *obstructed(r):- not supported(q_i).*   for all i $\in$ {1,2,...,n},

$d_8(r)$: *supported(p):- supported(q_1),...,supported(q_n), not defeated(r).*

- $d_3'(r,s_i)$ says that it is ok to apply r w.r.t. s_i is obstructed.
- $d_7(r,q_i)$ specifies the only way a rule can be obstructed: at least one of its antecedents must not be supported.
- $d_8(r)$ says that p is supported by applying r, if all the antecedents of r are supported, and r is not defeated.

For a defeasible theory with ambiguity propagation behavior D we define $P(D)$ to be the union of all clauses $a(p)$, $b(r)$, $c(p)$, $d_1(r)$, $d_2(r)$, $d_3'(r,s_i)$, $d_4(r,s_i)$, $d_5(r,q_i)$, $d_6(r,s_i)$, $d_7(r,q_i)$, $d_8(r)$, $e(r,s)$.

5   Translation into XML Files

Another interesting part of our work is the creation of a DTD which allows us to translate defeasible theories into XML files. This DTD is in fact an extension of the RuleML DTDs [25]. It covers both strict and defeasible rules, as well as the superiority relations between these rules. The elements of the RuleML DTD that we added / modified are:

- The "rulebase" root element which uses "imp" (strict) and "def" (defeasible) rules, "fact" assertions and "superiority" relations.
- The "imp" element, which consists of a "_head" and a "_body" element, accepts a "name" attribute, and refers to the strict rules of a theory.
- The "def" element which consists of a "_head" and a "_body" element, accepts a "name" attribute, and refers to the defeasible rules of a theory.
- The "superiority" empty element, which accepts the name of two rules as its attributes ("sup" & "inf"), and refers to the superity relation of these two rules.

Below we present the modified DTD:

```
<!ELEMENT rulebase ((imp|def|fact|superiority)*)>
<!ELEMENT imp ((_head, _body) | (_body, _head))>
<!ATTLIST imp
          name ID #IMPLIED>
<!ELEMENT def((_head, _body) | (_body, _head))>
<!ATTLIST def
          name ID #IMPLIED>
<!ELEMENT fact (_head) >
<!ELEMENT superiority EMPTY>
<!ATTLIST superiority
          sup IDREF #REQUIRED
          inf IDREF #REQUIRED>
<!ELEMENT _head (atom)>
```

```
<!ELEMENT _body (atom | and)>
<!ELEMENT and (atom*)>
<!ELEMENT atom ((_opr,(ind | var)*) | ((ind | var)+,
_opr))>
<!ELEMENT _opr (rel)>
<!ELEMENT ind  (#PCDATA)>
<!ELEMENT var  (#PCDATA)>
<!ELEMENT rel  (#PCDATA)>
```

6 Implementation

Our goal was to develop a system that supports not only the basics of defeasible logic, but also the two different behaviors (ambiguity blocking and ambiguity propagation) of this logic, and the use of conflicting literals. The system consists of five different tools: the *parser*, the *logic translator*, the *XML translator*, the *logic compiler*, and the *evaluator*. We employed *lex & yacc*, to create the parser and the two translators. We use XSB [28] as the logic compiler. The same system is responsible for evaluating the user's queries.

The system can be used either to translate a defeasible theory into an XML file, according to the DTD we described in section 5, or as a query evaluator. The queries that the user can make are of the form: "Can you conclude that the literal *p* of my defeasible theory *D* is / is not proved strictly / defeasibly?". The system can evaluate the answer of one query of this form at a time. It has not the ability to evaluate queries of the form: "Which literals of my defeasibly theory *D* are proved strictly / defeasibly?". The overall procedure is described in Fig.1.

In the follwing sections, we will describe the role of each of the tools that compose the architecture of the system.

6.1 The Parser

The parser is responsible for parsing the user's defeasible theory and for checking for the validity of this theory. The theory is considered to be valid, if it follows the standard syntax of defeasible logic, as described in section 3. If there are syntax errors in a defeasible theory, the system informs the user about these errors, and does not proceed to the translation of the theory. If the theory is valid, the parser creates a symbol table, which includes all the facts, rules and superiority relations of the user's defeasible theory. The symbol table will be later used by the translator.

Another important task of the parser is to check for the conflicting literals of the defeasible theory, and to augment the theory with the appropriate rules and superiority relations. If the user has defined two or more literals to be conflicting, the parser checks for the rules which have one of these literals as their head, and for the superiority relations among these rules, and creates new rules and superiority relations, following the way we described in Section 3.

The last task of the parser is to check for the validity of the user's queries. We have defined a standard syntax for these queries:

- +*D p* : is it concluded that literal *p* of the defeasible theory is proved strictly?
- -*D p* : is it concluded that literal *p* of the defeasible theory is not proved strictly?
- +*d p* : is it concluded that literal *p* of the defeasible theory is proved defeasibly?
- -*d p* :is it concluded that literal *p* of the defeasible theory is not proved defeasibly?

The syntax we use for the complementary of a literal *p* is ~*p*.

6.2 The Logic Translator

If the defeasible theory has been parsed with success, the translator creates the logic program which corresponds to the user's defeasible theory. The translator has two inputs and one output. The first input is the user's defeasible theory *D* (checked and possibly augmented with new rules and superiority relations by the parser). The second input is the user's choice of the behavior of the defeasible theory: ambiguity blocking / ambiguity propagation. The output is a logic program *P(D)*, which is in fact a Prolog file. The translation of each defeasible rule to the corresponding Prolog rule is described in section 4. The only difference is that, instead of *not* we use *tnot*, which is XSB's negation operator implementing well founded semantics. The translator parses the symbol table, which is created by the parser, and translates the defeasible rules one by one. In the course of this procedure, some searches of the symbol table are required. For example, if a translator meets a defeasible rule with head *p*, it searches the symbol table for defeasible rules with complementary head, ~*p*.

The translator is also responsible for transforming the user's queries into valid Prolog queries:

- +D p is translated into definitely(p).
- -D p is translated into not definitely(p).
- +d p is translated into defeasibly(p).
- -d p is translated into not defeasibly(p).

6.3 The XML Translator

The role of the XML translator is to translate the defeasible theory, which has already been checked for its validity by the parser, into a valid XML file. A valid defeasible theory acts as input of the translation. The output is an XML file, which is created according to the DTD that we described in section 5.

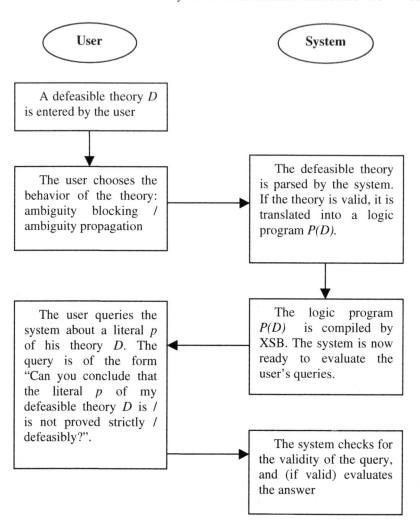

Fig. 1. The Interaction between the system and its users.

6.4 The Logic Program Compiler

The logic program compiler employs XSB to compile the logic program $P(D)$, created by the logic translator. We use XSB, as we need a powerful Prolog system for our needs. A defeasible theory which consists of n number of facts, rules and superiority relations, is translated into a logic program with $r*n$ Prolog rules, where $2<n<6$ in the case of ambiguity blocking behavior, and $3<n<8$ in the case of ambiguity propagation behavior.

XSB is appropriate for building integrated real-world systems, as it is easy to construct the communication module between XSB and the other parts of such systems. In our case, it was critical for the performance of the system, to find an easy and efficient way to communicate the logic program compiler with the parser and the translator. Only a small number of code was enough to construct this communication module.

6.5 The Evaluator

The role of the evaluator is to evaluate the answer to the user's queries. The queries are parsed by the parser, and translated into Prolog queries by the logic translator, before being passed to the evaluator. The Prolog queries are applied to the compiled Prolog file, and a positive ("yes") or a negative answer ("no") is produced by the evaluator.

7 Related Work

There exist several previous implementations of defeasible logics. [12] gives the historically first implementation, *D-Prolog*, a Prolog-based implementation. It was not declarative in certain aspects (because it did not use a declarative semantic for the not operator), therefore it did not correspond fully to the abstract definition of the logic. Also, D-Prolog supported only one variation thus it lacked the flexibility of the implementation we report on. Finally it did not provide any means of integration with Semantic Web layers and concepts.

Deimos [22] is a flexible, query processing system based on Haskell. It implements several variants, but not conflicting literals. Also, it does not integrate with Semantic Web (for example, there is no way to treat RDF data; nor does it use an XML-based or RDF-based syntax). Thus it is an isolated solution. Finally, it is propositional and does not support variables.

Delores [22] is another implementation, which computes all conclusions from a defeasible theory (the only system of its kind known to us). It is very efficient, exhibiting linear computational complexity. Delores only supports ambiguity blocking propositional defeasible logic; so, it does not support ambiguity propagation, nor conflicting literals and variables. Also, it does integrate with other Semantic Web languages and systems.

RD-DEVICE [27] is another effort on implementing defeasible reasoning, parallel to the present work albeit with a different approach. RD-DEVICE is implemented in Jess, and integrates well with RuleML and RDF. It is a system for query answering. Compared to the work of this paper, RD-DEVICE supports only one variant, ambiguity blocking, thus it does not offer the flexibility of this implementation.

SweetJess [17] is another implementation of a defeasible reasoning system (situated courteous logic programs) based on Jess. It integrates well with RuleML. Also, it allows for procedural attachments, a feature not supported by any of the above implementations, not by the system of this paper. However, SweetJess is more limited in flexibility, in that it implements only one reasoning variant (it corresponds to ambiguity blocking defeasible logic). Moreover, it imposes a number of restrictions on the programs it can map on Jess. In comparison, our system implements the full version of defeasible logic.

8 Conclusion

In this paper we described reasons why conflicts among rules arise naturally on the Semantic Web. To address this problem, we proposed to use defeasible reasoning which is known from the area of knowledge representation. And we reported on the implementation of a system for defeasible reasoning on the Web. It is Prolog-based, and supports RuleML syntax.

Planned future work includes:

- Comparing the speed of this implementation with other systems using the data and methodology of [22].

- Adding arithmetic capabilities to the rule language, and using appropriate constraint solvers in conjunction with logic programs.

- Implementing load/upload functionality in conjunction with an RDF repository, such as RDF Suite [1] and Sesame [10].

- Study in more detail integration of defeasible reasoning with description logic based ontologies. Starting point of this investigation will be the Horn definable part of OWL [18].

- Applications of defeasible reasoning and the developed implementation for brokering, bargaining, automated agent negotiation, and personalization.

References

1. S. Alexaki, V. Christophides, G. Karvounarakis, D. Plexousakis and K. Tolle (2001). The ICS-FORTH RDFSuite: Managing Voluminous RDF Description Bases. In *Proc. 2nd International Workshop on the Semantic Web*, Hongkong, May 1, 2001.
2. G. Antoniou (2002). Nonmonotonic Rule Systems on Top of Ontology Layers. In *Proc. 1st International Semantic Web Conference*. Springer, LNCS 2342, 394-398
3. G. Antoniou and M. Arief (2002). Executable Declarative Business rules and their use in Electronic Commerce. In *Proc. ACM Symposium on Applied Computing*
4. G. Antoniou, D. Billington and M.J. Maher (1999). On the analysis of regulations using defeasible rules. In *Proc. 32nd Hawaii International Conference on Systems Science*
5. G. Antoniou, D. Billington, G. Governatori and M.J. Maher (2001). Representation results for defeasible logic. ACM Transactions on Computational Logic 2, 2 (2001): 255 - 287
6. G. Antoniou, M. J. Maher and D. Billington (2000). Defeasible Logic versus Logic Programming without Negation as Failure. *Journal of Logic Programming* 41,1 (2000): 45-57
7. G. Antoniou, M.J. Maher (2002). Embedding Defeasible Logic into Logic Programs. In *Proc. ICLP 2002,* 393-404
8. R. Ashri, T. Payne, D. Marvin, M. Surridge and S. Taylor (2004). Towards a Semantic Web Security Infrastructure. In *Proc. of Semantic Web Services 2004 Spring Symposium Series*, Stanford University, California

9. T. Berners-Lee, J. Hendler, and O. Lassila (2001). The Semantic Web. *Scientific American*, 284, 5 (2001): 34-43
10. J. Broekstra, A. Kampman and F. van Harmelen (2003) Sesame: An Architecture for Storin gand Querying RDF Data and Schema Information. In: D. Fensel, J. A. Hendler, H. Lieberman and W. Wahlster (Eds.), *Spinning the Semantic Web*, MIT Press, 197-222
11. D. Connolly, F. van Harmelen, I. Horrocks, D. L. McGuinness, P. F. Patel-Schneider and L. A. Stein (2001). *DAML+OIL Reference Description*. www.w3.org/TR/daml+oil-reference
12. M. A. Covington, D. Nute and A. Vellino (1997). *Prolog Programming in Depth*, 2nd ed. Prentice-Hall
13. M. Dean and G. Schreiber (Eds.) (2004). *OWL Web Ontology Language Reference*. www.w3.org/TR/2004/REC-owl-ref-20040210/
14. A. van Gelder, K. Ross and J. Schlipf (1991). The well-founded semantics for general logic programs. *Journal of the ACM* 38 (1991): 620—650
15. G. Governatori, M. Dumas, A. ter Hofstede and P. Oaks (2001). A formal approach to legal negotiation. In *Proc. ICAIL 2001*, 168-177
16. B. N. Grosof (1997). Prioritized conflict handing for logic programs. In *Proc. of the 1997 International Symposium on Logic Programming*, 197-211
17. B. N. Grosof, M. D. Gandhe and T. W. Finin: SweetJess: Translating DAMLRuleML to JESS. RuleML 2002. In: *Proc. International Workshop on Rule Markup Languages for Business Rules on the Semantic Web*
18. B. N. Grosof, I. Horrocks, R. Volz and S. Decker (2003). Description Logic Programs: Combining Logic Programs with Description Logic". In: *Proc. 12th Intl. Conf. on the World Wide Web (WWW-2003)*, ACM Press
19. B. N. Grosof and T. C. Poon (2003). SweetDeal: representing agent contracts with exceptions using XML rules, ontologies, and process descriptions. In *Proc. 12th International Conference on World Wide Web*. ACM Press, 340 – 349
20. A. Levy and M.-C. Rousset (1998). Combining Horn rules and description logics in CARIN. *Artificial Intelligence* 104, 1-2 (1998):165 - 209
21. N. Li, B. N. Grosof and J. Feigenbaum (2003). Delegation Logic: A Logic-based Approach to Distributed Authorization. In: *ACM Transactions on Information Systems Security* 6,1 (2003)
22. M. J. Maher, A. Rock, G. Antoniou, D. Billington and T. Miller (2001). Efficient Defeasible Reasoning Systems. *International Journal of Tools with Artificial Intelligence* 10,4 (2001): 483-501
23. V.W. Marek and M. Truszczynski (1993). *Nonmonotonic Logics; Context Dependent Reasoning*. Springer Verlag
24. D. Nute (1994). Defeasible logic. In *Handbook of logic in artificial intelligence and logic programming (vol. 3): nonmonotonic reasoning and uncertain reasoning*. Oxford University Press
25. RuleML. *The Rule Markup Language Initiative*. www.ruleml.org
26. D.D. Touretzky, J.F. Horty and R.H. Thomason. (1987). A Clash of Intuitions: The Current State of Nonmonotonic Inheritance Systems. In *Proc. IJCAI-87*, 476-482, Morgan Kaufmann, 1987.
27. N. Vassiliades, G. Antoniou and Y. Vlahavas (2004). RD-DEVICE: A Defeasible Reasoning Systems for the Web. Submitted.
28. XSB, Logic Programming and Deductive Database System for Unix and Windows. xsb.sourceforge.net
29. Lex & Yacc, dinosaur.compilertools.net

Rule Learning for Feature Values Extraction from HTML Product Information Sheets*

Costin Bădică[1] and Amelia Bădică[2]

[1] University of Craiova, Software Engineering Department
Bvd.Decebal 107, Craiova, 200440, Romania
c_badica@hotmail.com
[2] University of Craiova, Business Information Systems Department
A.I.Cuza 13, Craiova, RO-1100, Romania
ameliabd@yahoo.com

Abstract. The Web is now a huge information repository with a rich semantic structure that, however, is primarily addressed to human understanding rather than automated processing by a computer. The problem of collecting product information from the Web and organizing it in an appropriate way for automated machine processing is a primary task of software shopping agents and has received a lot of attention during the last years. In this paper we assume that product information is represented as a set of feature-value pairs contained in an HTML product information sheet that is usually formatted using HTML tables. The paper presents a technique for learning extraction rules of product information from such product information sheets. The technique exploits the fact that the Web pages that represent product information of a certain producer are generated on the fly from the producer database and therefore they exhibit uniform structures. Consequently, while the extraction task is executed manually for a few information items by a human user, a general-purpose inductive learner (we have used FOIL in our experiments) can learn extraction rules that will be further applied to the current and other product information sheets to automatically extract other items. The input to the learning algorithm is a relational description of the HTML document tree that defines the HTML tree nodes types and the relationships between them. The approach is demonstrated with appropriate examples, experimental results, and software tools.

1 Introduction

The Web is now a huge information repository that is characterized by i) *high diversity*, i.e. the Web information covers almost any application area, ii) *disparity*, i.e. the Web information comes in many formats ranging from plain and structured text to multimedia documents and iii) *rapid growth*, i.e. old information is continuously being updated in form and content and new information is

---

* The research described here was partly supported with funding from Syncro Soft
http://www.oxygenxml.com

G. Antoniou and H. Boley (Eds.): RuleML 2004, LNCS 3323, pp. 37–48, 2004.

constantly being produced. The HTML markup language is the *lingua franca* for publishing information on the Web. In our opinion these facts explain the significant growth of the interest in the field of automatizing the tasks of information extraction (IE hereafter) from HTML information sources.

IE was developed as part of DARPA's MUC program and originally was concerned with locating specific pieces of information in text documents written in natural language ([8]). The field then expanded rapidly to cover extraction tasks from networked documents including HTML and XML.

Paper [10] identified two major types of IE: i) IE from unstructured texts that treat the document as a string of characters and ii) IE from (semi-)structured texts that treat the document as a tree.

Traditional IE from strings uses techniques from computational linguistics based on finite-state methodologies. Paper [3] cites two approaches: i) the *local approach* concerned with enhancing document parsers with a set of extraction patterns and ii) the *global approach* concerned with applying grammatical inference methods to identify the language of the target document.

IE from tree documents exploits the structural information conveyed by the document tree. An important advantage of this approach is that the extracted item can depend on its structural context in a document, while this information is lost in the event the tree document is treated linearly as a string ([6]). Two recent IE approaches in this class are: i) *tree automata induction* ([6]) and ii) *learning subtree delimiters* ([3]).

This paper presents a methodology and experimental results on the application of first order rule learning to extract information from HTML documents structured as trees. The experiments were carried out in the area of collecting product information from the Web, an important task in product data integration ([4,1]). However, the approach is general enough to be useful in other application areas that require IE from tree structured documents including XML and XHTML, as for example in wrapper development for querying bibliographic databases in digital libraries.

The rest of the paper is structured as follows. Section 2 contains an overview of the stages in the IE process. In section 3 we present the relational representation of HTML document trees. In section 4 we show how the task of learning IE rules from a tree document can be mapped to FOIL ([12]). Section 5 contains a brief description of the software tools we have used in our experiments. Section 6 presents the experiments performed and the results obtained in terms of precision and recall measures. Section 7 cites related work highlighting similarities with and differences from our work. Section 8 contains some conclusions and points to future research.

2   Overview of the Extraction Process

The IE process was structured as a linear sequence of stages:

i)   *Crawl or browse the Web and download HTML pages of interest.* This step is quite straightforward. Either a human user is browsing the Web to download interesting pages or the task of Web navigation and page download is automatized by means of a crawler component ([2]). The result of this step is a collection of pages that were fetched and stored locally on the user machine.

ii) *Preprocess and convert the document from HTML to XHTML.* In this step the input HTML document is cleaned and converted to a well-formed XML document written in XHTML and structured as a tree.

iii) *Manually extract a few examples.* In this step the user loads a few XHTML pages from the local repository and performs a few extraction tasks. The result is a set of annotated XHTML documents with the extracted fields.

iv) *Parse the annotated XHTML documents and generate a relational representation as input for the learner.* In this step the annotated XHTML documents are parsed and converted into input for the learning program. The result will contain the target relation, the sets of positive and negative examples and the background relations.

v) *Apply the learning algorithm and obtain the IE rules.* In this step the learning program is executed on the input generated in the previous step. The result is a set of first order IE rules.

vi) *Apply the rules to extract information.* In this step the user applies the learnt IE rules to new XHTML pages in order to automatically extract new information. In principle there are two possibilities to perform this task: i) the target document is converted to a relational representation in Prolog and the first order IE rules are applied to the Prolog representation or ii) the first order IE rules are mapped to XSLT and the resulted XSLT is applied to the target XHTML document.

3   Relational Representation of Document Trees

An XHTML document is composed of a structural component and a content component.

The structural component consists of the set of document nodes or elements. The document elements are nested into a tree like structure. Each document element has assigned a specific tag from a given finite set of tags Σ. There is a special tag $text \in \Sigma$ that designates a text element.

The content component of a document consists of the actual text in the text elements and the attribute-value pairs attached to the other document elements.

The structure of XHTML documents can be represented as unranked ordered trees, also known as Σ-trees. According to [11], the set $\mathcal{T}_\Sigma$ of Σ-trees is defined inductively as follows:

i)   if $\sigma \in \Sigma$ then $\sigma \in \mathcal{T}_\Sigma$;
ii) if $\sigma \in \Sigma$ and $t_1, \ldots, t_n \in \mathcal{T}_\Sigma$, $n \geq 1$, then $\sigma(t_1, \ldots, t_n) \in \mathcal{T}_\Sigma$.

Note that there is no a priori bound on the number of children of a node in a Σ-tree, i.e. the tree is *unranked*, and note also that the set of children of a given node in a Σ-tree is ordered, i.e. the tree is *ordered*.

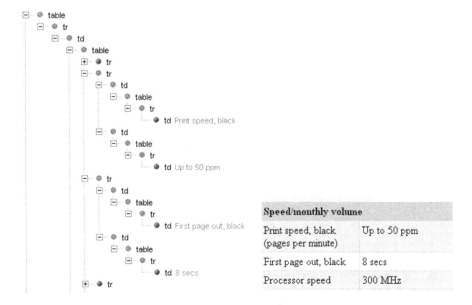

Fig. 1. An XHTML document fragment and its graphic view

Example 1. Consider the Hewlett Packard's site of electronic products[1] and the task of IE from a product information sheet for printers. The printer information is displayed in a two-column table as a set of feature-value pairs. Our task is to extract the names and/or the values of the printer features. This information is stored in the leaf elements of the page. Figure 1 displays in the left panel the XHTML tree of a fragment of this document and in the right panel the graphical view of this fragment as a two-column table. Figure 2 displays this XHTML document fragment as a Σ-tree. ∎

Recall that our task in this section was to devise a relational representation for an XHTML document tree. We assign a unique identifier (an integer value) to each node of the tree. Let $\mathcal{N}$ be the set of all node identifiers. This set can be partitioned into the set $\mathcal{N}_N$ of non-text node identifiers and the set $\mathcal{N}_T$ of text node identifiers. In what follows a node is identified by its unique identifier.

The structural component of an XHTML document tree can be represented using the following three relations:

i) $child \subseteq \mathcal{N}_N \times \mathcal{N}$ defined as $(child(P, C) = true) \Leftrightarrow (P$ is the parent of $C)$.
ii) $next \subseteq \mathcal{N} \times \mathcal{N}$ defined as $(next(L, N) = true) \Leftrightarrow (L$ is the left sibling of $N)$.
iii) $tag \subseteq \mathcal{N} \times \Sigma$ defined as $(tag(N, T) = true) \Leftrightarrow (T$ is the tag of node $N)$.

In order to be able to represent the content component of an XHTML document tree, we introduce two more sets: the set $\mathcal{S}$ of content elements, which are basically the strings attached to text elements and the values assigned to element attributes, and the set $\mathcal{A}$ of attributes. With these notations, the content

---
[1] http://www.hp.com

```
html( ...                          tag(0.html)
    table(                         tag(100, table)
                                                       child(100, 101)
        tr(...),                   tag(101, tr)
        tr(                        tag(102, tr)        child(100, 101)
                                                       child(100, 102)
            td(table(tr(td(text)))),   tag(103, tr)
            td(table(tr(td(text)))),   tag(107, td)    child(100, 103)
        ),                         tag(108, table)     child(101, 107)
        tr(                        tag(109, tr)        child(107, 108)
                                                       child(108, 109)
            td(table(tr(td(text)))),   tag(110, td)
            td(table(tr(td(text)))),   tag(111, text)  child(109, 110)
        ),                                             child(110, 111)
        tr(...),                   content(111,
        ...                          'Print speed, black' )  next(101, 102)
    )                                                  next(102, 103)
    ...                            attribute_value(108,     next(103, 104)
)                                    border,'0' )
```

Fig. 2. The structure of the XHTML fragment from figure 1 represented as a Σ-tree and a part of its relational representation

component of an XHTML document tree can be represented using the following two relations:

i) *content* $\subseteq \mathcal{N}_T \times \mathcal{S}$ defined as $(content(N, S) = true) \Leftrightarrow (S$ is the string contained by the text node N).

ii) *attribute_value* $\subseteq \mathcal{N}_N \times \mathcal{A} \times \mathcal{S}$ defined as $(attribute\_value(N, A, S) = true) \Leftrightarrow (S$ is the text value of the attribute A of the node N).

Example 2. The right panel of figure 2 displays a part of the relational representation of the XHTML document tree shown on the left panel. ∎

The relational representation of document trees introduced in this section makes convenient the definition of first-order IE rules. An IE rule defines a relation *extract* $\subseteq \mathcal{N}$ such that $(extract(N) = true) \Leftrightarrow (N$ is an extracted node). Usually, the extraction process is focused on text elements, so we can safely assume that *extract* $\subseteq \mathcal{N}_T$.

The definition of an IE rule consists of a set of clauses. The head of a clause is *extract(N)* and the body of a clause is a conjunction of positive and negative literals made of the relations *child*, *next*, and *tag* (*attribute_value* could be used as well to additionally check node attributes). The relation *content* can be used to find the actual content of the extracted nodes.

Example 3. Assuming that we want to extract all the text nodes of the XHTML document from figure 1 that have a grand-grand-parent of type *table* that has a parent that has a right sibling, we can use the following IE rule:

$$extract(A) \leftarrow$$
$$tag(A, text) \wedge child(B, A) \wedge child(C, B) \wedge child(D, C) \wedge tag(D, table) \wedge$$
$$child(E, D) \wedge next(E, F)$$

∎

Obviously, the manual writing of IE rules of this type is a slow and difficult process requiring a careful analysis of the structure of the target XHTML document. Fortunately, it is possible to learn first order IE rules with a general purpose relational learning program and this issue is the focus of the next section of the paper.

4   Using FOIL to Learn Extraction Rules

FOIL – First Order Inductive Learner is a general purpose first order (also known as relational) inductive learning program developed by John Ross Quinlan and his team at the beginning of the '90s ([12]). Even if it is not in the scope of the paper to give a detailed description of how FOIL works, we decided to give a brief overview of first order inductive learning in order to make the paper self contained. For more details see [12] and [9] (chapter 10).

In first order inductive learning the training data comprises the following two components:

i) The *target relation*, i.e. the relation that is learnt. It is defined extensionally as a set of tuples. Usually the tuples are partitioned into a set of positive tuples and a set of negative tuples.
ii) The *background relations*, usually defined extensionally as sets of tuples.

The goal of first order inductive learning is to construct a logic program that represents an appropriate intensional definition of the target relation in terms of the background relations and, optionally itself, if recursive definitions are allowed. The learnt definition must cover all the positive tuples (or a large fraction of them) and no negative tuples (or a small fraction of them) from its extensional definition.

FOIL requires as input the information about the target and the background relations, as mentioned above, and the definition of the relations arguments types, as sets of constants. FOIL's output is a set of clauses that represents a disjunctive definition of the target relation. The set of clauses is constructed iteratively, one clause at a time, removing all the covered positive tuples until an empty set remains. Every clause is constructed using an heuristic hill climbing search strategy that is guided by the information gain, determinate literals and the clause complexity (see [12] for details).

An important step in our IE experiments was to prepare the input for FOIL. In what follows we assume that during the training stage the user selects a single XHTML document – the training document, and performs a few extraction tasks on it. The problem is to map the training data into input for FOIL.

First, we must define the relations arguments types. We used a single type that represents the set $\mathcal{N}$ of all the nodes found in the training document.

Second, we must define the target relation *extract*. We used only the nodes extracted during the training stage from the training document, as the set of positive examples. FOIL uses the closed world assumption by considering all the other nodes in the training document as negative examples.

Third, we must define the background relations *next* and *tag*. For convenience, we have replaced the relation *tag* with a set of relations r_σ, for all $\sigma \in \Sigma$, defined as $r_\sigma = \{N | tag(N, \sigma) = true\}$.

Example 4. We consider a FOIL input example taken from our experiments. The input is split into the following sections: argument types (N), target relation (*extract*, only positive examples), and background relations (*child, next, table, ..., span*).

```
#N: 0,1,2,3,4, ..., 1096,1097.

extract(N)
1004
1006
...
1056
1058
.
*child(N,N)
0,1
0,2
1,3
1,4
...
1094,1097
.
*next(N,N)
1,2
3,4
...
1091,1092
.
*table(N)
26
27
...
991
.
...
*span(N)
250
251
...
980
.
```

∎

Additionally, FOIL can be parameterized from the command line. All the parameters have default values, but we found useful to control explicitly the following options:

i)   The use or not of negative literals in the body of a clause.
ii) The maximum variable depth in literals. Variables occurring in the clause head have depth 0 and a new variable in the literal has depth one greater than the maximum depth of its existing variables.
iii) And finally, to set the minimum clause accuracy to an appropriate value. The clause accuracy represents the percentage of the positive tuples from the set of all tuples covered by the relation. FOIL will not accept any clause with an accuracy lower than this value.

Example 5. This example shows a FOIL command-line used by our experiments.

```
foil -d8 -a40 -v3 <ex10.d >ex10.o
```

The parameter d8 is used for setting the maximum variable depth to 8. The parameter a40 is used for setting the minimum clause accuracy to 40 %. The parameter v3 is used to set the level of verbosity of FOIL's output to 3 (minimum is 0 and maximum is 4), i.e. the output will include quite detailed information about the FOIL's search process. The parameters ex10.d and ex10.o are the input and output files. ∎

5   Software Tools

We have developed a set of prototype software tools to support our experiments with rule learning for IE from HTML. The tool set implements the scenario outlined in section 2 with the restriction that the training stage is based on a single training document. The tool set incorporates the following on-the-shelf software components:

i)   The machine learning program FOIL. This component is called from the main program through a command line.
ii) The Xerces[2] library for XML processing. This component is used to read an XHTML document into a DOM tree. The DOM tree is then mapped onto the format required as input for FOIL using a breadth-first traversal.
iii) The Tidy[3] library for HTML document cleaning and pre-processing. This component is used in the pre-processing stage of HTML documents for converting them to XHTML. We have also developed a custom XSLT stylesheet to remove redundant HTML elements like *script* and *style*.

The development of a Java-based GUI shell for our set of tools is underway. It will support the user in performing the following operations: convert HTML files to XHTML, load an XHTML document for training, manually select with

---

[2] http://xml.apache.org/xerces2-j/index.html
[3] http://www.w3.org/People/Ragget/tidy/

the mouse some examples for extraction, generate the input for FOIL from the training document and the manually extracted information, run FOIL, visualize the learnt IE rules, convert the IE rules to XSLT, visualize the XSLT IE rules, run the XSLT IE rules on a target XHTML document and visualize the output.

6   Experimental Results

We ran a series of experiments of rule learning for IE from the Hewlett Packard's Web site. The task was to extract the printers feature values from their information sheets.

We selected an experimental set of 30 documents representing information sheets for HP printers. The printer information is represented in two column HTML tables (see figure 1). The feature values are stored in the second column. Each of the selected documents contains between 28 and 38 features.

We used training examples from a single document representing the information sheet of the HP Business Inkjet 2600 (C8109A) printer. This document contains 28 positive examples and a total of 1098 nodes. We performed learning experiments with 1, 2, 3, 4, 12, 24 and 28 positive examples selected from this set. The results of the learning stage were applied to all of the 30 documents, measuring the precision and recall indicators. These values were computed by averaging the precision and recall for each individual document.

The experiments were divided in two classes:

i) In the first class we have ignored the *next* relation as a background relation of FOIL's input.

ii) In the second class we have added the *next* relation to the set of background relations of FOIL's input.

In all the experiments we ignored the attribute information of HTML elements (i.e. the relation *attribute_value* introduced in section 3).

For each class of experiments we have varied explicitly the following parameters: the use or not of negated literals in rule bodies (FOIL parameter), the minimum clause accuracy (FOIL parameter), and the number of positive examples. We also set the maximum variable depth to 8 and used the closed world assumption to let FOIL generate the set of negative examples in all the experiments.

The results of the experiments in the first and second class are summarized in tables 1 and 2 respectively.

Example 6. This example shows the rule learnt for our printer data case in experiment 16 from table 2.

$extract(A) \leftarrow$
$child(B, A) \wedge tag(A, text) \wedge tag(B, td) \wedge \neg next(A, \_1) \wedge \neg next(\_1, A) \wedge$
$child(C, B) \wedge child(D, C) \wedge \neg next(\_1, C) \wedge child(E, D) \wedge child(F, E) \wedge$
$\neg next(F, \_1) \wedge \neg next(E, \_1)$

■

Table 1. Experiments without the use of the background relation *next*

Exper. no.	Neg. lit.	No. of pos. examples	Clause acc.	Precision	Recall
1	No	12	10 %	0.334	0.980
2	Yes	12	0 %	0.355	1
3	No	24	20 %	0.334	0.980
4	Yes	24	0 %	0.409	0.970
5	No	28	20 %, 30 %	0.334	0.980
6	Yes	28	0 %, 20 %	0.409	0.970

Table 2. Experiments with the use of the background relation *next*

Exper. no.	Neg. lit.	No. of pos. examples	Clause acc.	Precision	Recall
1	No	1	0 %	0.332	1
2	Yes	1	0 %	0.411	1
3	No	2	0 %	0.730	0.800
4	Yes	2	0 %	0.440	1
5	No	3	0 %, 5 %	0.698	1
6	Yes	3	0 %	0.440	1
7	No	4	0 %	0.332	1
8	No	4	10 %	0.730	0.800
9	Yes	4	0 %	0.448	1
10	No	12	20 %, 40 %	0.855	0.800
11	Yes	12	20 %	1	0.800
12	No	24	20 %	0.698	1
13	No	24	60 %	0.855	0.800
14	Yes	24	80 % (default)	1	0.800
15	No	28	80 % (default)	0.855	0.800
16	Yes	28	80 % (default)	1	1

Note that if X is an unbound variable and Y is a bound variable then $\neg next(X, Y) = true$ means that Y is instantiated with the first child node of its parent node. Therefore we can introduce the relation $first$ defined as $(first(X) = true) \Leftrightarrow (X$ is the first child node of its parent node) and replace $\neg next(X, Y)$ with $first(Y)$. Similarly, if X is a bound variable and Y is an unbound variable then $\neg next(X, Y) = true$ means that Y is instantiated with the last child node of its parent node. Therefore we can introduce the relation $last$ defined as $(last(X) = true) \Leftrightarrow (X$ is the last child node of its parent node) and replace $\neg next(X, Y)$ with $last(X)$.

Example 7. The rule from example 6 can be rewritten without negations:
$extract(A) \leftarrow$
    $child(B, A) \wedge tag(A, text) \wedge tag(B, td) \wedge last(A) \wedge first(A) \wedge child(C, B) \wedge$
    $child(D, C) \wedge first(C) \wedge child(E, D) \wedge child(F, E) \wedge last(F) \wedge last(E)$

Note that this rule can be easily mapped to the following XPath expression:

```
//*/*[position()=last()]/*[position()=last()]/*/*[position()=1]/
td/node()[last()=1]/self::text()
```

■

After a careful analysis of the results of our experiments, the following conclusions were drawn:

i) In all the experiments with the precision lower than 0.500 the learnt IE rule also extracted the feature name of every extracted feature value. This explains the low values of the precision in these experiments.

ii) The low precision values in the experiments of the first class clearly shows the importance of exploiting the information conveyed by the *next* relation for IE from tree structured documents.

iii) The use of negated literals in rule bodies improves significantly the precision of the IE rules in the case of using the *next* relation. But note that in all the experiments the use of ¬ could be replaced with predicates *last* and *first*.

iv) The learnt IE rules were able to extract all the feature values (i.r. recall was 1) even when for training was used a single positive example. This indicates a minimum user effort to manually extract a single item from the training document.

v) In the case when we used for training as positive examples all the fields that must be extracted from the training document and we allowed the presence of negated literals in rule bodies, the precision and recall were 1.

7 Related Work

With the rapid expansion of the Internet and the Web, the field of IE from IITML attracted a lot of researchers during the last decade. Clearly, it is impossible to mention all of their work here. However, at least two papers that are more closely related to the work reported in our paper, can be cited – [5] and [3].

Paper [5] describes the relational learner SRV that uses a FOIL-like algorithm for learning first order IE rules from a text document represented as a sequence of lexical tokens. The relations used in the rule bodies check various token features like: length, position in the text fragment, if they are numeric or capitalized, a.o. SRV has been adapted to learn IE rules from HTML. For this purpose new token features have been added to check the HTML context in which a token occurs. The most important similarity between SRV and our approach is the use of relational learning and a FOIL-like algorithm. The difference is that our approach has been explicitly devised to cope with tree structured documents, rather than string documents.

Paper [3] describes a generalization of the notion of string delimiters developed for IE from string documents ([7]) to subtree delimiters for IE from tree documents. The paper describes a special purpose learner that constructs a structure called candidate index based on trie data structures, which is very different from FOIL's approach. Note however that the tree leaf delimiters described in that paper are quite similar to our IE rules. Moreover, the representation of reverse paths using the symbols $Up(\uparrow)$, $Left(\leftarrow)$ and $Right(\rightarrow)$ can be easily simulated in our IE rules using the relations *child* and *next*.

8 Conclusions

This paper brings experimental evidence in support of the usefulness of first order rule induction for IE from HTML documents. As future research directions we would like to mention: i) the development of a GUI support for the IE approach outlined in this paper, in order to make it feasible for real users, ii) the investigation into the possibility of automatic translation of first order IE rules to XSLT or other XML query language and iii) experimenting with our approach in other application areas and for significantly larger collection of Web pages in order to asses its scalability and generality.

References

1. Bădică, C., Bădică, A., Liţoiu, V.: Enhancing WWW E-Commerce by Acquiring and Managing Product Knowledge. In: *Proceedings of TAINN'03*, vol.E-7, Çanakkale, Turkey (2003) 684–692.
2. Chakrabarti, S.: *Mining the Web. Discovering Knowledge from Hypertext Data.* Morgan Kaufmann Publishers, (2003).
3. Chidlovskii, B.: Information Extraction from Tree Documents by Learning Subtree Delimiters. In: *Proceedings of IJCAI-03 Workshop on Information Integration on the Web* (IIWeb-03), Acapulco, Mexico (2003), 3–8.
4. Fensel, D., Ding, Y., Omelayenko, B., Schulten, E., Botquin, G., Brown, M., Flet, A.: Product Data Integration. *IEEE Intelligent Systems*, Vol. 16, No.4, IEEE Computer Society (2001) 54–59.
5. Freitag, D.: Information extraction from HTML: application of a general machine learning approach. In: *Proceedings of AAAI'98*, (1998), 517–523.
6. Kosala, R., Bussche, J. van den, Bruynooghe, M., Blockeel, H.: Information Extraction in Structured Documents using Tree Automata Induction. In: *Principles of Data Mining and Knowledge Discovery, 6th European Conference*, Helsinki, Finland, LNAI 2431, (2002), 299–310.
7. Kushmerick, N.: Wrapper induction: Efficiency and expressiveness. *Artificial Intelligence*, No.118, Elsevier Science (2000), 15–68.
8. Lenhert, W., Sundheim, B.: A Performance Evaluation of Text-Analysis Technologies. In: *AI Magazine*, 12(3) (1991), 81–94.
9. Mitchell, T.M.: *Machine Learning*, McGraw-Hill, (1997).
10. Muşlea, I.: Extraction Patterns for Information Extraction Tasks: A Survey. In: *AAAI-99 Workshop on Machine Learning for Information Extraction*, (1999).
11. Neven, F.: Automata Theory for XML Researchers. *SIGMOD Record*, 31(3) (2002), 39–46.
12. Quinlan, J. R., Cameron-Jones, R. M.: Induction of Logic Programs: FOIL and Related Systems, *New Generation Computing*, 13, (1995), 287–312.

A Defeasible Logic Reasoner for the Semantic Web

Nick Bassiliades[1], Grigoris Antoniou[2], and Ioannis Vlahavas[1]

[1]Department of Informatics, Aristotle University of Thessaloniki
GR-54124 Thessaloniki, Greece
{nbassili, vlahavas}@csd.auth.gr
[2]Institute of Computer Science, FO.R.T.H.
P.O. Box 1385, GR-71110, Heraklion, Greece
antoniou@ics.forth.gr

Abstract. Defeasible reasoning is a rule-based approach for efficient reasoning with incomplete and inconsistent information. Such reasoning is, among others, useful for ontology integration, where conflicting information arises naturally; and for the modeling of business rules and policies, where rules with exceptions are often used. This paper describes these scenarios in more detail, and reports on the implementation of a system for defeasible reasoning on the Web. The system is called DR-DEVICE and is capable of reasoning about RDF metadata over multiple Web sources using defeasible logic rules. The system is implemented on top of CLIPS production rule system and builds upon R-DEVICE, an earlier deductive rule system over RDF metadata that also supports derived attribute and aggregate attribute rules. Rules can be expressed either in a native CLIPS-like language, or in an extension of the OO-RuleML syntax. The operational semantics of defeasible logic are implemented through compilation into the generic rule language of R-DEVICE. The paper also briefly presents a semantic web broker example for apartment renting.

1 Introduction

The development of the Semantic Web [16] proceeds in layers, each layer being on top of other layers. At present, the highest layer that has reached sufficient maturity is the ontology layer in the form of the description logic based languages of DAML+OIL [20] and OWL [37].

The next step in the development of the Semantic Web will be the logic and proof layers, and rule systems appear to lie in the mainstream of such activities. Moreover, rule systems can also be utilized in ontology languages. So, in general rule systems can play a twofold role in the Semantic Web initiative: (a) they can serve as extensions of, or alternatives to, description logic based ontology languages; and (b) they can be used to develop declarative systems on top of (using) ontologies. Reasons why rule systems are expected to play a key role in the further development of the Semantic Web include the following:

- Seen as subsets of predicate logic, monotonic rule systems (Horn logic) and description logics are orthogonal; thus they provide additional expressive power to ontology languages.

G. Antoniou and H. Boley (Eds.): RuleML 2004, LNCS 3323, pp. 49–64, 2004.

- Efficient reasoning support exists to support rule languages.
- Rules are well known in practice, and are reasonably well integrated in mainstream information technology.

Possible interactions between description logics and monotonic rule systems were studied in [26]. Based on that work and on previous work on hybrid reasoning [29] it appears that the best one can do at present is to take the intersection of the expressive power of Horn logic and description logics; one way to view this intersection is the Horn-definable subset of OWL.

This paper is devoted to a different problem, namely conflicts among rules. Here we just mention the main sources of such conflicts, which are further expanded in section 2. At the ontology layer: (a) default inheritance within ontologies, (b) ontology merging; and at the logic and reasoning layers: (a) rules with exceptions as a natural representation of business rules, (b) reasoning with incomplete information.

Defeasible reasoning is a simple rule-based approach to reasoning with incomplete and inconsistent information. It can represent facts, rules, and priorities among rules. This reasoning family comprises defeasible logics ([35], [6]) and Courteous Logic Programs [25]. The main advantage of this approach is the combination of two desirable features: enhanced representational capabilities allowing one to reason with incomplete and contradictory information, coupled with low computational complexity compared to mainstream nonmonotonic reasoning.

In this paper we report on the implementation of DR-DEVICE which is a defeasible reasoning system for the Semantic Web. The system's main concepts and design have been presented in [11]. The most important features of DR-DEVICE are the following:

- It supports multiple rule types of defeasible logic, such as strict rules, defeasible rules, and defeaters. Furthermore, it supports priorities among rules.
- Its user interface is compatible with RuleML [17], the main standardization effort for rules on the Semantic Web.
- It supports direct import from the Web of RDF ontologies and data as input facts to the defeasible logic program.
- It supports direct export to the Web of the results (conclusions) of the logic program as an RDF document.
- It is built on-top of a CLIPS-based implementation of deductive rules ([12], [13]). The core of the system consists of a translation of defeasible knowledge into a set of deductive rules, including derived and aggregate attributes. However, the implementation is declarative because it interprets the not operator using Well-Founded Semantics [22].

In the rest of this paper we detail on various motivating cases for using conflicting rules on the Semantic Web in section 2; in section 3 we briefly introduce the syntax and semantics of defeasible logics; in section 4 we present the architecture of the DR-DEVICE system, including a brief description of the R-DEVICE system which lies at the core. Section 5 describes the syntax of defeasible logic rules in DR-DEVICE and its RuleML syntax; Section 6 details the translation scheme from the defeasible logic rule language of DR-DEVICE into the deductive rule language of R-DEVICE; Section 7 presents a use case of a semantic web broker that reasons about apartment renting, using defeasible logic rules. Finally, section 8 briefly overviews related work and section 9 concludes this paper and poses future research directions.

2   Motivation for Conflicting Rules on the Semantic Web

Reasoning with Incomplete Information. In [3] a scenario is described where business rules have to deal with incomplete information: in the absence of certain information some assumptions have to be made which lead to conclusions not supported by classical predicate logic. In many applications on the Web such assumptions must be made because other players may not be able (e.g. due to communication problems) or willing (e.g. because of privacy or security concerns) to provide information. This is the classical case for the use of nonmonotonic knowledge representation and reasoning [33].

Rules with Exceptions. Rules with exceptions are a natural representation for policies and business rules [5]. And priority information is often implicitly or explicitly available to resolve conflicts among rules. Potential applications include security policies ([10], [30]), business rules [2], personalization, brokering, bargaining, and automated agent negotiations [23].

Default Inheritance in Ontologies. Default inheritance is a well-known feature of certain knowledge representation formalisms. Thus it may play a role in ontology languages, which currently do not support this feature. In [24] some ideas are presented for possible uses of default inheritance in ontologies. A natural way of representing default inheritance is rules with exceptions, plus priority information. Thus, nonmonotonic rule systems can be utilized in ontology languages.

Ontology Merging. When ontologies from different authors and/or sources are merged, contradictions arise naturally. Predicate logic based formalisms, including all current Semantic Web languages, cannot cope with inconsistencies. If rule-based ontology languages are used (e.g. DLP [26]) and if rules are interpreted as defeasible (that is, they may be prevented from being applied even if they can fire) then we arrive at nonmonotonic rule systems. A skeptical approach, as adopted by defeasible reasoning, is sensible because it does not allow for contradictory conclusions to be drawn. Moreover, priorities may be used to resolve some conflicts among rules, based on knowledge about the reliability of sources or on user input). Thus, nonmonotonic rule systems can support ontology integration.

3   Defeasible Logics

The basic characteristics of defeasible logics are:
- Defeasible logics are rule-based, without disjunction.
- Classical negation is used in the heads and bodies of rules, but negation-as-failure is not used in the object language (it can easily be simulated, if necessary [6], [9]).
- Rules may support conflicting conclusions.
- The logics are skeptical in the sense that conflicting rules do not fire. Thus consistency is preserved.
- Priorities on rules may be used to resolve some conflicts among rules.
- The logics take a pragmatic view and have low computational complexity.

A *defeasible theory* D is a couple $(R,>)$ where R a finite set of rules, and $>$ a superiority relation on R. In expressing the proof theory we consider only propositional rules. Rules containing free variables are interpreted as the set of their variable-free instances.

There are three kinds of rules: *Strict rules* are denoted by $A \rightarrow p$, and are interpreted in the classical sense: whenever the premises are indisputable then so is the conclusion. An example of a strict rule is "Professors are faculty members". Written formally: `professor(X)` $\rightarrow$ `faculty(X)`. Inference from strict rules only is called *definite inference*. Strict rules are intended to define relationships that are definitional in nature, for example ontological knowledge.

Defeasible rules are denoted by $A \Rightarrow p$, and can be defeated by contrary evidence. An example of such a rule is `faculty(X)` $\Rightarrow$ `tenured(X)` which reads as follows: "Professors are typically tenured".

Defeaters are denoted as $A \leadsto p$ and are used only to prevent some conclusions, not to actively support conclusions. An example of such a defeater is `assistant-Prof(X)` $\leadsto$ `¬tenured(X)` which reads as follows: "Assistant professors may be not tenured".

A *superiority relation* on R is an acyclic relation > on R (that is, the transitive closure of > is irreflexive). When $r_1 > r_2$, then r_1 is called *superior* to r_2, and r_2 *inferior* to r_1. This expresses that r_1 may override r_2. For example, given the defeasible rules

```
r:  professor(X) =>  tenured(X)
r': visiting(X)  =>  ¬tenured(X)
```

which contradict one another, no conclusive decision can be made about whether a visiting professor is tenured. But if we introduce a superiority relation > with r' > r, then we can indeed conclude that a visiting professor is not tenured.

A formal definition of the proof theory is found in [6]. A model theoretic semantics is found in [31].

4   DR-DEVICE System Architecture

The DR-DEVICE system consists of two major components (Fig. 1): the RDF loader/translator and the rule loader/translator. The former accepts from the latter (or the user) requests for loading specific RDF documents. The RDF triple loader downloads the RDF document from the Internet and uses the ARP parser [34] to translate it to triples in the N-triple format. Both the RDF/XML and N-triple files are stored locally for future reference. Furthermore, the RDF document is recursively scanned for namespaces which are also parsed using the ARP parser. The rationale for translating namespaces is to obtain a complete RDF Schema in order to minimize the number of OO schema redefinitions. Fetching multiple RDF schema files will aggregate multiple RDF-to-OO schema translations into a single OO schema redefinition. Namespace resolution is not guaranteed to yield an RDF schema document; therefore, if the namespace URI is not an RDF document, then the ARP parser will not produce triples and DR-DEVICE will make assumptions, based on the RDF semantics [28], about non-resolved properties, resources, classes, etc.

All N-triples are loaded into memory, while the resources that have a `URI#anchorID` or `URI/anchorID` format are transformed into a `ns:anchorID` format if URI belongs to the initially collected namespaces, in order to save memory space. The transformed RDF triples are fed to the RDF triple translator which maps them into COOL objects and then deletes them.

The rule loader accepts from the user a URI (or a local file name) that contains a defeasible logic rule program in RuleML notation [17]. The RuleML document may also contain the URI of the input RDF document on which the rule program will run, which is forwarded to the RDF loader. The RuleML program is translated into the native DR-DEVICE rule notation using the Xalan XSLT processor [38] and an XSLT stylesheet. The DR-DEVICE rule program is then forwarded to the rule translator.

The rule translator accepts from the rule loader (or directly from the user) a set of rules in DR-DEVICE notation and translates them into a set of CLIPS production rules. The translation of the defeasible logic rules is performed in two steps: first, the defeasible logic rules are translated into sets of deductive, derived attribute and aggregate attribute rules of the basic R-DEVICE rule language (section 6), and then, all these rules are translated into CLIPS production rules. All compiled rule formats are kept into local files, so that the next time they are needed they can be directly loaded, increasing speed. When the translation ends, CLIPS runs the production rules and generates the objects that constitute the result of the initial rule program or query. Finally, the result-objects are exported to the user as an RDF/XML document through the RDF extractor.

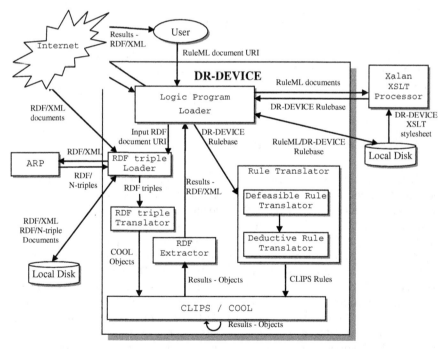

Fig. 1. Architecture of the DR-DEVICE system.

The R-DEVICE system is a deductive object-oriented knowledge base system, which transforms RDF triples into objects [12] and uses a deductive rule language [13] for querying and reasoning about them. R-DEVICE imports RDF data into the CLIPS production rule system [19] as COOL objects. The main difference between the established RDF triple-based data model and our OO model is that we treat properties both as first-class objects and as normal encapsulated attributes of resource objects. In this way properties of resources are not scattered across several triples as in most other RDF querying/inferencing systems, resulting in increased query performance due to less joins. The main features of this mapping scheme are the following:

- Resource *classes* are represented both as COOL classes and as direct or indirect instances of the `rdfs:Class` class. This binary representation is due to the fact that COOL does not support meta-classes.
- All *resources* are represented as COOL objects, direct or indirect instances of the `rdfs:Resource` class.
- Finally, *properties* are instances of the class `rdf:Property`. Furthermore, properties are defined as slots (attributes) of their domain class(es). The values of properties are stored inside resource objects as slot values.

The descriptive semantics of RDF data may call for dynamic redefinitions of the OO schema, which are effectively handled by R-DEVICE. One example for such a redefinition is when a new property is defined for an existing class.

Furthermore, R-DEVICE features a powerful deductive rule language which is able to express complex inferences both on the RDF schema and data, including recursion, stratified negation, ground and generalized path expressions over the objects, derived attributes and aggregate, grouping, and sorting functions, mainly due to the second-order syntax of the rule language which is efficiently translated into sets of first-order logic rules using metadata. R-DEVICE rules define views which are materialized and, optionally, incrementally maintained. Finally, users can use and define functions using the CLIPS host language. R-DEVICE belongs to a family of previous such deductive object-oriented rule languages ([15], [14]). Deductive rules are implemented as CLIPS production rules and their syntax is a variation of the CLIPS syntax. Examples of rules can be found in the next section, as well as in [36].

5   The Syntax of the Rule Language of DR-DEVICE

There are three types of rules in DR-DEVICE, closely reflecting defeasible logic: strict rules, defeasible rules, and defeaters. Rule type is declared with keywords `strictrule`, `defeasiblerule`, and `defeater`, respectively. For example, the following rule construct represents the defeasible rule `r4: bird(X) => flies(X)`.

```
(defeasiblerule r4
  (bird (name ?X))
=>
  (flies (name ?X)))
```

Predicates have named arguments, called slots, since they represent CLIPS objects. DR-DEVICE has also a RuleML-like syntax [17]. The same rule is represented in RuleML notation (version 0.85) as follows:

```
<imp>
  <_rlab ruleID="r4" ruletype="defeasiblerule"><ind>r4</ind></_rlab>
  <_head>   <atom>    <_opr><rel>bird</rel></_opr>
                      <_slot name="name"><var>X</var></_slot>
            </atom>
  </_head>
  <_body>   <atom>    <_opr><rel href="flies"/></_opr>
                      <_slot name="name"><var>X</var></_slot>
            </atom>
  </_body>
</imp>
```

We have tried to re-use as many features of RuleML syntax as possible. However, several features of the DR-DEVICE rule language could not be captured by the existing RuleML DTDs (0.85[1]); therefore, we have developed a new DTD (Fig. 2) using the modularization scheme of RuleML, extending the Datalog with strong negation DTD. For example, rules have a unique (ID) ruleID attribute in their _rlab element, so that superiority of one rule over the other can be expressed through an IDREF attribute of the superior rule. For example, the following rule r5 is superior to rule r4 that has been presented above.

```
(defeasiblerule r5
  (declare (superior r4))
  (penguin (name ?X))
 =>
  (not (flies (name ?X))))
```

In RuleML notation, there is a superiority attribute in the rule label.

```
<imp>
  <_rlab ruleID="r5" ruletype="defeasiblerule" superior="r4">
    <ind>r5</ind>
  </_rlab>
...
</imp>
```

```
<!ENTITY % LABELs "IDREFS">                  <!ENTITY % CLASSes "NMTOKENS">
<!ATTLIST _rlab     ruleID ID #REQUIRED
                    ruletype (strictrule | defeasiblerule | defeater) #REQUIRED
                    superior %LABELs; #IMPLIED>
<!ENTITY % _calc.cont "(function+)">         <!ELEMENT calc %_calc.cont;>
<!ENTITY % _head.content " (calc?, (atom | neg))">
<!ENTITY % _body.content "(atom | neg | and | or)">
<!ENTITY % _fname.cont "(#PCDATA)">          <!ELEMENT fname %_fname.cont;>
<!ENTITY % pos_term "(ind | var | function)">
<!ELEMENT function (fname, (%pos_term;)*)>
<!ENTITY % term "(_not | %pos_term;)">
<!ELEMENT _not (ind | var)>
<!ELEMENT _or (%term;, (%term;)+)>      <!ELEMENT _and (%term;, (%term;)+)>
<!ENTITY % constraint "(_not | _or | _and)">
<!ENTITY % _slot.content "(ind | var | %constraint;)">
<!ENTITY % negurdatalog_include SYSTEM
                    " http://www.ruleml.org/0.85/dtd/neg/negurdatalog.dtd">
%negurdatalog_include;
<!ATTLIST rulebase   rdf_import CDATA #IMPLIED
                     rdf_export_classes %CLASSes; #IMPLIED
                     rdf_export CDATA #IMPLIED>
```

Fig. 2. DTD for the RuleML syntax of the DR-DEVICE rule language.

***

[1] In the future we will upgrade to newer XSD-based versions of RuleML (e.g. 0.87).

Classes and objects (facts) can also be declared in DR-DEVICE; however, the focus in this paper is the use of RDF data as facts. The input RDF file(s) are declared in the `rdf_import` attribute of the `rulebase` (root) element of the RuleML document. There exist two more attributes in the `rulebase` element: the `rdf_export` attribute that declares the address of the RDF file with the results of the rule program to be exported, and the `rdf_export_classes` attribute that declares the derived classes whose instances will be exported in RDF/XML format. Further extensions to the RuleML syntax, include function calls that are used either as constraints in the rule body or as new value calculators at the rule head. Furthermore, multiple constraints in the rule body can be expressed through the logical operators: `_not`, `_and`, `_or`. Examples of all these can be found in the section 7 (Fig. 6, Fig. 7).

6   The Translation of DR-DEVICE Rules into R-DEVICE Rules

The translation of defeasible rules into R-DEVICE rules is based on the translation of defeasible theories into logic programs through the well-studied meta-program of [7]. However, instead of directly using the meta-rpogram at run-time, we have used it to guide defeasible rule compilation. Therefore, at run-time only first-order rules exist.

Before going into the details of the translation we briefly present the auxiliary system attributes (in addition to the user-defined attributes) that each defeasibly derived object in DR-DEVICE has in order to support our translation scheme:

- `pos`, `neg`: These numerical slots hold the proof status of the defeasible object. A value of 1 at the `pos` slot denotes that the object has been defeasibly proven; whereas 2 denotes definite proof. Equivalent `neg` slot values denote an equivalent proof status for the negation of the defeasible object. A 0 value for both slots denotes that there has been no proof for either the positive or the negative conclusion.
- `pos-sup`, `neg-sup`: These attributes hold the rule ids of the rules that can *potentially* prove positively or negatively the object.
- `pos-over`, `neg-over`: These attributes hold the rule ids of the rules that have overruled the positive or the negative proof of the defeasible object. For example, in the rules r4 and r5 that were presented above, rule r5 has a negative conclusion that overrides the positive conclusion of rule r4. Therefore, if the condition of rule r5 is satisfied then its rule id is stored at the `pos-over` slot of the corresponding derived object.
- `pos-def`, `neg-def`: These attributes hold the rule ids of the rules that can defeat overriding rules when the former are superior to the latter. For example, rule r5 is superior to rule r4. Therefore, if the condition of rule r5 is satisfied then its rule id is stored at the `neg-def` slot of the corresponding derived object along with the rule id of the defeated rule r4. Then, even if the condition of rule r4 is satisfied, it cannot overrule the negative conclusion derived by rule r5 (as it is suggested by the previous paragraph) because it has been defeated by a superior rule.

Each *defeasible rule* in DR-DEVICE is translated into a set of 5 R-DEVICE rules:

- A *deductive* rule that generates the derived defeasible object when the condition of the defeasible rule is met. The proof status slots of the derived objects are initially set to 0. For example, for rule r5 the following deductive rule is generated:

```
(deductiverule r5-deductive
  (penguin (name ?X))
 =>
  (flies (name ?X) (pos 0) (neg 0)))
```

Rule r5-deductive states that if an object of class penguin with slot name equal to ?X exists, then create a new object of class flies with a slot name with value ?X. The derivation status of the new object (according to defeasible logic) is unknown since both its positive and negative truth status slots are set to 0. Notice that if a flies object already exists with the same name, it is not created again. This is ensured by the value-based semantics of the R-DEVICE deductive rules.

- An aggregate attribute "*support*" rule that stores in -sup slots the rule ids of the rules that can potentially prove positively or negatively the object. For example, for rule r5 the following "support" rule is generated (list is an aggregate function that just collects values in a list):

```
(aggregateattrule r5-sup
  (penguin (name ?X))
  ?gen23 <- (flies (name ?X))
 =>
  ?gen23 <- (flies (neg-sup (list r5))))
```

Rule r5-sup states that if there is a penguin object named ?X, and there is a flies object with the same name, then derive that rule r5 could potentially support the defeasible negation of the flies object (slot neg-sup).

- A derived attribute "*defeasibly*" rule that defeasibly proves either positively or negatively an object by storing the value of 1 in the pos or neg slots, if the rule condition has been at least defeasibly proven, if the opposite conclusion has not been definitely proven and if the rule has not been overruled by another rule. For example, for rule r5 the following "defeasibly" rule is generated:

```
(derivedattrule r5-defeasibly
  (penguin (name ?X) (pos ?gen29&:(>= ?gen29 1)))
  ?gen23 <- (flies (name ?X) (pos ~2)
                   (neg-over $?gen25&:(not (member$ r5 $?gen25))))
 =>
  ?gen23 <- (flies (neg 1)))
```

Rule r5-defeasibly states that if it has been defeasibly proven that a penguin object named ?X exists, and there is a flies object with the same name that is not already strictly-positively proven and rule r5 has not been overruled (check slot neg-over), then derive that the flies object is defeasibly-negatively proven.

- A derived attribute "*overruled*" rule that stores in -over slots the rule id of the rule that has overruled the positive or the negative proof of the defeasible object, along with the ids of the rules that support the opposite conclusion, if the rule condition has been at least defeasibly proven, and if the rule has not been defeated by a superior rule. For example, for rule r4 the following "overruled" rule is generated (through calc expressions, arbitrary user-defined calculations are performed):

```
(derivedattrule r4-over
  (bird (name ?X) (pos ?gen22&:(>= ?gen22 1)))
  ?gen16 <- (flies (name ?X) (neg-sup $?gen19) (neg-over $?gen20)
                   (pos-def $?gen18&:(not (member$ r4 $?gen18)))))
=>
  (calc (bind $?gen21 (create$ r4-over $?gen19 $?gen20)))
  ?gen16 <- (flies (neg-over $?gen21)))
```

Rule r4-over actually overrules all rules that can support the negative derivation of flies, including rule r5. Specifically, it states that if it has been defeasibly proven that a bird object named ?X exists, and there is a flies object with the same name that its negation can be potentially supported by rules in the slot neg-sup, then derive that rule r4-over overruled those "negative supporters" (slot neg-over), unless it has been defeated (check slot pos-def).

- A derived attribute "*defeated*" rule that stores in -def slots the rule id of the rule that has defeated overriding rules (along with the defeated rule ids) when the former is superior to the latter, if the rule condition has been at least defeasibly proven. A "defeated" rule is generated only for rules that have a superiority relation, i.e. they are superior to others. For example, for rule r5 the following "defeated" rule is generated:

```
(derivedattrule r5-def
  (penguin (name ?X) (pos ?gen29&:(>= ?gen29 1)))
  ?gen23 <- (flies (name ?X) (pos-def $?gen26))
=>
  (calc (bind $?gen25 (create$ r5-def r4 $?gen26)))
  ?gen23 <- (flies (pos-def $?gen25)))
```

Rule r5-def actually defeats rule r4, since r5 is superior to r4. Specifically, it states that if it has been defeasibly proven that a penguin object named ?X exists, and there is a flies object with the same name then derive that rule r5-def defeats rule r4 (slot pos-def).

Strict rules are handled in the same way as defeasible rules, with an addition of a derived attribute rule (called *definitely* rule) that definitely proves either positively or negatively an object by storing the value of 2 in the pos or neg slots, if the condition of the strict rule has been definitely proven, and if the opposite conclusion has not been definitely proven. For example, for the strict rule r3: penguin(X) → bird(X), the following "definitely" rule is generated:

```
(derivedattrule r3-definitely
  (penguin (name ?X) (pos 2))
  ?gen9 <- (bird (name ?X) (pos ~2))
  =>
  ?gen9 <- (bird (pos 2)))
```

Defeaters are much weaker rules that can only overrule a conclusion. Therefore, for a defeater only the "overruled" rule is created, along with a deductive rule to allow the creation of derived objects, even if their proof status cannot be supported by defeaters.

Execution Order. The order of execution of all the above rule types is as follows: "deductive", "support", "definitely", "defeated", "overruled", "defeasibly". Moreover, rule priority for stratified defeasible rule programs is determined by stratification. Finally, for non-stratified rule programs rule execution order is not determined. However, in order to ensure the correct result according to the defeasible logic theory for each derived attribute rule of the rule types "definitely", "defeated", "overruled" and "defeasibly" there is an opposite "truth maintenance" derived attribute rule that un-does (retracts) the conclusion when the condition is no longer met. In this way, even if rules are not executed in the correct order, the correct result will be eventually de-duced because conclusions of rules that should have not been executed can be later undone. For example, the following rule undoes the "defeasibly" rule of rule r5 when either the condition of the defeasible rule is no longer defeasibly satisfied, or the op-posite conclusion has been definitely proven, or if rule r5 has been overruled.

```
(derivedattrule r5-defeasibly-dot
   ?gen23 <- (flies (name ?X) (neg 1) (neg-sup $? r5 $?))
   (not (and (penguin (name ?X) (pos ?gen29&:(>= ?gen29 1)))
     ?gen23 <- (flies (pos ~2) (neg-over $?g&:(not (member$ r5 $?g)))))))
   =>
   ?gen23 <- (flies (neg 0)))
```

DR-DEVICE has been extensively tested for correctness using a tool that generates scalable test defeasible logic theories that comes with Deimos, a query answering de-feasible logic system [32].

7 A Brokered Trade Example

In this section we present a full example of using DR-DEVICE rules in a brokered trade application that takes place via an independent third party, the broker. The bro-ker matches the buyer's requirements and the sellers' capabilities, and proposes a transaction when both parties can be satisfied by the trade. In our case, the concrete application (which has been adopted from [8]) is apartment renting and the landlord takes the role of the abstract seller.

Available apartments reside in an RDF document (Fig. 4). The requirements of a potential renter, called e.g. Carlo, are shown in Fig. 3. These requirements are ex-pressed in DR-DEVICE's defeasible logic rule language as shown in Fig. 5 (in native CLIPS-like syntax). Rule r2 covers one of the first set of requirements in Fig. 3, rules r7 and r9 represent requirements from the second set and rule r10, from the third. Rule r7 is shown in Fig. 6 in the RuleML-like syntax of DR-DEVICE. Things to no-tice here is the expression of complex constraints on the value of a slot based on functions calls and logical operators, and the calculation of the values of the slots in the rule head, through again the use of function calls, which are directly expressed in XML.

After the rule document in Fig. 6 is loaded into DR-DEVICE, it is transformed into the native DR-DEVICE syntax (Fig. 5). DR-DEVICE rules are further translated into R-DEVICE rules, as presented in the previous section, which in turn are translated into CLIPS production rules. Then the RDF document(s) of Fig. 4 is loaded and trans-formed into CLIPS (COOL) objects. Finally, the reasoning can begin, which ends up with 3 acceptable apartments and one suggested apartment for renting, according to Carlo's requirements and the available apartments [8].

1. *Carlos is looking for an apartment of at least 45m² with at least 2 bedrooms. If it is on the 3rd floor or higher, the house must have an elevator. Also, pet animals must be allowed.*
2. *Carlos is willing to pay $300 for a centrally located 45m² apartment, and $250 for a similar flat in the suburbs. In addition, he is willing to pay an extra $5 per m² for a larger apartment, and $2 per m² for a garden.*
3. *He is unable to pay more than $400 in total. If given the choice, he would go for the cheapest option. His 2nd priority is the presence of a garden; lowest priority is additional space.*

Fig. 3. Verbal description of Carlo's (a potential renter) requirements.

```
<!DOCTYPE rdf:RDF [...<!ENTITY carlo "http://.../dr-device/carlo/carlo.rdf#">
]>
<rdf:RDF ... xmlns:carlo="&carlo;">
 <carlo:apartment rdf:about="&carlo;a1">
    <carlo:bedrooms rdf:datatype="&xsd;integer">1</carlo:bedrooms>
    <carlo:central>yes</carlo:central>
    <carlo:floor rdf:datatype="&xsd;integer">1</carlo:floor>
    <carlo:gardenSize rdf:datatype="&xsd;integer">0</carlo:gardenSize>
    <carlo:lift>no</carlo:lift>
    <carlo:name>a1</carlo:name>
    <carlo:pets>yes</carlo:pets>
    <carlo:price rdf:datatype="&xsd;integer">300</carlo:price>
    <carlo:size rdf:datatype="&xsd;integer">50</carlo:size>
 </carlo:apartment>
 ...
</rdf:RDF>
```

Fig. 4. RDF document for available apartments

```
 (import-rdf "http://.../dr-device/carlo/carlo.rdf")
 (export-rdf "http://.../dr-device/carlo/export-carlo.rdf" acceptable rent)
...
(defeasiblerule r2
 (declare (superior r1))
 (carlo:apartment (carlo:name ?x) (carlo:bedrooms  ?y&:(< ?y 2)))
 =>
 (not (acceptable (apartment ?x))))
...
(defeasiblerule r7
 (carlo:apartment (carlo:name ?x) (carlo:size ?y&:(>= ?y 45))
                  (carlo:gardenSize ?z) (carlo:central "yes"))
 =>
 (calc (bind ?a (+ 300 (* 2 ?z) (* 5 (- ?y 45)))))
 (offer (apartment ?x) (amount ?a)))
...
(defeasiblerule r9
 (declare (superior r1))
 (offer (apartment ?x) (amount ?y))
 (carlo:apartment (carlo:name ?x) (carlo:price ?z&:(< ?y ?z)))
 =>
 (not (acceptable (apartment ?x))))
...
(defeasiblerule r10
 (cheapest (apartment ?x))
 =>
 (rent (apartment ?x)))
...
```

Fig. 5. Part of Carlo's requirements in native (CLIPS-like) DR-DEVICE syntax

```
<!DOCTYPE rulebase SYSTEM "http://.../dr-device/defeasible-dr-device.dtd">
<rulebase rdf_import="http://.../dr-device/carlo/carlo.rdf#"
          rdf_export_classes="acceptable rent"
          rdf_export="http://.../dr-device/carlo/export-carlo.rdf">
 <_rbaselab><ind type="defeasible">carlo-rules</ind></_rbaselab>
 ...
<imp>
    <_rlab><ind type="defeasiblerule">r7</ind></_rlab>
    <_head> <calc><function><fname>bind</fname>
                         <var>a</var>
                         <function><fname>+</fname>
                                   <ind>300</ind>
                                   <function><fname>*</fname>
                                             <ind>2</ind>
                                             <var>z</var>
                                   </function>
                                   <function><fname>*</fname>
                                             <ind>5</ind>
                                             <function><fname>-</fname>
                                                       <var>y</var>
                                                       <ind>45</ind>
                                             </function>
                                   </function>
                         </function>
                </function>
            </calc>
            <atom>  <_opr><rel>offer</rel></_opr>
                    <_slot name="apartment"><var>x</var></_slot>
                    <_slot name="amount"><var>a</var></_slot>
            </atom>
    </_head>
    <_body><atom><_opr><rel href="carlo:apartment"/></_opr>
                <_slot name="carlo:name"><var>x</var></_slot>
                <_slot name="carlo:size"><_and><var>y</var>
                                              <function><fname>>=</fname>
                                                        <var>y</var>
                                                        <ind>45</ind>
                                              </function>
                                         </_and>
                </_slot>
                <_slot name="carlo:gardenSize"><var>z</var></_slot>
                <_slot name="carlo:central"><ind>"yes"</ind></_slot>
            </atom>
    </_body>
 </imp>
 ...
</rulebase>
```

Fig. 6. Part of Carlo's requirements in RuleML-like DR-DEVICE syntax

```
<!DOCTYPE rdf:RDF [ ...
    <!ENTITY dr-device "http://.../dr-device/export/export-carlo.rdf#"> ]>
<rdf:RDF ... xmlns:dr-device='&dr-device;'>
...
 <dr-device:acceptable rdf:about="&dr-device;acceptable2">
    <dr-device:apartment>a2</dr-device:apartment>
    <dr-device:truthStatus>defeasibly-not-proven</dr-device:truthStatus>
 </dr-device:acceptable>
...
 <dr-device:rent rdf:about="&dr-device;rent1">
    <dr-device:apartment>a5</dr-device:apartment>
    <dr-device:truthStatus>defeasibly-proven</dr-device:truthStatus>
 </dr-device:rent>
...
</rdf:RDF>
```

Fig. 7. Results of defeasible reasoning exported as an RDF document

The results (i.e. objects of derived classes) are exported in an RDF file according to the specifications posed in the RuleML document (Fig. 6). Fig. 7 shows an example of the result exported for class `acceptable` (acceptable or not apartments) and class `rent` (suggestions to rent a house or not). Notice that both the positively and negatively proven (defeasibly or definitely) objects are exported. Objects that cannot be at least defeasibly proven, either negatively or positively, are not exported, although they exist inside DR-DEVICE. Furthermore, the RDF schema of the derived classes is also exported.

8   Related Work

There exist several previous implementations of defeasible logics. In [21] the historically first implementation, D-Prolog, a Prolog-based implementation is given. It was not declarative in certain aspects (because it did not use a declarative semantic for the not operator), therefore it did not correspond fully to the abstract definition of the logic. Finally it did not provide any means of integration with Semantic Web layers and concepts.

Deimos [32] is a flexible, query processing system based on Haskell. It does not integrate with Semantic Web (for example, there is no way to treat RDF data; nor does it use an XML-based or RDF-based syntax). Thus it is an isolated solution.

Delores [32] is another implementation, which computes all conclusions from a defeasible theory (the only system of its kind known to us). It is very efficient, exhibiting linear computational complexity. However, it does not integrate with other Semantic Web languages and systems.

Another Prolog-based implementation of defeasible logics is in [4], which places emphasis on completeness (covering full defeasible logic) and flexibility (covering all important variants). However, at present it lacks the ability of processing RDF data.

SweetJess [27] is another implementation of a defeasible reasoning system (situated courteous logic programs) based on Jess. It integrates well with RuleML. However, SweetJess rules can only express reasoning over ontologies expressed in DAMLRuleML (a DAML-OIL like syntax of RuleML) and not on arbitrary RDF data, like DR-DEVICE. Furthermore, SweetJess is restricted to simple terms (variables and atoms). This applies to DR-DEVICE to a large extent. However, the basic R-DEVICE language [12] can support a limited form of functions in the following sense: (a) path expressions are allowed in the rule condition, which can be seen as complex functions, where allowed function names are object referencing slots; (b) aggregate and sorting functions are allowed in the conclusion of aggregate rules. Finally, DR-DEVICE can also support conclusions in non-stratified rule programs due to the presence of truth-maintenance rules (section 6).

9   Conclusions and Future Work

In this paper we described reasons why conflicts among rules arise naturally on the Semantic Web. To address this problem, we proposed to use defeasible reasoning which is known from the area of knowledge representation. And we reported on the implementation of a system for defeasible reasoning on the Web. It is based on CLIPS production rules, and supports RuleML syntax.

Currently, we are working on extending the rule language with support for negation-as-failure in addition to classical (strong) negation and support for conflicting literals, i.e. derived objects that exclude each other.

Planned future work includes:

- Implementing load/upload functionality in conjunction with an RDF repository, such as RDF Suite [1] and Sesame [18].
- Developing a visual editor for the RuleML-like rule language.
- Deploying the reasoning system as a Web Service.
- Study in more detail integration of defeasible reasoning with description logic based ontologies. Starting point of this investigation will be the Horn definable part of OWL [26].
- Applications of defeasible reasoning and the developed implementation for brokering, bargaining, automated agent negotiation, and personalization.

References

[1] Alexaki S., Christophides V., Karvounarakis G., Plexousakis D. and Tolle K., "The ICS-FORTH RDFSuite: Managing Voluminous RDF Description Bases", *Proc. 2nd Int. Workshop on the Semantic Web*, Hong-Kong, 2001.

[2] Antoniou G. and Arief M., "Executable Declarative Business rules and their use in Electronic Commerce", *Proc. ACM Symposium on Applied Computing*, 2002.

[3] Antoniou G., "Nonmonotonic Rule Systems on Top of Ontology Layers", *Proc. 1st Int. Semantic Web Conference*, Springer, LNCS 2342, pp. 394-398, 2002.

[4] Antoniou G., Bikakis A., "A System for Nonmonotonic Rules on the Web", *Submitted*, 2004.

[5] Antoniou G., Billington D. and Maher M.J., "On the analysis of regulations using defeasible rules", *Proc. 32nd Hawaii International Conference on Systems Science*, 1999.

[6] Antoniou G., Billington D., Governatori G. and Maher M.J., "Representation results for defeasible logic", *ACM Trans. on Computational Logic*, 2(2), 2001, pp. 255-287.

[7] Antoniou G., Billington D., Governatori G., Maher M.J, "A Flexible Framework for Defeasible Logics", *Proc. AAAI/IAAI 2000*, AAAI/MIT Press, pp. 405-410.

[8] Antoniou G., Harmelen F. van, *A Semantic Web Primer*, MIT Press, 2004.

[9] Antoniou G., Maher M. J., Billington D., "Defeasible Logic versus Logic Programming without Negation as Failure", *Journal of Logic Programming*, 41(1), 2000, pp. 45-57.

[10] Ashri R., Payne T., Marvin D., Surridge M. and Taylor S., "Towards a Semantic Web Security Infrastructure", *Proc. of Semantic Web Services*, 2004 Spring Symposium Series, Stanford University, California, 2004.

[11] Bassiliades N., Antoniou G. and Vlahavas I., "DR-DEVICE: A Defeasible Logic System for the Semantic Web", *Proc. 2nd Workshop on Principles and Practice of Semantic Web Reasoning (PPSWR04)*, LNCS 3208, Springer-Verlag, 2004.

[12] Bassiliades N., Vlahavas I., "Capturing RDF Descriptive Semantics in an Object Oriented Knowledge Base System", *Proc. 12th Int. WWW Conf. (WWW2003)*, Budapest, 2003.

[13] Bassiliades N., Vlahavas I., "R-DEVICE: A Deductive RDF Rule Language", accepted for presentation at *Workshop on Rules and Rule Markup Languages for the Semantic Web (RuleML 2004)*, Hiroshima, Japan, 8 Nov. 2004.

[14] Bassiliades N., Vlahavas I., and Sampson D., "Using Logic for Querying XML Data", *Web-Powered Databases*, Ch. 1, pp. 1-35, Idea-Group Publishing, 2003.

[15] Bassiliades N., Vlahavas I., Elmagarmid A.K., "E-DEVICE: An extensible active knowledge base system with multiple rule type support", *IEEE TKDE*, 12(5), pp. 824-844, 2000.

[16] Berners-Lee T., Hendler J., and Lassila O., "The Semantic Web", *Scientific American*, 284(5), 2001, pp. 34-43.

[17] Boley H., Tabet S., *The Rule Markup Initiative*, www.ruleml.org/

[18] Broekstra J., Kampman A. and Harmelen F. van, "Sesame: An Architecture for Storing and Querying RDF Data and Schema Information", *Spinning the Semantic Web*, Fensel D., Hendler J. A., Lieberman H. and Wahlster W., (Eds.), MIT Press, pp. 197-222, 2003.

[19] *CLIPS Basic Programming Guide* (v. 6.21), www.ghg.net/clips/CLIPS.html

[20] Connolly D., Harmelen F. van, Horrocks I., McGuinness D.L., Patel-Schneider P.F., Stein L.A., DAML+OIL Reference Description, 2001, www.w3c.org/TR/daml+oil-reference

[21] Covington M.A., Nute D., Vellino A., *Prolog Programming in Depth*, 2nd ed., Prentice-Hall, 1997.

[22] Gelder A. van, Ross K. and Schlipf J., "The well-founded semantics for general logic programs", *Journal of the ACM*, Vol. 38, 1991, pp. 620-650.

[23] Governatori G., Dumas M., Hofstede A. ter and Oaks P., "A formal approach to legal negotiation", *Proc. ICAIL 2001*, pp. 168-177, 2001.

[24] Grosof B. N. and Poon T. C., "SweetDeal: representing agent contracts with exceptions using XML rules, ontologies, and process descriptions", *Proc. 12th Int. Conf. on World Wide Web.*, ACM Press, pp. 340-349, 2003.

[25] Grosof B. N., "Prioritized conflict handing for logic programs", *Proc. of the 1997 Int. Symposium on Logic Programming*, pp. 197-211, 1997.

[26] Grosof B. N., Horrocks I., Volz R. and Decker S., "Description Logic Programs: Combining Logic Programs with Description Logic", *Proc. 12th Intl. Conf. on the World Wide Web (WWW-2003)*, ACM Press, 2003, pp. 48-57.

[27] Grosof B.N., Gandhe M.D., Finin T.W., "SweetJess: Translating DAMLRuleML to JESS", *Proc. Int. Workshop on Rule Markup Languages for Business Rules on the Semantic Web (RuleML 2002)*.

[28] Hayes P., "RDF Semantics", *W3C Recommendation*, Feb. 2004, www.w3c.org/TR/rdf-mt/

[29] Levy A. and Rousset M.-C., "Combining Horn rules and description logics in CARIN", *Artificial Intelligence*, Vol. 104, No. 1-2, 1998, pp. 165-209.

[30] Li N., Grosof B. N. and Feigenbaum J.,"Delegation Logic: A Logic-based Approach to Distributed Authorization", *ACM Trans. on Information Systems Security*, 6(1), 2003.

[31] Maher M.J., "A Model-Theoretic Semantics for Defeasible Logic", *Proc. Workshop on Paraconsistent Computational Logic*, pp. 67-80, 2002.

[32] Maher M.J., Rock A., Antoniou G., Billington D., Miller T., "Efficient Defeasible Reasoning Systems", *Int. Journal of Tools with Artificial Intelligence*, 10(4), 2001, pp. 483-501.

[33] Marek V.W., Truszczynski M., *Nonmonotonic Logics; Context Dependent Reasoning*, Springer-Verlag, 1993.

[34] McBride B., "Jena: Implementing the RDF Model and Syntax Specification", *Proc. 2nd Int. Workshop on the Semantic Web*, 2001.

[35] Nute D., "Defeasible logic", *Handbook of logic in artificial intelligence and logic programming (vol. 3): nonmonotonic reasoning and uncertain reasoning*, Oxford University Press, 1994.

[36] Seaborne A., and Reggiori A., "RDF Query and Rule languages Use Cases and Examples survey", rdfstore.sourceforge.net/2002/06/24/rdf-query/

[37] *Web Ontology Language (OWL)*, http://www.w3.org/2004/OWL/

[38] *Xalan-Java XSLT processor*, xml.apache.org/xalan-j/

R-DEVICE: A Deductive RDF Rule Language

Nick Bassiliades and Ioannis Vlahavas

Dept. of Informatics
Aristotle University of Thessaloniki
54124 Thessaloniki, Greece
{nbassili,vlahavas}@csd.auth.gr

Abstract. In this paper we present R-DEVICE, a deductive rule language for reasoning about RDF metadata. R-DEVICE includes features such as normal and generalized path expressions, stratified negation, aggregate, grouping, and sorting, functions. The rule language supports a second-order syntax, where variables can range over classes and properties. Users can define views which are materialized and, optionally, incrementally maintained by translating deductive rules into CLIPS production rules. Users can choose between an OPS5/CLIPS-like or a RuleML-like syntax. R-DEVICE is based on a OO RDF data model, different than the established graph model, which maps resources to objects and encapsulates properties inside resource objects, as traditional OO attributes. In this way, less joins are required to access the properties of a single resource resulting in better inferencing/querying performance. The descriptive semantics of RDF may call for dynamic re-definitions of resource classes and objects, which are handled by R-DEVICE effectively.

1   Introduction

Semantic Web is the next step of evolution for the Web [7], where information is given well-defined meaning, enabling computers and people to work in better cooperation. Currently information found on the Web is mainly built around visualization, and is not machine-understandable. It is difficult to automate things on the Web, and because of the volume of information the Web contains, it is even more difficult to manage it manually. The solution that has been proposed by the WWW Consortium was to use metadata to describe the data contained on the Web. The Resource Description Framework (RDF) is a foundation for processing metadata; it provides interoperability between applications that exchange machine-understandable information on the Web [24].

Conveying the content of documents is just a first step for achieving the full potential of the Semantic Web. Additionally, it is mandatory to be able to reason with and about information spread across the WWW. Rules provide the natural and wide-accepted mechanism to perform automated reasoning, with mature and available theory and technology. This has been identified as a Design Issue for the Semantic Web, as clearly stated in [7].

Rules and rule markup languages, such as RuleML [8], will play an important role for the success of the Semantic Web. Rules will act as a means to draw inferences, to

G. Antoniou and H. Boley (Eds.): RuleML 2004, LNCS 3323, pp. 65–80, 2004.
© Springer-Verlag Berlin Heidelberg 2004

express constraints, to specify policies, to react to events/changes, to transform data, etc. Rule markup languages will allow to enrich web ontologies by adding definitions of derived concepts, to publish rules on the web, to exchange rules between different systems and tools, etc. The applications range from electronic commerce applications, data integration and sharing, information gathering, security access and control, law, diagnosis, B2B, and of course, to modeling of business rules and processes.

It seems natural to add rules "on top" of web ontologies. However, as it is argued in [2], putting rules and description logics together poses many problems, and may be an overkill, both computationally and linguistically. Another possibility is to start with RDF/RDFS, and extend it by adding rules.

In this paper we present R-DEVICE, a deductive rule language for reasoning about RDF metadata. R-DEVICE is able to draw inferences both on the RDF schema and data. R-DEVICE includes features such as ground and generalized path expressions, stratified negation, aggregate, grouping, and sorting, functions. All these can be combined with a second-order syntax, where variables can range over classes and properties. Such variables are grounded at compile-time using metadata so second-order rules are safely and efficiently translated into sets of first-order rules. Furthermore, users can define views with R-DEVICE rules which are materialized and, optionally, incrementally maintained by translating deductive rules into CLIPS production rules [10]. Users can use built-in functions of CLIPS or can define their own arbitrary functions. The syntax of R-DEVICE rules follows the OPS5/CLIPS paradigm. Furthermore, an XML syntax is provided that extends RuleML [8] and especially the version that supports OO features and negation-as-failure.

R-DEVICE employs a novel OO-RDF data model [4] that maps RDF documents into COOL objects inside the CLIPS production rule system. The main difference between the RDF graph model and our data model is that we treat properties mainly as attributes encapsulated inside resource objects, as in traditional OO programming languages. In this way properties about a single resource are gathered together in one object, resulting in superior inference/query performance than the performance of a triple-based model, as it has been experimentally shown elsewhere [5]. Most other RDF inferencing/querying systems that are based on a triple model scatter resource properties across several triples and they require several joins to access the properties of a single resource. The descriptive semantics of RDF data may call for dynamic re-definitions of resource classes and objects, which are handled by R-DEVICE.

In the rest of this paper we briefly review related work in RDF rule languages in section 2; Section 3 presents the architecture of the R-DEVICE system, including the OO RDF model of R-DEVICE; Section 4 describes the R-DEVICE rule language, including its RuleML syntax and how inference results are exported as RDF documents. Finally, section 5 concludes this paper and discusses future work.

2   Related Work

Many RDF rule languages exist in the literature. Some on-line surveys of RDF Inference and Query systems can be found in [25] and [23]. In this section, we will refer to some of the most representative ones and we will compare them to R-DEVICE.

TRIPLE [26], an extension of the SiLRI system [11], is an RDF rule (query, inference, and transformation) language, with a layered and modular nature, that is based on Horn Logic and F-Logic and aims to support applications in need of RDF reasoning and transformation, i.e., to provide mechanisms to query web resources in a declarative way. However, in contrast with many other RDF rule/query languages, TRIPLE allows the semantics of languages on top of RDF to be defined with rules, instead of supporting the same functionality with built-in semantics. Wherever the definition of language semantics is not easily possible with rules (e.g., OWL [27]), TRIPLE provides access to external programs, like description logic classifiers.

TRIPLE permits the usage of path expressions, but not generalized path expressions, i.e. the path length and composition must be entirely known. Furthermore, compared to R-DEVICE, TRIPLE does not support aggregate, grouping, sorting and user-defined functions. Rules in TRIPLE are used for transient querying and cannot be used for defining and maintaining views. As its name implies, the query and data model of TRIPLE is triples, therefore TRIPLE requires multiple joins for collecting all the properties of a resource, since property instances and resource instances are stored in different database relations (or in different tuples of the same relation). In [5] we have shown that the OO-RDF data model of R-DEVICE is superior in performance compared to the triple-based data model of most RDF query and rule languages. Finally, TRIPLE does not have a RuleML compatible syntax.

SweetJess [17] is an implementation of a defeasible reasoning system (situated courteous logic programs) based on Jess. R-DEVICE is a deductive rule language that supports non-monotonicity in terms of negation-as-failure. Furthermore, recently we have developed a defeasible logic extension to R-DEVICE [3]. SweetJess integrates well with RuleML, as R-DEVICE. However, SweetJess rules can only express reasoning over ontologies expressed in DAMLRuleML (a DAML-OIL like syntax of RuleML) and not on arbitrary RDF data, like R-DEVICE. Furthermore, SweetJess is restricted to simple terms (variables and atoms). R-DEVICE can support a limited form of functions in the following sense: (a) path expressions are allowed in the rule condition, which can be seen as complex functions, where allowed function names are object referencing slots; (b) aggregate and sorting functions are allowed in the conclusion of aggregate rules. Finally, R-DEVICE can also support conclusions in non-stratified rule programs due to the presence of truth-maintenance rules.

SWRL [19] is a rule language based on a combination of the OWL DL and Lite sublanguages of OWL [27] with the Unary/Binary Datalog sublanguages of RuleML [8]. SWRL enables Horn-like rules to be combined with an OWL knowledge base. SWRL provides several types of syntaxes, including RuleML and RDF-like. SWRL is also based on the triple model of RDF and is a first-order, negation free logic language specification with no concrete implementation. Its main purpose is to provide a formal meaning of OWL ontologies and extend OWL DL.

The Edutella project [22] provides a family of Datalog like languages, called RDF-QEL-i, that support different levels of query capabilities among distributed, heterogeneous RDF repositories. The highest level language RDF-QEL-5 is equivalent to stratified Datalog. Furthermore, aggregation and foreign functions are supported. Actually, the RDF-QEL-i languages provide a common query and inference syntax and semantics for the heterogeneous peers and are translated into the base rule/query language of each peer. Several query language wrappers have been implemented, such as RQL, TRIPLE, etc. The common data model of Edutella is based on triples and an RDF-like syntax is provided. Path expressions and view maintenance are not supported.

CWM [6] is a general-purpose data processor for the semantic web. It is a forward chaining reasoner which can be used for querying, checking, transforming and filtering information. Its core language is RDF, extended to include rules, and it uses RDF/XML or RDF/N3. CWM supports path expressions, like TRIPLE, but only concrete ones, i.e. the path length should be known in advance and every step in the path should be ground. Furthermore, CWM does not support negation. CWM allows aggregated functions but not grouping and sorting.

Jena [21] is based on the RDF triple data model has an inference subsystem that allows a range of inference engines or reasoners to be plugged into Jena. The inference mechanism is designed to be quite general and it includes a generic rule engine that can be used for many RDF processing or transformation tasks. The generic rule reasoner supports user defined rules under forward chaining, tabled backward chaining and hybrid execution strategies. The rule language allows a limited form of functors, but does not support either negation, aggregation or path expressions. Jena rules do not have a RuleML-like syntax, but the extensibility of the system allows for different syntaxes. Finally, the Jena rule system allows maintenance of asserted conclusions, which however is trivial due to the lack of negation.

ROWL [12] is a system that enables users to express rules in RDF/XML syntax using an ontology in OWL. Using XSLT stylesheets, the rules in RDF/XML are transformed into forward-chaining production rules in JESS. ROWL also uses stylesheets to transform ontology and instance files into Jess unordered triple facts, which is also the model followed by the rules. ROWL does not maintain the assertions derived by the rules and does not support either negation, path expressions or aggregate functions. The rule language has been used in a Semantic Web environment for pervasive computing where agents reason about context and privacy concerns of the user [14].

Bossam [20] is a RETE-based forward-chaining production rule engine that has an RDF logic-like rule language, called Buchingae. Bossam has an RDF-like knowledge representation scheme and supports both strong and weak negation and second-order typed predicates. The Bossam data model is based on triples, therefore second order syntax is actually translated into first-order querying over property and/or type definition triples. Negation is supported by the rule language; however, no hint on how it is implemented by the rule engine is given. Bossam also provides a RuleML-like language, called LogicML, which however overrides several of the RuleML elements, hindering compatibility with standard RuleML. Finally, inference results exported by Bossam are flat, i.e. there is no notion of derived classes and properties.

3   R-DEVICE Architecture

The R-DEVICE system consists of two major components (Fig. 1): the RDF loader/translator and the rule loader/translator. The former accepts from the user requests for loading specific RDF documents. The RDF triple loader downloads the

RDF document from the Internet and uses the ARP parser [21] to translate it to triples in the N-triple format. Both the RDF/XML and RDF/N-triple files are stored locally for future reference.

The RDF document is scanned for namespaces that have not already been imported/translated into the system. Some of the untranslated namespaces may already exist on the local disk, while others are fetched from the Internet. All namespaces (both fetched and locally existing) are recursively scanned for namespaces, which are also fetched if not locally stored. Finally, all untranslated namespaces are also parsed using the ARP parser. The reason for doing this is explained below.

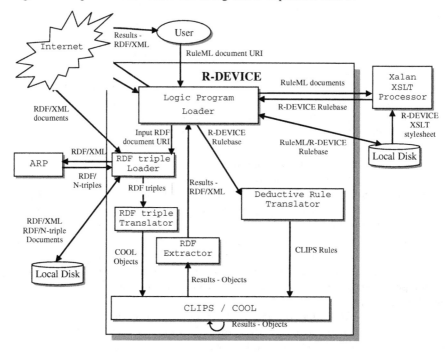

Fig. 1. Architecture of the R-DEVICE system.

RDF documents usually refer to existing RDF Schema documents through the namespace mechanism. Although the semantics of an RDF document is precisely defined by [18], the knowledge of the RDF Schema that an RDF document follows provides better understanding of its content both for the human and the machine (reasoning engine). Furthermore, the knowledge of the schema allows for more knowledgeable (and thus more efficient) rules/queries over the contents of the RDF document.

The rationale for recursively translating all namespaces is to minimize the number of OO schema redefinitions. Fetching multiple RDF schema files will aggregate multiple RDF-to-OO schema translations into a single OO schema redefinition. Namespace resolution is not guaranteed to yield an RDF schema document; therefore, if the namespace URL is not an RDF document, then the ARP parser will not produce triples and R-DEVICE will make assumptions, based on the RDF semantics, about non-resolved properties, resources, classes, etc.

Notice that the scheme we use is "nondeterministic", because if a resource is temporarily unavailable, then when loading an RDF document its namespace (i.e. RDF Schema) will not be fetched and the RDF descriptions will be translated differently than if the schema were available. However, we find that this "nondeterminism" is compatible with the unstable nature of the Web.

If the automatic namespace/schema handling is not desired by the user, the feature can be simply turned off. Users can then manually and explicitly import RDF Schema documents before the loading of the actual RDF instance documents. This explicit import of a schema is not available in RDF/S, but the issue is resolved in OWL [27], where explicit import of remote ontologies is supported.

All N-triples are loaded into memory, while the resources that have a URI#anchorID format are transformed into a namespace:anchorID format if URI belongs to the initially collected namespaces, in order to save memory space. The transformed RDF triples are fed to the RDF triple translator which maps them into COOL objects, according to the mapping schema that is briefly sketched in the following subsection. Notice that when an RDF triple is consumed it is deleted.

The rule loader accepts from the user a URI (or a local file name) that contains a deductive rule program in RuleML notation [8]. The RuleML document may also contain the URI of the input RDF document on which the rule program will run, which is forwarded to the RDF loader. The RuleML program is translated into the native R-DEVICE rule notation using the Xalan XSLT processor [28] and an XSLT stylesheet. The R-DEVICE rule program is then forwarded to the rule translator.

The rule translator accepts from the user a set of R-DEVICE rules and translates them into a set of CLIPS production rules. When the translation ends, CLIPS runs the production rules and generates the objects that constitute the result of the initial rule program. Finally, the result-objects are exported to the user as an RDF/XML document through the RDF extractor. An example of the results produced by R-DEVICE inferencing can be found in Fig. 4.

3.1   The Object-Oriented RDF Model

In this subsection we briefly describe how the RDF data model is mapped onto the COOL object-oriented model of the CLIPS language. More details can be found at [4], [5]. The main features of this mapping scheme are the following:

Resource *classes* are represented both as COOL classes and as direct or indirect instances of the rdfs:Class class. This binary representation is due to the fact that COOL does not support meta-classes. Class names follow the namespace:anchorID format, while their corresponding instances have an object identifier with the same name, surrounded by square brackets.

All *resources* are represented as COOL objects, direct or indirect instances of the rdfs:Resource class. The identifier of a resource object is either in namespace:anchorID format, if its URI can be resolved in this way, or its complete address otherwise.

The specific class of each resource object depends on the `rdf:type` property of the resource. When a resource has multiple `rdf:type` properties then the resource object belongs to multiple classes. This cannot be handled directly in COOL (and in most OO programming languages), therefore a dummy class is generated which is a subclass of all the classes that the object should belong to. Then the resource object is made an instance of this class. The slot `source` indicates whether an object is a proper RDF resource or a system-generated object.

Properties are direct or indirect instances of the class `rdf:Property`. Furthermore, properties whose domain is a single class are defined as slots (attributes) of this class. The values of properties are stored inside resource objects as slot values. Actually, RDF properties are multislots, i.e. they store lists of values, because a resource can have multiple times the same property attached to it (with a different value, of course). When a property has multiple domains, then a dummy class is generated which is a subclass of all the classes of the property domain. The property is then made a slot of this dummy class, since resource objects that have this property must be instances of all the classes in the domain.

Properties with no domain constraint become slots of the `rdfs:Resource` class. However, this class is already defined, which means that it should be dynamically re-defined. This is a consequence of RDF descriptive semantics which may add new properties to already existing classes and is treated in R-DEVICE by re-defining classes at run-time. Dynamic class re-definition requires backing-up to a file all CLIPS constructs (functions, rules, instances, sub-classes) that depend on the re-defined class, un-defining these constructs (including the class), re-defining the class adding the new property(-ies), and re-inserting the backed-up constructs into the knowledge base. Similar dynamic re-definitions occur in several other occasions in R-DEVICE, because new triples can be added at any time. In general, R-DEVICE does not reject any RDF triple because every asserted triple is considered to be true. In [5] a performance comparison between having and not having dynamic class re-definition can be found, which shows that schema re-definition does not incur a very high overhead at the total triple import time.

The `rdfs:range` constraint of properties defines the type of the values of slots. When this constraint is absent, there is no type constraint for the slots. If the value of the constraint is `rdfs:Literal` then the corresponding slot is of type STRING. Some of the XML Schema data types have been mapped to COOL data types through the `rdfs:Datatype` class. Specifically, `xsd:integer`, `xsd:long`, etc. are casted to INTEGER, `xsd:float`, `xsd:decimal`, etc. are casted to FLOAT, while all other data types are treated as strings. Finally, when the range of a property is a class, the type of the slot is INSTANCE, i.e. slot values are OIDs of resource objects. When there are multiple range constraints, R-DEVICE creates a dummy class (similarly to the case of multiple domain constraints) which becomes the type of the slot.

The RDF triple translator is actually implemented as a CLIPS production rule program. Some production rules consume RDF triples and create COOL resource objects, filling up their slots with properties, while other rules examine these resource objects and enforce RDF model theory, i.e. they create COOL classes and they treat property hierarchies using an aliasing mechanism.

4   The Deductive Rule Language of R-DEVICE

The deductive rule language of R-DEVICE supports inferencing over RDF data represented as objects and defines materialized views over them. Views can be maintained incrementally or not, based on users' preferences. The conclusions of deductive rules represent derived classes, i.e. classes whose objects are generated by evaluating these rules over the current set of objects. Furthermore, the language supports recursion, stratified negation, path expressions over the objects, generalized path expressions (i.e. path expressions with an unknown number of intermediate steps), derived and aggregate attributes. Finally, users can call out to arbitrary built-in or user-defined functions of the implementation language, i.e. CLIPS.

Each deductive rule in R-DEVICE is implemented as a pair of CLIPS production rules: one for inserting a derived object when the condition of the deductive rule is satisfied and one for deleting the derived object when the condition is no more satisfied, due to base object deletions and/or slot modifications. The latter is only generated when the user prefers the derived class to be maintainable. R-DEVICE uses RETE algorithm to match production rule conditions against the objects. More details on the translation algorithm can be found in [5].

Below is an example of a deductive rule that finds the latest published articles on a Web site whose title contains the word 'RDQL'. We notice that most of the rule examples have been obtained from [25].

```
(deductiverule q5
   (rss:item (rss:title ?title&:(str-index "RDQL" ?title))
             (rss:link ?link))
=>
   (result (link ?link)))
```

We notice that the assertion of a derived object is based on a counter mechanism which counts how many derivations exist for a certain derived object, based on the values of its slots. The latter also define the identifier of the derived object. Derived objects are created only when not already exist, otherwise their counter is just increased by one. Furthermore, derived objects are deleted when their counter is one, otherwise their counter is decreased by one. Production rules that watch out for possible deletion of derived objects, have the negation of the original deductive rule condition in their condition. Finally, derived objects also keep the OIDs of their derivators, i.e. the base objects to which they owe their existence, and the name of the rule that derived them. This is needed to correctly maintain the derived view.

4.1   Rule Syntax

The syntax of R-DEVICE deductive rules is a variation of the syntax for CLIPS production rules [10] and can be found in [5]. Although R-DEVICE uses COOL objects, the syntax of rules is as if deductive rules query over CLIPS templates, because the syntax is simpler. Specifically, each condition element follows the following format:

```
?OID <- (classname (path-expr value-expr) …)
```

where ?OID is the (optional) object identifier (or instance name, *not* address) of an object of class classname, and (path-expression value-expression) are zero, one, or more conditions to be tested on each object that matches this pattern.

When the name of the class is unknown, a variable can be used instead. Classnames can consist of a namespace prefix followed by a colon and a local part name. R-DEVICE allows the use of variables in both the place of the namespace prefix and the local part name. The following condition element applies to instances of classes of the rss namespace: (rss:?c (rss:title ?t)).

A value expression can be a constant or a variable or a constraint or a combination of those, as defined by CLIPS rule syntax. A path expression is an extension of CLIPS's single ground slot expression. Specifically, in R-DEVICE a path expression can be one of the following:

- A single slot of the class classname. The following single condition element accesses slots rss:title and rss:link of objects of class rss:item:

```
(rss:item (rss:title ?t) (rss:link ?l))
```

- A single variable denoting *any* slot of class classname. The following condition element searches for a resource object with an unknown slot whose value is "Smith": (rdfs:Resource (?s "Smith")).

- A ground path that consists of a list of multiple slots surrounded by brackets. The following rule shows an example of such a path:

```
(deductiverule path-example
  (dmoz:Topic (dc:title "Arts") ((dc:title dmoz:link) ?t)
  =>
  (art-titles (title ?t)))
```

The right-most slot should be a slot of the "departing" class. Moving to the left, slots belong to classes that represent the range of the predecessor slots. The value expression in such a pattern (e.g. variable ?t) actually describes a value of the left-most slot of the path.

- A path that contains one or more single-field variables, i.e. a path whose length is known but some of the steps are not. The above ground path can be turned into such a path: ((dc:title ?x) ?t).

- A generalized path that contains one or more multi-field variables, i.e. variables that their value is a list. These non-ground paths have an unknown length. The path below can have at least zero steps and at most 1 (given the specific example): ((dc:title $?p) ?t).

- A path that contains an encapsulated recursive sub-path, i.e. a sub-path that is traversed an unknown number of times. The following path contains the recursive sub-path (dcq:references) which recursively follows resources that reference each other: ((dc:title (dcq:references)) ?t).

Recursive paths can be used to express transitive closure queries. The following rule collects all resources (pages) recursively referenced by a certain resource. Notice that URIs that are reachable following many paths will only be included once in the result and that infinite loops will be avoided, due to the counter mechanism.

```
(deductiverule collect_refs
  (? (uri "http://lpis.csd.auth.gr")
    ((uri (dcq:references)) ?uri))
```

```
=>
  (result (uri ?uri)))
```

Recursive sub-paths can be implicitly included in a path of unknown length. For example in the following generalized path, the multifield variable $?p can represent both linear and recursive sub-paths: ((dc:title $?p) ?t).

Multifield variables can also occur at the place of value expressions, since all RDF properties are treated as multislots. The following pattern retrieves in a list $?l all the values for the rss:link property of a resource object: (rss:link $?l). On the other hand, if we know that a resource object has many values for one property and we want to iterate over them, the pattern should be: (rss:link $? ?l $?), which means that variable ?l will eventually become instantiated with all the values of the property rss:link. This retrieval pattern is so common that a shortcut (rss:link ??l) is provided which expands to the above pattern during a macro expansion phase.

When the value of a specific variable is of no interest then an anonymous variable '?' can be used, which is replaced by a singleton system-generated variable during the macro expansion phase.

Selection conditions can be placed inside value expressions, as in CLIPS. For example, the following pattern retrieves the family name in a variable and, at the same time, tests if the slot value does not equal "Smith":

```
(vcard:Family ?last&~"Smith")
```

Conditions can also express disjunction and negation. Only stratified negation is allowed. Rule conclusion can also contain a set of function calls that calculate the values to be stored at the slots of the derived object. Such calls are placed inside a calc construct before the derived class template. For example, the following variation of rule q9 retrieves the given and family name of a resource object and using a CLIPS function concatenates them into a single string that is stored in the slot full-name of the derived objects of class person.

```
(deductiverule q9-variation
  (? (vcard:Family ?f) (vcard:Given ?v))
 =>
  (calc (bind ?full (str-cat ?v " " ?f)))
  (person (full-name ?full)))
```

Finally, R-DEVICE supports aggregate functions and grouping in the form of aggregate attribute rules. These rules express how values are accumulated and combined into attributes of existing objects. For example, the following rule iterates over all resources and generates one object for each distinct creator, which holds in the URIs slot all the resources that he/she has created.

```
(deductiverule ex1-aggregate
  (? (dcq:creator ?c) (uri ?uri))
 =>
  (pages (author ?c) (URIs (list ?uri))))
```

Function list is an aggregate function that just collects values in a list. There are several other aggregate functions, such as sum, count, avg, etc. Notice that in the above example a grouping is performed because the conclusion contains the slot author in addition to the aggregate slot URIs.

4.2   RuleML Syntax of R-DEVICE Rules

R-DEVICE rule language has also a RuleML [8] compatible syntax. We have tried to keep as close as possible to the DTD-based RuleML version 0.85[1]. However, several features of R-DEVICE could not be captured by the latest RuleML DTDs, so we have developed a new DTD (see Fig. 2) using the modularization scheme of RuleML, extending the Datalog with negation as failure DTD with OO features.

Rule q5 that has been presented above is represented in RuleML notation as:

```
<imp>
  <_rlab ruletype="deductiverule" maintainable="yes">
    <ind>q5</ind>
  </_rlab>
  <_head>
    <atom>
      <_opr><rel><ind>result</ind></rel></_opr>
      <_slot name="link">  <var type="single">link</var>
      </_slot>
    </atom>
  </_head>
  <_body>
    <atom>
      <_opr><rel><ind>rss:item</ind></rel></_opr>
      <_slot name="rss:title">
        <_and>  <var type="single">title</var>
                <function_call name="str-index">
                  <ind>"RDQL"</ind>
                  <var type="single">title</var>
                </function_call>
        </_and>
      </_slot>
      <_slot name="rss:link">  <var type="single">link</var>
      </_slot>
    </atom>
  </_body>
</imp>
```

There are three types of rules: deductive rules, derived attribute rules and aggregate attribute rules. Classes and objects (facts) can also be declared in R-DEVICE; however, the focus in this paper is the use of RDF data as facts. The input RDF file(s) are declared in the `rdf_import` attribute of the `rulebase` (root) element of the RuleML document. There exist two more attributes in the `rulebase` element: the `rdf_export` attribute that declares the address of the RDF file with the results of the rule program to be exported, and the `rdf_export_classes` attribute that declares the derived classes whose instances will be exported in RDF/XML format.

Further extensions to the RuleML syntax, include function calls that are used either as constraints in the rule body or as new value calculators at the rule head. Furthermore, multiple constraints in the rule body can be expressed through the logical operators: `_not`, `_and`, `_or`. Variables belong to three types, single, multi, and a combined form to reflect variables expressions in the previous subsection.

---

[1] In the future we will upgrade to newer XSD-based versions of RuleML (e.g. 0.87).

Finally, simple slot expressions have been augmented with the ability to declare path expressions according to the R-DEVICE abilities, i.e. simple ground path expressions, simple path expressions with variables, generalized path expressions, recursive path expressions, etc. Notice that the relation name of the operator can be either a constant (class name) or a variable, since R-DEVICE allows variable to range over class and slot names. Furthermore, each `atom` element has been augmented with an optional `_id` element to represent the OID of the corresponding resource object.

```
<!ENTITY % CLASSes "NMTOKENS">
<!ATTLIST _rlab
        ruletype (deductiverule | derivedattrule | aggregateattrule) #REQUIRED
        maintainable (yes | no) "yes">
<!ATTLIST var type (single | multi | single-multi) #REQUIRED>
<!ENTITY % recpath.content "(slotname+)">  <!ELEMENT recpath %recpath.content;>
<!ENTITY % genpath.content "(var)">        <!ELEMENT genpath %genpath.content;>
<!ENTITY % slotname.content "(ind|var)"> <!ELEMENT slotname %slotname.content;>
<!ELEMENT _varslot %_slot.content;>
<!ENTITY % _path.content "(slotname|genpath|recpath)+">
<!ELEMENT _path (%_path.content;, %_slot.content;)>
<!ENTITY % rel.content "(ind | var)">
<!ENTITY % _id.content "(ind | var)">      <!ELEMENT _id %_id.content;>
<!ENTITY % atom.content "((_id?,_opr,(_path|_slot|_varslot)*, ...))">
<!ENTITY % _calc.cont "(function_call+)">   <!ELEMENT calc %_calc.cont;>
<!ENTITY % _head.content "(calc?, atom)">
<!ELEMENT aggregate_function_call (var)>
<!ATTLIST aggregate_function_call
        name (sum|count|list|avg|max|min|ord_list|set|string|phrase) #REQUIRED>
<!ELEMENT function_call (%pos_term;)*>
<!ATTLIST function_call name CDATA #REQUIRED>
<!ENTITY % pos_term "(ind | var | function_call)">
<!ENTITY % term "(_not | %pos_term;)">     <!ELEMENT _not (ind | var)>
<!ELEMENT _or (%term;, (%term;)+)>          <!ELEMENT _and (%term;, (%term;)+)>
<!ENTITY % constraint "(_not | _or | _and)">
<!ENTITY % _slot.content "(ind | var | %constraint;|aggregate_function_call)">
<!ENTITY % nafurdatalog_include SYSTEM
                      "http://www.ruleml.org/0.85/dtd/naf/nafurdatalog.dtd">
%nafurdatalog_include;
<!ATTLIST rulebase  xmlns %URI; #IMPLIED  xsi:schemaLocation %URI; #IMPLIED
             xmlns:xsi %URI; #IMPLIED  rdf_import CDATA #IMPLIED
             rdf_export_classes %CLASSes; #IMPLIED rdf_export CDATA #IMPLIED>
```

Fig. 2. DTD for the RuleML syntax of the R-DEVICE rule language.

4.3 Extracting Inference Results as RDF Documents

After production rules have been executed and all the derived objects have been generated, the RDF extractor generates an RDF/XML document and returns it to the user through a Web server, as the result of the user's program. The document contains both RDF definitions for the schema of the desired derived classes and, of course, for the instances of the derived classes.

Initially the result document contains namespace definitions for rdf/rdfs and for the exported document. Then the derived classes are defined as `rdfs:Class` elements, followed by `rdfs:Property` elements for each of their slot that was defined at the deductive rule conclusion. Domains and ranges of the properties are obtained from the COOL definition of each derived class. The domain for all the properties of a class is the class itself, while the range can be one of the following:

- If the slot is of type STRING, the property range is rdfs:Literal.
- If the slot is of type INTEGER, the property range is xsd:integer.
- If the slot is of type FLOAT, the property range is xsd:float.
- If the slot is of type INSTANCE, the property range is a class whose name is obtained by the metadata. When the referenced class is a dummy class that was generated from the system to cater for multi-range properties, then multiple property ranges are generated for each one of the superclasses of the dummy class.
- If the slot has any other combination of types, then there is no range constraint.

Notice that in the fourth case the RDF schema for the referenced class(es) must be included in the result document, unless it is not a derived but a base RDF class, i.e. an RDF class whose definition has been imported from a namespace. In this case, the document header is enriched with the namespace address and no further schema definition is included. Otherwise, definitions for the referenced class and its properties are included in the RDF result document. The same actions are recursively repeated for all classes, that are reachable by reference slots from the initial class.

Below all class and property definitions, appear RDF statements about the instances of those classes. For each of the initial derived classes, all its objects are included using class names as outside elements and property names as inside elements. Only slots/properties that do have a value are included. Properties with multiple values are represented as multiple consecutive elements. Finally, objects recursively referenced from the above objects are also included in the result document. When instances of base RDF classes are included the outside element is rdf:Description, because type information is included as one or more rdf:type properties. The URIs of the derived objects are constructed from the URI of the R-DEVICE system (http://startrek.csd.auth.gr/r-device/export/), the name of the exported file and a uniquely generated anchor ID, constructed from the class name and consecutive integers. The URIs of instances of base classes are taken from the uri slot of each object.

```
<!DOCTYPE rdf:RDF [
    <!ENTITY dmoz "http://directory.mozilla.org/rdf/">
]>
<rdf:RDF xmlns:rdf="http://www.w3c.org/1999/02/22-rdf-syntax-ns#"
         xmlns:dc="http://purl.org/dc/elements/1.1/"
         xmlns:dmoz="&dmoz;">
  <dmoz:Topic rdf:about="&dmoz;Top">
    <dmoz:catid>1</dmoz:catid>
    <dc:title>Top</dc:title>
    <dmoz:narrow rdf:resource="&dmoz;Top/Arts"/>
  </dmoz:Topic>
  <dmoz:Topic rdf:about="&dmoz;Top/Arts">
    <dmoz:catid>2</dmoz:catid>
    <dc:title>Arts</dc:title>
    <dmoz:link rdf:resource="http://www3.bc.sympatico.ca/GlassPage.html"/>
  </dmoz:Topic>
  <dmoz:ExternalPage rdf:about="http://www3.bc.sympatico.ca/GlassPage.html">
    <dc:title>John Phillips Blown glass</dc:title>
    <dc:description>A small display of glass by John Phillips</dc:description>
  </dmoz:ExternalPage>
</rdf:RDF>
```

Fig. 3. Sample RDF/XML document.

The following R-DEVICE rule `example` retrieves the title of an ODP topic that has at least one associated page, along with the titles of all associated pages, and when applied on the RDF document of Fig. 3, exports the results shown in Fig. 4.

```
(deductiverule example
  (dmoz:Topic (dc:title ?t) (dmoz:link $? ?l $?))
  ?l <- (dmoz:ExternalPage (dc:title ?lt))
 =>
  (result (title ?t) (link_title ?lt)))
```

```
<!DOCTYPE rdf:RDF [
    <!ENTITY rdf "http://www.w3c.org/1999/02/22-rdf-syntax-ns#">
    <!ENTITY rdfs "http://www.w3c.org/2000/01/rdf-schema#">
    <!ENTITY r_device
           "http://startrek.csd.auth.gr/r-device/export/example-result.rdf#">
]>
<rdf:RDF  xmlns:rdf='&rdf;'  xmlns:rdfs='&rdfs;'
          xmlns:r_device='&r_device;'>
  <rdfs:Class rdf:about='&r_device;result'> </rdfs:Class>
  <rdf:Property rdf:about='&r_device;title'>
    <rdfs:domain rdf:resource='&r_device;result'/>
  </rdf:Property>
  <rdf:Property rdf:about='&r_device;link_title'>
    <rdfs:domain rdf:resource='&r_device;result'/>
  </rdf:Property>
  <r_device:result rdf:about=" r_device;result1">
    <r_device:title>Arts</r_device:title>
    <r_device:link_title>John phillips Blown glass</r_device:link_title>
  </r_device:result>
</rdf:RDF>
```

Fig. 4. Exported results for R-DEVICE rule `example`.

5   Conclusions and Future Work

In this paper we have presented R-DEVICE, a deductive rule language for reasoning about RDF metadata. R-DEVICE includes features such as normal and generalized path expressions, stratified negation, aggregate, grouping, and sorting, functions. The rule language supports a second-order syntax, where variables can range over classes and properties. Users can define views which are materialized and, optionally, incrementally maintained. Users can also choose between an OPS5/CLIPS-like or a RuleML-like syntax. R-DEVICE is based on a OO RDF data model, different than the established graph model, which maps resources to objects and encapsulates properties inside resource objects, as traditional OO attributes. In this way, less joins are required to access the properties of a single resource resulting in better inferencing/querying performance. The descriptive semantics of RDF may call for dynamic re-definitions of resource classes and objects, which are handled by R-DEVICE effectively.

Regarding potential applications, R-DEVICE could be used as an inference mechanism on top of an RDF repository. The RDF data would be pre-loaded and external users would submit rule programs into the system either through a form-based HTML interface or using R-DEVICE remotely as a Web-service through SOAP messaging. Changes to the base RDF metadata of the repository would be incrementally propagated to R-DEVICE, as well. Another use for R-DEVICE could be an on-the-fly RDF inferencing service, provided that the input RDF documents are not very large, since parsing very large RDF/XML documents into triples at run-time and then importing them in R-DEVICE would not be very efficient.

We are currently developing a defeasible logic extension of R-DEVICE [3] which will be used as a backend reasoning mechanism of negotiating agents to express and apply various negotiation strategies [15]. Among our plans for further developing R-DEVICE is to extend the system to handle ontologies in OWL [27], by using the R-DEVICE rule language to define the extended semantics of OWL, rather than building-in the semantics into the system, from scratch. Of course, the starting point of this investigation will be the Horn definable part of OWL [16]. Furthermore, we are planning to develop a visual editor for the RuleML-like rule language. Another extension would be to turn R-DEVICE into a Web Service. Finally, we aim to develop an interface to RDF storage systems, such as ICS-FORTH RDFSuite [1] or Sesame [9].

References

[1] Alexaki S., Christophides V., Karvounarakis G., Plexousakis D., and Tolle K., "The ICSFORTH RDFSuite: Managing Voluminous RDF Description Bases", *Proc. 2nd Int. Workshop on the Semantic Web*, pp. 1-13, Hong Kong, 2001.

[2] Antoniou G., Wagner G., "Rules and Defeasible Reasoning on the Semantic Web", in *Proc. RuleML Workshop 2003*, Springer-Verlag, LNCS 2876, pp. 111–120, 2003.

[3] Bassiliades N., Antoniou G., Vlahavas I., "A Defeasible Logic Reasoner for the Semantic Web", accepted for presentation at *Workshop on Rules and Rule Markup Languages for the Semantic Web (RuleML 2004)*, Hiroshima, Japan, 8 Nov. 2004.

[4] Bassiliades N., Vlahavas I., "Capturing RDF Descriptive Semantics in an Object Oriented Knowledge Base System", *Proc. 12th Int. WWW Conf. (WWW2003)*, Budapest.

[5] Bassiliades N., Vlahavas I., "R-DEVICE: An Object-Oriented Knowledge Base System for RDF Metadata", *Technical Report TR-LPIS-141-03*, LPIS Group, Dept. of Informatics, Aristotle University of Thessaloniki, Greece, 2003.

[6] Berners-Lee T., "CWM - closed world machine", http://www.w3c.org/2000/10/swap/doc/cwm.html, 2000.

[7] Berners-Lee T., Hendler J., Lassila O., "The Semantic Web", Scientific American, May 2001.

[8] Boley, H., Tabet, S., Wagner, G., "Design Rationale of RuleML: A Markup Language for Semantic Web Rules", *Proc. Int. Semantic Web Working Symp.*, pp. 381-402, 2001.

[9] Broekstra J., Kampman A., van Harmelen F., "Sesame: A Generic Architecture for Storing and Querying RDF and RDF Schema", *Proc. 1st Int. Semantic Web Conf.*, Springer-Verlag, LNCS 2342, pp. 54-68, 2002.

[10] *CLIPS Basic Programming Guide*, Version 6.20, March 31st 2002, http://www.ghg.net/clips/Download.html.

[11] Decker S., Brickley D., Saarela J., Angele J., "A query and inference service for RDF", in *QL'98 - The Query Languages Workshop*, Boston, USA, 1998.

[12] Gandon F. L., Sheshagiri M., Sadeh N. M., "ROWL: Rule Language in OWL and Translation Engine for JESS",

[13] http://mycampus.sadehlab.cs.cmu.edu/public_pages/ROWL/ROWL.html

[14] Gandon F., Sadeh N., "Semantic Web Technologies to Reconcile Privacy and Context Awareness", *Web Semantics Journal*, Vol. 1, No. 3, 2004.

[15] Governatori G., Dumas M., Hofstede A. ter and Oaks P., "A formal approach to legal negotiation", *Proc. ICAIL 2001*, pp. 168-177.

[16] Grosof B. N., Horrocks I., Volz R. and Decker S., "Description Logic Programs: Combining Logic Programs with Description Logic", *Proc. 12th Intl. Conf. on the World Wide Web (WWW-2003)*, ACM Press, 2003, pp. 48-57.

[17] Grosof B.N., Gandhe M.D., Finin T.W., "SweetJess: Translating DAMLRuleML to JESS", *Proc. RuleML Workshop*, 2002.

[18] Hayes P., "RDF Semantics", *W3C Recommendation*, 10 Feb. 2004,
http://www.w3c.org/TR/rdf-mt/

[19] Horrocks I., Patel-Schneider P. F., Boley H., Tabet S., Grosof B., Dean M., "SWRL: A Semantic Web Rule Language Combining OWL and RuleML", Version 0.5, 19 Nov 2003, http://www.daml.org/2003/11/swrl/

[20] Jang M., "Bossam - A Java-based Rule Processor for the Semantic Web", http://mknows.etri.re.kr/bossam

[21] McBride B., "Jena: A Semantic Web Toolkit", *IEEE Internet Computing*, 6(6), pp. 55-59, 2002.

[22] Nejdl W., Wolf B., Qu C., Decker S., Sintek M., Naeve A., Nilsson M., Palmer M., Risch T., "Edutella: A P2P networking infrastructure based on RDF", in *Proc. of WWW-2002*, ACM Press, 2002, pp. 604-615.

[23] Prud'hommeaux E., "RDF Query and Rules Status",
http://www.w3c.org./2001/11/13-RDF-Query-Rules/

[24] *Resource Description Framework (RDF)*, http://www.w3c.org/RDF/

[25] Seaborne A., Reggiori A., "RDF Query and Rule languages Use Cases and Examples survey", http://rdfstore.sourceforge.net/2002/06/24/rdf-query/

[26] Sintek M., Decker S., "TRIPLE-A Query, Inference, and Transformation Language for the Semantic Web", *Proc. 1st Int. Semantic Web Conf.*, Springer-Verlag, LNCS 2342, pp. 364-378, 2002.

[27] *Web Ontology Language (OWL)*, http://www.w3c.org/2004/OWL/

[28] *Xalan-Java XSLT processor*, xml.apache.org/xalan-j/

Well-Founded Semantics for Description Logic Programs in the Semantic Web[*]

Thomas Eiter[1], Thomas Lukasiewicz[1,2], Roman Schindlauer[1], and Hans Tompits[1]

[1] Institut für Informationssysteme, Technische Universität Wien
Favoritenstraße 9-11, A-1040 Vienna, Austria
{eiter,roman,tompits}@kr.tuwien.ac.at
[2] Dipartimento di Informatica e Sistemistica, Università di Roma "La Sapienza"
Via Salaria 113, I-00198 Rome, Italy
lukasiewicz@dis.uniroma1.it

Abstract. In previous work, towards the integration of rules and ontologies in the Semantic Web, we have proposed a combination of logic programming under the answer set semantics with the description logics $\mathcal{SHIF}(\mathbf{D})$ and $\mathcal{SHOIN}(\mathbf{D})$, which underly the Web ontology languages OWL Lite and OWL DL, respectively. More precisely, we have introduced *description logic programs* (or *dl-programs*), which consist of a description logic knowledge base L and a finite set of description logic rules P, and we have defined their answer set semantics. In this paper, we continue this line of research. Here, as a central contribution, we present the well-founded semantics for dl-programs, and we analyze its semantic properties. In particular, we show that it generalizes the well-founded semantics for ordinary normal programs. Furthermore, we show that in the general case, the well-founded semantics of dl-programs is a partial model that approximates the answer set semantics, whereas in the positive and the stratified case, it is a total model that coincides with the answer set semantics. Finally, we also provide complexity results for dl-programs under the well-founded semantics.

1 Introduction

The *Semantic Web* [6,7,14] aims at extending the current World Wide Web by standards and techniques that enable the *automated processing* of Web content. Among other issues, the main ideas to achieve this goal is to add a machine-readable meaning to Web pages, to use ontologies for a precise definition of shared information terms, and to make use of KR technology for automated reasoning from Web resources.

The Semantic Web is conceived in hierarchical layers, where the *Ontology layer*, in form of the *OWL Web Ontology Language* [35,21] (recommended by the W3C),

---

[*] This work was partially supported by the Austrian Science Fund under grants Z29-N04 and P17212-N04, by the European Commission through the IST REWERSE Network of Excellence and the Marie Curie Individual Fellowship HPMF-CT-2001-001286 (disclaimer: The authors are solely responsible for information communicated and the European Commission is not responsible for any views or results expressed), and by the German Research Foundation through a Heisenberg Fellowship. We thank Ulrike Sattler for providing valuable information on complexity-related issues about OWL-DL related description logics.

is currently the highest layer of sufficient maturity. OWL consists of three increasingly expressive sublanguages, namely *OWL Lite*, *OWL DL*, and *OWL Full*. OWL Lite and OWL DL are essentially very expressive description logics with an RDF syntax [21]. As shown in [19], ontology entailment in OWL Lite (resp., OWL DL) reduces to knowledge base (un)satisfiability in the description logic $\mathcal{SHIF}(\mathbf{D})$ (resp., $\mathcal{SHOIN}(\mathbf{D})$).

On top of the Ontology layer, the *Rules*, *Logic*, and *Proof layers* of the Semantic Web will be developed next, which should offer sophisticated representation and reasoning capabilities. As a first effort in this direction, *RuleML* (Rule Markup Language) [8] is an XML-based markup language for rules and rule-based systems, while the OWL Rules Language [20] is a first proposal for extending OWL by Horn clause rules.

A key requirement of the layered architecture of the Semantic Web is to integrate the Rules and the Ontology layer. In particular, it is crucial to allow for building rules on top of ontologies, that is, for rule-based systems that use vocabulary from ontology knowledge bases. Another type of combination is to build ontologies on top of rules, which means that ontological definitions are supplemented by rules or imported from rules.

Towards this goal, in [13], we have proposed a combination of logic programs under the answer set semantics with description logics, introducing *description logic programs* (or *dl-programs*), which are of the form $KB = (L, P)$, where L is a knowledge base in a description logic and P is a finite set of description logic rules (or *dl-rules*).

Such dl-rules are similar to usual rules in logic programs with negation as failure, but may also contain *queries to L* in their bodies which are given by special atoms (on which possibly default negation may apply). For example, a rule

$$cand(X, P) \leftarrow paperArea(P, A), DL[Referee](X), DL[expert](X, A)$$

may express that X is a candidate reviewer for a paper P, if the paper is in area A, and X is known to be a referee and an expert for area A. Here, the latter two are queries to the description logic knowledge base L, which has a concept *Referee* and role *expert* in its signature. For the evaluation, the precise definition of *Referee* and *expert* within L is fully transparent, and only the logical contents at the level of inference counts. Thus, dl-programs fully support encapsulation and privacy of L—this is needed if parts of L should not be accessible (for example, if L contains an ontology about risk assessment in credit assignment), and only extensional reasoning services are available.

Another important feature of dl-rules is that queries to L also allow for specifying an input from P, and thus for a *flow of information from P to L*, besides the flow of information from L to P, given by any query to L. Hence, description logic programs allow for building rules on top of ontologies, but also (to some extent) building ontologies on top of rules. This is achieved by dynamic update operators through which the extensional part of L can be modified for subjunctive querying. For example, the rule

$$paperArea(P, A) \leftarrow DL[keyword \uplus kw; inArea](P, A)$$

intuitively says that paper P is in area A, if P is in A according to the description logic knowledge base L, where the extensional part of the *keyword* role in L (which is known to influence *inArea*) is augmented by the facts of a binary predicate *kw* from the program. In this way, additional knowledge (gained in the program) can be supplied to L before querying. Using this mechanism, also more involved relationships between concepts and/or roles in L can be defined and exploited.

The semantics of dl-programs was defined in [13] as an extension of the answer set semantics [15] for ordinary normal programs, which is one of the most widely used semantics for nonmonotonic logic programs. More precisely, in [13], we defined the notions of *weak* and *strong answer sets* of dl-programs, which coincide with usual answer sets in the case of ordinary normal programs. The description logic knowledge bases in dl-programs are specified in the well-known description logics $\mathcal{SHIF}(\mathbf{D})$ and $\mathcal{SHOIN}(\mathbf{D})$.

In this paper, we continue our work on description logic programs and extend the *well-founded semantics* to this class of programs. Introduced by Van Gelder, Ross, and Schlipf [34], the well-founded semantics is another most widely used semantics for ordinary nonmonotonic logic programs. It is a skeptical approximation of the answer set semantics in the sense that every well-founded consequence of a given ordinary normal program P is contained in every answer set of P. While the answer set semantics resolves conflicts by virtue of permitting multiple intended models as alternative scenarios, the well-founded semantics remains agnostic in the presence of conflicting information, assigning the truth value *false* to a maximal set of atoms that cannot become true during the evaluation of a given program. Furthermore, well-founded semantics assigns a coherent meaning to *all* programs, while some programs are not consistent under answer set semantics, i.e., lack an answer set.

Another important aspect of the well-founded semantics is that it is geared towards efficient *query answering* and also plays a prominent role in deductive databases (see, e.g., [26] for a proposal for object-oriented deductive databases, which is applied to the Florid system implementing F-logic). As an important computational property, a query to an ordinary normal program is evaluable under well-founded semantics in polynomial time (under data complexity), while query answering under the answer set semantics is intractable in general. Finally, efficient implementations of the well-founded semantics exist, such as the XSB system [28] and Smodels [27].

The main contributions of this paper can be summarized as follows:

(1) We define the well-founded semantics for dl-programs by generalizing Van Gelder *et al.*'s [34] fixpoint characterization of the well-founded semantics for ordinary normal programs based on *greatest unfounded sets*. We then prove some appealing semantic properties of the well-founded semantics for dl-programs. In particular, it generalizes the well-founded semantics for ordinary normal programs. Furthermore, for general dl-programs, the well-founded semantics is a partial model, and for positive (resp., stratified) dl-programs, it is a total model and the canonical least (resp., iterative least) model. Finally, the well-founded semantics also tolerates abbreviations for dl-atoms.

(2) Generalizing a result by Baral and Subrahmanian [5], we then show that the well-founded semantics for dl-programs can be characterized in terms of the least and the greatest fixpoint of an operator γ^2_{KB}, which is defined using a generalized Gelfond-Lifschitz transform of dl-programs relative to an interpretation.

(3) We also show that, similarly as for ordinary normal programs, the well-founded semantics for dl-programs approximates the strong answer set semantics for dl-programs. That is, every *well-founded* ground atom is true in every answer set, and every *unfounded* ground atom is false in every answer set. Hence, every well-founded ground atom and no unfounded ground atom is a cautious (resp., brave) consequence of a dl-

program under the strong answer set semantics. Furthermore, we prove that when the well-founded semantics of a dl-program is total, then it is the only strong answer set.

(4) Finally, we give a precise characterization of the complexity of the well-founded semantics for dl-programs, over both $\mathcal{SHIF}(\mathbf{D})$ and $\mathcal{SHOIN}(\mathbf{D})$. Like for ordinary normal programs, literal inference under the well-founded semantics has a lower complexity than under the answer set semantics. More precisely, relative to program complexity [11], literal inference under the well-founded semantics for dl-programs over $\mathcal{SHIF}(\mathbf{D})$ (resp., $\mathcal{SHOIN}(\mathbf{D})$) is complete for EXP (resp., P^{NEXP}), while cautious literal inference under the strong answer set semantics for dl-programs over $\mathcal{SHIF}(\mathbf{D})$ (resp., $\mathcal{SHOIN}(\mathbf{D})$) is complete for co-NEXP (resp., co-NP^{NEXP}) [13].

2   Preliminaries

In this section, we recall normal programs under the answer set semantics and the well-founded semantics, as well as the description logics $\mathcal{SHIF}(\mathbf{D})$ and $\mathcal{SHOIN}(\mathbf{D})$.

Normal Programs. We assume a function-free first-order vocabulary Φ with nonempty finite sets of constant and predicate symbols, and a set $\mathcal{X}$ of variables. A *classical literal* (or *literal*) l is an atom a or a negated atom $\neg a$. A *negation-as-failure* (NAF) literal is an atom a or a default-negated atom $not\ a$. A *normal rule* (or *rule*) r is of the form

$$a \leftarrow b_1, \dots, b_k, not\ b_{k+1}, \dots, not\ b_m\ ,\quad m \geq k \geq 0\ , \tag{1}$$

where $a, b_1, \dots, b_m$ are atoms. We refer to a as the *head* of r, denoted $H(r)$, while the conjunction $b_1, \dots, b_k, not\ b_{k+1}, \dots, not\ b_m$ is the *body* of r; its *positive* (resp., *negative*) part is $b_1, \dots, b_k$ (resp., $not\ b_{k+1}, \dots, not\ b_m$). We define $B(r) = B^+(r) \cup B^-(r)$, where $B^+(r) = \{b_1, \dots, b_k\}$ and $B^-(r) = \{b_{k+1}, \dots, b_m\}$. A *normal program* (or *program*) P is a finite set of rules. We say P is *positive* iff no rule in P contains default-negated atoms.

The well-founded semantics has many different equivalent definitions [34,5]. We recall here the one based on unfounded sets.

Let P be a program. *Ground terms, atoms, literals*, etc., are defined as usual. We denote by HB_P the *Herbrand base* of P, i.e., the set of all ground atoms with predicate and constant symbols from P (if P contains no constant, then choose an arbitrary one from Φ), and by $ground(P)$ the set of all ground instances of rules in P (w.r.t. HB_P).

For literals $l = a$ (resp., $l = \neg a$), we use $\neg .l$ to denote $\neg a$ (resp., a), and for sets of literals S, we define $\neg .S = \{\neg .l \mid l \in S\}$ and $S^+ = \{a \in S \mid a$ is an atom$\}$. We use $Lit_P = HB_P \cup \neg .HB_P$ to denote the set of all ground literals with predicate and constant symbols from P. A set $S \subseteq Lit_P$ is *consistent* iff $S \cap \neg .S = \emptyset$. A *three-valued interpretation* relative to P is any consistent $I \subseteq Lit_P$.

A set $U \subseteq HB_P$ is an *unfounded set* of P relative to I, if for every $a \in U$ and every $r \in ground(P)$ with $H(r) = a$, either (i) $\neg b \in I \cup \neg .U$ for some atom $b \in B^+(r)$, or (ii) $b \in I$ for some atom $b \in B^-(r)$. There exists the greatest unfounded set of P relative to I, denoted $U_P(I)$. Intuitively, if I is compatible with P, then all atoms in $U_P(I)$ can be safely switched to false and the resulting interpretation is still compatible with P.

The operators T_P and W_P on consistent $I \subseteq Lit_P$ are then defined by:

- $T_P(I) = \{H(r) \mid r \in ground(P),\ B^+(r) \cup \neg.B^-(r) \subseteq I\};$
- $W_P(I) = T_P(I) \cup \neg.U_P(I).$

The operator W_P is monotonic, and thus has a least fixpoint, denoted $lfp(W_P)$, which is the *well-founded semantics* of P, denoted $WFS(P)$. An atom $a \in HB_P$ is *well-founded* (resp., *unfounded*) w.r.t. P, if a (resp., $\neg a$) is in $lfp(W_P)$. Intuitively, starting with $I = \emptyset$, rules are applied to obtain new positive and negated facts (via $T_P(I)$ and $\neg.U_P(I)$, respectively). This process is repeated until no longer possible.

Example 2.1 Consider the propositional program $P = \{p \leftarrow not\ q;\ q \leftarrow p;\ p \leftarrow not\ r\}$. For $I = \emptyset$, we have $T_P(I) = \emptyset$ and $U_P(\emptyset) = \{r\}$: p cannot be unfounded because of the first rule and Condition (ii), and hence q cannot be unfounded because of the second rule and Condition (i). Thus, $W_P(\emptyset) = \{\neg r\}$. Since $T_P(\{\neg r\}) = \{p\}$ and $U_P(\{\neg r\}) = \{r\}$, it follows $W_P(\{\neg r\}) = \{p, \neg r\}$. Since $T_P(\{p, \neg r\}) = \{p, q\}$ and $U_P(\{p, \neg r\}) = \{r\}$, it then follows $W_P(\{p, \neg r\}) = \{p, q, \neg r\}$. Thus, $lfp(W_P) = \{p, q, \neg r\}$. That is, r is unfounded relative to P, and the other atoms are well-founded.

$\mathcal{SHIF}(\mathbf{D})$ **and** $\mathcal{SHOIN}(\mathbf{D})$**.** We first describe $\mathcal{SHOIN}(\mathbf{D})$. We assume a set $\mathbf{D}$ of *elementary datatypes*. Every $d \in \mathbf{D}$ has a set of *data values*, called the *domain* of d, denoted $\mathrm{dom}(d)$. We use $\mathrm{dom}(\mathbf{D})$ to denote $\bigcup_{d \in \mathbf{D}} \mathrm{dom}(d)$. A *datatype* is either an element of $\mathbf{D}$ or a subset of $\mathrm{dom}(\mathbf{D})$ (called *datatype oneOf*). Let $\mathbf{A}$, $\mathbf{R}_A$, $\mathbf{R}_D$, and $\mathbf{I}$ be nonempty finite and pairwise disjoint sets of *atomic concepts*, *abstract roles*, *datatype roles*, and *individuals*, respectively. We use $\mathbf{R}_A^-$ to denote the set of all inverses R^- of abstract roles $R \in \mathbf{R}_A$.

A *role* is an element of $\mathbf{R}_A \cup \mathbf{R}_A^- \cup \mathbf{R}_D$. *Concepts* are inductively defined as follows. Every $C \in \mathbf{A}$ is a concept, and if $o_1, o_2, \ldots \in \mathbf{I}$, then $\{o_1, o_2, \ldots\}$ is a concept (called *oneOf*). If C and D are concepts and if $R \in \mathbf{R}_A \cup \mathbf{R}_A^-$, then $(C \sqcap D)$, $(C \sqcup D)$, and $\neg C$ are concepts (called *conjunction*, *disjunction*, and *negation*, respectively), as well as $\exists R.C$, $\forall R.C$, $\geq nR$, and $\leq nR$ (called *exists*, *value*, *atleast*, and *atmost restriction*, respectively) for an integer $n \geq 0$. If $d \in \mathbf{D}$ and $U \in \mathbf{R}_D$, then $\exists U.d$, $\forall U.d$, $\geq nU$, and $\leq nU$ are concepts (called *datatype exists*, *value*, *atleast*, and *atmost restriction*, respectively) for an integer $n \geq 0$. We write $\top$ and $\bot$ to abbreviate $C \sqcup \neg C$ and $C \sqcap \neg C$, respectively, and we eliminate parentheses as usual.

An *axiom* is of one of the following forms: (1) $C \sqsubseteq D$, where C and D are concepts (*concept inclusion*); (2) $R \sqsubseteq S$, where either $R, S \in \mathbf{R}_A$ or $R, S \in \mathbf{R}_D$ (*role inclusion*); (3) $\mathrm{Trans}(R)$, where $R \in \mathbf{R}_A$ (*transitivity*); (4) $C(a)$, where C is a concept and $a \in \mathbf{I}$ (*concept membership*); (5) $R(a, b)$ (resp., $U(a, v)$), where $R \in \mathbf{R}_A$ (resp., $U \in \mathbf{R}_D$) and $a, b \in \mathbf{I}$ (resp., $a \in \mathbf{I}$ and $v \in \mathrm{dom}(\mathbf{D})$) (*role membership*); and (6) $a = b$ (resp., $a \neq b$), where $a, b \in \mathbf{I}$ (*equality* (resp., *inequality*)). A *knowledge base* L is a finite set of axioms. (For decidability, number restrictions in L are restricted to simple $R \in \mathbf{R}_A$ [22]).

The syntax of $\mathcal{SHIF}(\mathbf{D})$ is as the above syntax of $\mathcal{SHOIN}(\mathbf{D})$, but without the oneOf constructor and with the *atleast* and *atmost* constructors limited to 0 and 1.

For the semantics of $\mathcal{SHIF}(\mathbf{D})$ and $\mathcal{SHOIN}(\mathbf{D})$, we refer the reader to [19].

Example 2.2 A small computer store obtains its hardware from several vendors. It uses the following description logic knowledge base L_1, which contains information about the product range that is provided by each vendor and about possible rebate conditions (we assume here that choosing two or more parts from the same seller causes a discount). For some parts, a shop may already be contracted as supplier.

> ≥ 1 *supplier* $\sqsubseteq$ *Shop*; $\top \sqsubseteq \forall supplier.Part$; ≥ 2 *supplier* $\sqsubseteq$ *Discount*;
> *Part(harddisk)*; *Part(cpu)*; *Part(case)*;
> *Shop*(s_1); *Shop*(s_2); *Shop*(s_3);
> *provides*(s_1, *case*); *provides*(s_2, *cpu*); *provides*(s_3, *case*);
> *provides*(s_1, *cpu*); *provides*(s_2, *harddisk*); *provides*(s_3, *harddisk*);
> *supplier*(s_3, *case*).

Here, the first two axioms determine *Shop* and *Part* as domain and range of the property *supplier*, respectively, while the third axiom constitutes the concept *Discount* by putting a cardinality constraint on *supplier*.

3   Description Logic Programs

In this section, we recall *description logic programs* (or simply *dl-programs*) from [13], which combine description logics and normal programs. They consist of a knowledge base L in a description logic and a finite set of description logic rules P. Such rules are similar to usual rules in logic programs with negation as failure, but may also contain *queries to* L, possibly default negated. In [13], we considered dl-programs that may also contain classical negation and not necessarily monotonic queries to L. Here, we consider only the case where classical negation is absent and all queries to L are monotonic. The former is only for ease of presentation, since every dl-program with classical negation can be translated into one without, like in the ordinary case. The latter, however, is a technical necessity for the well-founded semantics of dl-programs, but not a severe restriction, since most queries to L are in fact monotonic (naturally, a dl-program may still contain NAF-literals).

A dl-program consists of a description logic knowledge base L and a generalized normal program P, which may contain queries to L. Roughly, in such a query, it is asked whether a certain description logic axiom or its negation logically follows from L or not. Formally, a *dl-query* $Q(\mathbf{t})$ is either

(a) a concept inclusion axiom F or its negation $\neg F$; or
(b) of the forms $C(t)$ or $\neg C(t)$, where C is a concept and t is a term; or
(c) of the forms $R(t_1, t_2)$ or $\neg R(t_1, t_2)$,[1] where R is a role and t_1, t_2 are terms.

A *dl-atom* has the form

$$DL[S_1 op_1 p_1, \ldots, S_m op_m\, p_m; Q](\mathbf{t}), \qquad m \geq 0, \tag{2}$$

where each S_i is a concept or role, $op_i \in \{\uplus, \cup\}$, p_i is a unary resp. binary predicate symbol, and $Q(\mathbf{t})$ is a dl-query. We call $p_1, \ldots, p_m$ its *input predicate symbols*. Intuitively,

---

[1] Note that $\mathcal{SHOIN}(\mathbf{D})$ does not provide terminological role negation; we use the expression $\neg(\exists R.\{b\})(a)$ in order to add and query $\neg R(a, b)$ for a specific pair of individuals.

$op_i = \uplus$ (resp., $op_i = \cup$) increases S_i (resp., $\neg S_i$) by the extension of p_i. A *dl-rule* r is of form (1), where any $b \in B(r)$ may be a dl-atom. A *dl-program* $KB = (L, P)$ consists of a description logic knowledge base L and a finite set of dl-rules P. We say $KB = (L, P)$ is *positive* iff P is positive.

Example 3.1 Consider the dl-program $KB_1 = (L_1, P_1)$, with L_1 as in Example 2.2 and P_1 given as follows, choosing vendors for needed parts w.r.t. possible rebates:

(1) $vendor(s_2); \quad vendor(s_1); \quad vendor(s_3);$
(2) $needed(cpu); \quad needed(harddisk); \quad needed(case);$
(3) $avoid(V) \leftarrow vendor(V), not\ rebate(V);$
(4) $rebate(V) \leftarrow vendor(V), DL[supplier \uplus buy\_cand; Discount](V);$
(5) $buy\_cand(V, P) \leftarrow vendor(V), not\ avoid(V), DL[provides](V, P), needed(P),$
$\qquad\qquad\qquad not\ exclude(P)$
(6) $exclude(P) \leftarrow buy\_cand(V_1, P), buy\_cand(V_2, P), V_1 \neq V_2;$
(7) $exclude(P) \leftarrow DL[supplier](V, P), needed(P);$
(8) $supplied(V, P) \leftarrow DL[supplier \uplus buy\_cand; supplier](V, P), needed(P).$

Rules (3)–(5) choose a possible vendor (buy_cand) for each needed part, taking into account that the selection might affect the rebate condition (by feeding the possible vendor back to L_1, where the discount is determined). Rules (6) and (7) assure that each hardware part is bought only once, considering that for some parts a supplier might already be chosen. Rule (8) eventually summarizes all purchasing results.

Answer Set Semantics. In the sequel, let $KB = (L, P)$ be a dl-program. The *Herbrand base* of P, denoted HB_P, is the set of all ground atoms with a standard predicate symbol that occurs in P and constant symbols in Φ. An *interpretation I relative to P* is any subset of HB_P. We say that I is a *model* of $a \in HB_P$ under L, denoted $I \models_L a$, iff $a \in I$. We say that I is a *model* of a ground dl-atom $a = DL[S_1 op_1 p_1, \ldots, S_m op_m p_m; Q](\mathbf{c})$ under L, denoted $I \models_L a$, iff $L \cup \bigcup_{i=1}^{m} A_i(I) \models Q(\mathbf{c})$, where

- $A_i(I) = \{S_i(\mathbf{e}) \mid p_i(\mathbf{e}) \in I\}$, for $op_i = \uplus$; and
- $A_i(I) = \{\neg S_i(\mathbf{e}) \mid p_i(\mathbf{e}) \in I\}$, for $op_i = \cup$.

We say I is a *model* of a ground dl-rule r iff $I \models_L H(r)$ whenever $I \models_L B(r)$, that is, $I \models_L a$ for all $a \in B^+(r)$ and $I \not\models_L a$ for all $a \in B^-(r)$. We say I is a *model* of a dl-program $KB = (L, P)$, denoted $I \models KB$, iff $I \models_L r$ for all $r \in ground(P)$. We say KB is *satisfiable* (resp., *unsatisfiable*) iff it has some (resp., no) model.

A ground dl-atom a is *monotonic* relative to $KB = (L, P)$ iff $I \subseteq I' \subseteq HB_P$ implies that if $I \models_L a$ then $I' \models_L a$. In this paper, we consider only ground dl-atoms which are monotonic relative to a dl-program, but one can also define dl-atoms that are not monotonic; see [13].

Like ordinary positive programs, every positive dl-program KB is satisfiable and has a unique least model, denoted M_{KB}, which naturally characterizes its semantics.

The *strong answer set semantics* of general dl-programs is then defined by a reduction to the least model semantics of positive ones as follows, using a generalized transformation that removes all default-negated atoms in dl-rules.

For dl-programs $KB = (L, P)$, the *strong dl-transform* of P w.r.t. L and an interpretation $I \subseteq HB_P$, denoted sP_L^I, is the set of all dl-rules obtained from $ground(P)$ by (i) deleting every dl-rule r such that $I \models_L a$ for some $a \in B^-(r)$, and (ii) deleting from each remaining dl-rule r the negative body. Notice that sP_L^I generalizes the Gelfond-Lifschitz reduct P^I [15].

Let KB^I denote the dl-program (L, sP_L^I). Since KB^I is positive, it has the least model M_{KB^I}. A *strong answer set* (or simply *answer set*) of KB is an interpretation $I \subseteq HB_P$ such that $I = M_{KB^I}$.

Example 3.2 The dl-program $KB_1 = (L_1, P_1)$ of Example 3.1 has the following three strong answer sets (only relevant atoms are shown):

$\{supplied(s_3, case); supplied(s_2, cpu); supplied(s_2, harddisk); rebate(s_2); \dots \};$
$\{supplied(s_3, case); supplied(s_3, harddisk); rebate(s_3); \dots \};$
$\{supplied(s_3, case); \dots \}.$

Since the supplier s_3 was already fixed for the part *case*, two possibilities for a discount remain ($rebate(s_2)$ or $rebate(s_3)$); s_1 is not offering the needed part *harddisk*, and the shop will not give a discount only for the part *cpu*).

The strong answer set semantics of dl-programs $KB = (L, P)$ without dl-atoms coincides with the ordinary answer set semantics of P [15]. Furthermore, strong answer sets of a general dl-program KB are also minimal models of KB. Finally, positive and stratified dl-programs have exactly one strong answer set, which coincides with their canonical minimal model. Note that *stratified dl-programs* are composed of hierarchic layers of positive dl-programs that are linked via default negation [13].

4   Well-Founded Semantics

In this section, we define the well-founded semantics for dl-programs. We do this by generalizing the well-founded semantics for ordinary normal programs. More specifically, we generalize the definition based on unfounded sets as given in Section 2.

In the sequel, let $KB = (L, P)$ be a dl-program. We first define the notion of an unfounded set for dl-programs. Let $I \subseteq Lit_P$ be consistent. A set $U \subseteq HB_P$ is an *unfounded set* of KB relative to I iff the following holds:

($*$) for every $a \in U$ and every $r \in ground(P)$ with $H(r) = a$, either (i) $\neg b \in I \cup \neg.U$ for some ordinary atom $b \in B^+(r)$, or (ii) $b \in I$ for some ordinary atom $b \in B^-(r)$, or (iii) for some dl-atom $b \in B^+(r)$, it holds that $S^+ \not\models_L b$ for every consistent $S \subseteq Lit_P$ with $I \cup \neg.U \subseteq S$, or (iv) $I^+ \models_L b$ for some dl-atom $b \in B^-(r)$.

What is new here are Conditions (iii) and (iv). Intuitively, (iv) says that *not b* is for sure false, regardless of how I is further expanded, while (iii) says that b will never become true, if we expand I in a way such that all unfounded atoms are false. The following examples illustrate the concept of an unfounded set for dl-programs.

Example 4.1 Consider $KB_2 = (L_2, P_2)$, where $L_2 = \{S \sqsubseteq C\}$ and P_2 is as follows:

$$p(a) \leftarrow DL[S \uplus q; C](a); \qquad q(a) \leftarrow p(a); \qquad r(a) \leftarrow not\ q(a),\ not\ s(a).$$

Here, $S_1 = \{p(a), q(a)\}$ is an unfounded set of KB_2 relative to $I = \emptyset$, since $p(a)$ is unfounded due to (iii), while $q(a)$ is unfounded due to (i). The set $S_2 = \{s(a)\}$ is trivially an unfounded set of KB_2 relative to I, since no rule defining $s(a)$ exists.

Relative to $J = \{q(a)\}$, S_1 is not an unfounded set of KB_2 (for $p(a)$, the condition fails) but S_2 is. The set $S_3 = \{r(a)\}$ is another unfounded set of KB_2 relative to J.

Example 4.2 Consider the dl-program $KB_3 = (L_2, P_3)$ where P_3 results by negating the dl-literal in P_2. Then $S_1 = \{p(a), q(a)\}$ is not an unfounded set of KB_3 relative to $I = \emptyset$ (Condition (iv) fails for $p(a)$), but $S_2 = \{s(a)\}$ is. Relative to $J = \{q(a)\}$, however, both S_1 and S_2 as well as $S_3 = \{r(a)\}$ are unfounded sets of KB_3.

Example 4.3 The unfounded set of $KB_1 = (L_1, P_1)$ in Example 3.1 relative to $I_0 = \emptyset$ contains $buy\_cand(s_1, harddisk)$, $buy\_cand(s_2, case)$, and $buy\_cand(s_3, cpu)$ due to (iii), since the dl-atom in Rule (5) of P_1 will never evaluate to true for these pairs. It reflects the intuition that the concept *provides* narrows the choice for buying candidates.

The following lemma implies that KB has a greatest unfounded set relative to I.

Lemma 4.4 *Let $KB = (L, P)$ be a dl-program, and let $I \subseteq Lit_P$ be consistent. Then, the set of unfounded sets of KB relative to I is closed under union.*

We now generalize the operators T_P, U_P, and W_P to dl-programs as follows. We define the operators T_{KB}, U_{KB}, and W_{KB} on all consistent $I \subseteq Lit_P$ by:

- $a \in T_{KB}(I)$ iff $a \in HB_P$ and some $r \in ground(P)$ exists such that (a) $H(r) = a$, (b) $I^+ \models_L b$ for all $b \in B^+(r)$, (c) $\neg b \in I$ for all ordinary atoms $b \in B^-(r)$, and (d) $S^+ \not\models_L b$ for each consistent $S \subseteq Lit_P$ with $I \subseteq S$, for all dl-atoms $b \in B^-(r)$;
- $U_{KB}(I)$ is the greatest unfounded set of KB relative to I; and
- $W_{KB}(I) = T_{KB}(I) \cup \neg.U_{KB}(I)$.

The following result shows that the three operators are all monotonic.

Lemma 4.5 *Let KB be a dl-program. Then, T_{KB}, U_{KB}, and W_{KB} are monotonic.*

Thus, in particular, W_{KB} has a least fixpoint, denoted $lfp(W_{KB})$. The well-founded semantics of dl-programs can thus be defined as follows.

Definition 4.6 Let $KB = (L, P)$ be a dl-program. The *well-founded semantics* of KB, denoted $WFS(KB)$, is defined as $lfp(W_{KB})$. An atom $a \in HB_P$ is *well-founded* (resp., *unfounded*) relative to KB iff a (resp., $\neg a$) belongs to $WFS(KB)$.

The following examples illustrate the well-founded semantics of dl-programs.

Example 4.7 Consider KB_2 of Example 4.1. For $I_0 = \emptyset$, we have $T_{KB_2}(I_0) = \emptyset$ and $U_{KB_2}(I_0) = \{p(a), q(a), s(a)\}$. Hence, $W_{KB_2}(I_0) = \{\neg p(a), \neg q(a), \neg s(a)\}$ $(=I_1)$. In the next iteration, $T_{KB_2}(I_1) = \{r(a)\}$ and $U_{KB_2} = \{p(a), q(a), s(a)\}$. Thus, $W_{KB_2}(I_1) = \{\neg p(a), \neg q(a), r(a), \neg s(a)\}$ $(=I_2)$. Since I_2 is total and W_{KB_2} is monotonic, it follows $W_{KB_2}(I_2) = I_2$ and hence $WFS(KB_2) = \{\neg p(a), \neg q(a), r(a), \neg s(a)\}$. Accordingly, $r(a)$ is well-founded and all other atoms are unfounded relative to KB_2. Note that KB_2 has the unique answer set $I = \{r(a)\}$.

Example 4.8 Now consider KB_3 of Example 4.2. For $I_0 = \emptyset$, we have $T_{KB_3}(I_0) = \emptyset$ and $U_{KB_3}(I_0) = \{s(a)\}$. Hence, $W_{KB_3}(I_0) = \{\neg s(a)\}$ $(=I_1)$. In the next iteration, we have $T_{KB_3}(I_1) = \emptyset$ and $U_{KB_3}(I_1) = \{s(a)\}$. Then, $W_{KB_3}(I_1) = I_1$ and $WFS(KB_3) = \{\neg s(a)\}$; atom $s(a)$ is unfounded relative to KB_3. Note that KB_3 has no answer set.

Example 4.9 Consider again $U_{KB_1}(I_0 = \emptyset)$ of Example 4.3. $W_{KB_1}(I_0)$ consists of $\neg U_{KB_1}(I_0)$ and all facts of P_1. This input to the first iteration along with (iii) applied to Rule (8) adds those *supplied* atoms to $U_{KB_1}(I_1)$ that correspond to the (negated) *buy_cand* atoms of $U_{KB_1}(I_0)$. Then, $T_{KB_1}(I_1)$ contains *exclude(case)* which forces additional *buy_cand* atoms into $U_{KB_1}(I_2)$, regarding (i) and Rule (5). The same unfounded set thereby includes *rebate(s_1)*, stemming from Rule (4). As a consequence, *avoid(s_1)* is in $T_{KB_1}(I_3)$. Eventually, the final $WFS(KB_1)$ is not able to make any positive assumption about choosing a new vendor (*buy_cand*), but it is clear about s_1 being definitely not able to contribute to a discount situation, since a supplier for *case* is already chosen in L_1, and s_1 offers only a single further part.

5   Semantic Properties

In this section, we describe some semantic properties of the well-founded semantics for dl-programs. An immediate result is that it conservatively extends the well-founded semantics for ordinary normal programs.

Theorem 5.1 *Let* $KB = (L, P)$ *be a dl-program without dl-atoms. Then, the well-founded semantics of KB coincides with the well-founded semantics of P.*

The next result shows that the well-founded semantics of a dl-program $KB = (L, P)$ is a partial model of KB. Here, a consistent $I \subseteq Lit_P$ is a *partial model* of KB iff some consistent $J \subseteq Lit_P$ exists such that (i) $I \subseteq J$, (ii) J^+ is a model of KB, and (iii) J is *total*, i.e., $J^+ \cup (\neg.J)^+ = HB_P$. Intuitively, the three-valued I can be extended to a (two-valued) model $I' \subseteq HB_P$ of KB.

Theorem 5.2 *Let KB be a dl-program. Then, $WFS(KB)$ is a partial model of KB.*

Like in the case of ordinary normal programs, the well-founded semantics for positive and stratified dl-programs is total and coincides with their least model semantics and iterative least model semantics, respectively. This result can be elegantly proved using a characterization of the well-founded semantics given in the next section.

Theorem 5.3 *Let* $KB = (L, P)$ *be a dl-program. If KB is positive (resp., stratified), then (a) every ground atom* $a \in HB_P$ *is either well-founded or unfounded relative to KB, and (b)* $WFS(KB) \cap HB_P$ *is the least model (resp., the iterative least model) of KB, which coincides with the unique strong answer set of KB.*

Example 5.4 The dl-program KB_2 in Example 4.1 is stratified (intuitively, the recursion through negation is acyclic) while KB_3 in Example 4.2 is not. The result computed in Example 4.7 verifies the conditions of Theorem 5.3.

The following result shows that we can limit ourselves to dl-programs in *dl-query form*, where dl-atoms equate designated predicates. Formally, a dl-program $KB = (L, P)$ is in *dl-query form*, if each $r \in P$ involving a dl-atom is of the form $a \leftarrow b$, where b is a dl-atom. Any dl-program $KB = (L, P)$ can be transformed into a dl-program $KB^{dl} = (L, P^{dl})$ in dl-query form. Here, P^{dl} is obtained from P by replacing every dl-atom $a(\mathbf{t}) = DL[S_1 op_1 p_1, \ldots, S_m op_m \, p_m; Q](\mathbf{t})$ by $p_a(\mathbf{t})$, and by adding the dl-rule $p_a(\mathbf{X}) \leftarrow a(\mathbf{X})$ to P, where p_a is a new predicate symbol and $\mathbf{X}$ is a list of variables corresponding to $\mathbf{t}$. Informally, p_a is an abbreviation for a. The following result now shows that KB^{dl} and KB are equivalent under the well-founded semantics. Intuitively, the well-founded semantics tolerates abbreviations in the sense that they do not change the semantics of a dl-program.

Theorem 5.5 *Let* $KB = (L, P)$ *be a dl-program. Then,* $WFS(KB) = WFS(KB^{dl}) \cap Lit_P$.

6   Relationship to Strong Answer Set Semantics

In this section, we show that the well-founded semantics for dl-programs can be characterized in terms of the least and greatest fixpoint of a monotone operator γ^2_{KB} similar as the well-founded semantics for ordinary normal programs [5]. We then use this characterization to derive further properties of the well-founded semantics for dl-programs.

For a dl-program $KB = (L, P)$, define the operator γ_{KB} on interpretations $I \subseteq HB_P$ by

$$\gamma_{KB}(I) = M_{KB^I},$$

i.e., as the least model of the positive dl-program $KB^I = (L, sP^I_L)$. The next result shows that γ_{KB} is anti-monotonic, like its counterpart for ordinary normal programs [5]. Note that this result holds only if all dl-atoms in P are monotonic.

Proposition 6.1 *Let* $KB = (L, P)$ *be a dl-program. Then,* γ_{KB} *is anti-monotonic.*

Hence, the operator $\gamma^2_{KB}(I) = \gamma_{KB}(\gamma_{KB}(I))$, for all $I \subseteq HB_P$, is monotonic and thus has a least and a greatest fixpoint, denoted $lfp(\gamma^2_{KB})$ and $gfp(\gamma^2_{KB})$, respectively. We can use these fixpoints to characterize the well-founded semantics of KB.

Theorem 6.2 *Let* $KB = (L, P)$ *be a dl-program. Then, an atom* $a \in HB_P$ *is well-founded (resp., unfounded) relative to KB iff* $a \in lfp(\gamma^2_{KB})$ *(resp.,* $a \notin gfp(\gamma^2_{KB})$*).*

Example 6.3 Consider the dl-program KB_1 from Example 3.1. The set $lfp(\gamma^2_{KB_1})$ contains the atoms $avoid(s_1)$ and $supplied(s_3, case)$, while $gfp(\gamma^2_{KB_1})$ does not contain $rebate(s_1)$. Thus, $WFS(KB_1)$ contains the literals $avoid(s_1)$, $supplied(s_3, case)$, and $\neg rebate(s_1)$, corresponding to the result of Example 4.9 (and, moreover, to the intersection of all answer sets of KB_1).

The next theorem shows that the well-founded semantics for dl-programs approximates their strong answer set semantics. That is, every well-founded ground atom is true in every answer set, and every unfounded ground atom is false in every answer set.

Theorem 6.4 *Let $KB = (L, P)$ be a dl-program. Then, every strong answer set of KB includes all atoms $a \in HB_P$ that are well-founded relative to KB and no atom $a \in HB_P$ that is unfounded relative to KB.*

A ground atom a is a *cautious* (resp., *brave*) *consequence under the strong answer set semantics* of a dl-program KB iff a is true in every (resp., some) strong answer set of KB. Hence, under the strong answer set semantics, every well-founded and no unfounded ground atom is a cautious (resp., brave) consequence of KB.

Corollary 6.5 *Let $KB = (L, P)$ be a dl-program. Then, under the strong answer set semantics, every well-founded atom $a \in HB_P$ relative to KB is a cautious (resp., brave) consequence of KB, and no unfounded atom $a \in HB_P$ relative to KB is a cautious (resp., brave) consequence of a satisfiable KB.*

If the well-founded semantics of a dl-program $KB=(L, P)$ is total, i.e., contains either a or $\neg a$ for every $a \in HB_P$, then it specifies the only strong answer set of KB.

Theorem 6.6 *Let $KB = (L, P)$ be a dl-program. If every atom $a \in HB_P$ is either well-founded or unfounded relative to KB, then the set of all well-founded atoms $a \in HB_P$ relative to KB is the only strong answer set of KB.*

7   Computation and Complexity

For any positive dl-program $KB = (L, P)$, its least model M_{KB} is the least fixpoint of $T_{KB}(I)$ [13]. Thus, $\gamma_{KB}(I) = M_{KB^I}$ (with $KB^I = (L, sP^I_L)$) can be computed as

$$lfp(T_{KB^I}) = \bigcup_{i \geq 0} T^i_{KB^I}(\emptyset) \quad (= \bigcup_{i=0}^{|HB_P|} T^i_{KB^I}(\emptyset)).$$

The least and greatest fixpoint of γ^2_{KB} can be constructed as the limits

$$U_\infty = \bigcup_{i \geq 0} U_i, \text{ where } U_0 = \emptyset, \text{ and } U_{i+1} = \gamma^2_{KB}(U_i), \text{ for } i \geq 0, \text{ and}$$
$$O_\infty = \bigcap_{i \geq 0} O_i, \text{ where } O_0 = HB_P, \text{ and } O_{i+1} = \gamma^2_{KB}(O_i), \text{ for } i \geq 0,$$

respectively, which are both reached within $|HB_P|$ many steps.

We recall that for a given ordinary normal program, computing the well-founded model needs exponential time in general (measured in the program size [11]), and also reasoning from the well-founded model has exponential time complexity.

Furthermore, evaluating a ground dl-atom a for $KB = (L, P)$ of the form (2) given an interpretation I_p of its input predicates $p = p_1, \ldots, p_m$ (i.e., deciding $I \models_L a$ for each I that coincides on p with I_p) is complete for EXP (resp., co-NEXP) for L from $\mathcal{SHIF}(\mathbf{D})$ (resp., $\mathcal{SHOIN}(\mathbf{D})$) [13], where EXP (resp., NEXP) denotes exponential (resp., nondeterministic exponential) time; this is inherited from the complexity of the satisfiability problem for $\mathcal{SHIF}(\mathbf{D})$ (resp., $\mathcal{SHOIN}(\mathbf{D})$) [31,19].

The following result implies that the complexity of the well-founded semantics for dl-programs over $\mathcal{SHIF}(\mathbf{D})$ does not increase over the one of ordinary logic programs.

Theorem 7.1 *Given Φ and a dl-program $KB=(L, P)$ with L in $\mathcal{SHIF}(\mathbf{D})$, computing $WFS(KB)$ is feasible in exponential time. Furthermore, deciding whether for a given literal l it holds that $l \in WFS(KB)$ is* EXP*-complete.*

For dl-programs over $\mathcal{SHOIN}(\mathbf{D})$, the computation of $WFS(KB)$ and reasoning from it is expected to be more complex than for $\mathcal{SHIF}(\mathbf{D})$ knowledge bases, since already evaluating a single dl-atom is co-NEXP-hard. Computing WFS can be done, in a similar manner as in the case of $\mathcal{SHIF}(\mathbf{D})$, in exponential time using an oracle for evaluating dl-atoms; to this end, an NP oracle is sufficient. As for the reasoning problem, this means that deciding $l \in WFS(KB)$ is in $\mathrm{EXP}^{\mathrm{NP}}$.

A more precise account reveals the following strict characterization of the complexity, which is believed to be lower.

Theorem 7.2 *Given Φ, a dl-program $KB = (L, P)$ with L in $\mathcal{SHOIN}(\mathbf{D})$, and a literal l, deciding $l \in WFS(KB)$ is* $\mathrm{P}^{\mathrm{NEXP}}$*-complete.*

The results in Theorems 7.1 and 7.2 also show that, like for ordinary normal programs, inference under the well-founded semantics is computationally less complex than under the answer set semantics, since cautious reasoning from the strong answer sets of a dl-programs using a $\mathcal{SHIF}(\mathbf{D})$ (resp., $\mathcal{SHOIN}(\mathbf{D})$) description logic knowledge base is complete for co-NEXP (resp., co-$\mathrm{NP}^{\mathrm{NEXP}}$) [13].

We leave an account of the data complexity of dl-programs $KB = (L, P)$ (i.e., L and the rules of P are fixed, while facts in P may vary) for further work. However, we note that whenever the evaluation of dl-atoms is polynomial (i.e., in description logic terminology, A-Box reasoning is polynomial), then also the computation of the well-founded semantics for dl-programs is polynomial. Most recent results in [23] suggest that for $\mathcal{SHIF}(\mathbf{D})$, the problem is solvable in polynomial time with an NP oracle (and, presumably, complete for that complexity).

8   Related Work

Related work can be divided into (a) hybrid approaches using description logics as input to logic programs, (b) approaches reducing description logics to logic programs, (c) combinations of description logics with default and defeasible logic, and (d) approaches to rule-based well-founded reasoning in the Semantic Web. Below we discuss some representatives for (a)–(d). Further works are discussed in [13].

The works by Donini *et al.* [12], Levy and Rousset [24], and Rosati [29] are representatives of hybrid approaches using description logics as input. Donini *et al.* [12] introduce a combination of (disjunction-, negation-, and function-free) datalog with the description logic $\mathcal{ALC}$. An integrated knowledge base consists of a structural component in $\mathcal{ALC}$ and a relational component in datalog, where the integration of both components lies in using concepts from the structural component as constraints in rule bodies of the relational component.

The closely related work by Levy and Rousset [24] presents a combination of Horn rules with the description logic $\mathcal{ALCNR}$. In contrast to Donini *et al.* [12], Levy and Rousset also allow for roles as constraints in rule bodies, and do not require the safety condition that variables in constraints in the body of a rule r must also appear in ordinary atoms in the body of r. Finally, Rosati [29] presents a combination of disjunctive datalog (with classical and default negation, but without function symbols) with $\mathcal{ALC}$, which is based on a generalized answer set semantics.

Some approaches reducing description logic reasoning to logic programming are the works by Van Belleghem *et al.* [32], Alsaç and Baral [1], Swift [30], Grosof *et al.* [17], and Hufstadt *et al.* [23]. In detail, Van Belleghem *et al.* [32] analyze the close relationship between description logics and open logic programs, and present a mapping of description logic knowledge bases in $\mathcal{ALCN}$ to open logic programs. Alsaç and Baral [1] and Swift [30] reduce inference in the description logic $\mathcal{ALCQI}$ to query answering from normal logic programs (with default negation, but without disjunctions and classical negations) under the answer set semantics. Grosof *et al.* [17] show how inference in a subset of the description logic $\mathcal{SHOIQ}$ can be reduced to inference in a subset of function-free Horn programs (where negations and disjunctions are disallowed), and vice versa. The type of inference follows traditional minimal model semantics, thus not allowing for nonmonotonic reasoning. In contrast to a mapping between description logics and logic programs, we presented a full-fledged coupling under the well-founded semantics. Hufstadt *et al.* [23] show how $\mathcal{SHIQ}(\mathbf{D})$ can be reduced to disjunctive datalog and exploit this for efficient query answering. As a byproduct of their reduction, they obtain a decidable extension of $\mathcal{SHIQ}(\mathbf{D})$ with positive rules in which variables are bound to objects occurring in the extensional part of the description logic knowledge base. These rules, however, have classical first-order semantics; this can be easily emulated within the strong answer set semantics of [13]. Handling negation is not addressed in [23].

Early work on dealing with default information in description logics is the approach due to Baader and Hollunder [4], where Reiter's default logic is adapted to terminological knowledge bases, differing significantly from our approach. Antoniou [2] combines defeasible reasoning with description logics for the Semantic Web. In [3], Antoniou and Wagner summarize defeasible and strict reasoning in a single rule formalism, building on the idea of using rules as a uniform basis for the Ontology, Logic, and Proof layers. Like in other work above, the considered description logics serve only as an input for the nonmonotonic reasoning mechanism running on top of it. Note that defeasible logic is in general different from well-founded semantics, the latter being able to draw more conclusions in certain situations [9]. Maher and Governatori [25] present a well-founded defeasible logic, based on the definition of unfounded sets by Van Gelder *et al.* [34], which reconstructs the well-founded semantics.

An important approach to rule-based reasoning under the well-founded semantics for the Semantic Web is due to Damásio [10]. He aims at developing Prolog tools for implementing different semantics for RuleML [8]. So far, an XML parser library as well as a RuleML compiler have been developed, providing routines to convert RuleML rule bases to Prolog and vice versa. Currently, the compiler supports paraconsistent well-founded semantics with explicit negation; it is planned to be extended to use XSB. However, as a crucial difference to our work, the approach of [10] does not address interfacing to ontologies and ontology reasoning, and thus provides no direct support for integrating rule-based and ontology reasoning, which we have done in this paper.

9   Summary and Outlook

We have presented the well-founded semantics for dl-programs, which generalizes the well-founded semantics for ordinary normal programs [34]. We have given a definition via greatest unfounded sets for dl-programs as well as an equivalent characterization using a generalized Gelfond-Lifschitz transform. We have then analyzed the semantic properties of the well-founded semantics for dl-programs. In particular, we have shown that it generalizes the well-founded semantics for ordinary normal programs. Moreover, in the general case, the well-founded semantics for dl-programs is a partial model that approximates the answer set semantics, while in the positive and stratified case, it is a total model that coincides with the answer set semantics. Finally, we have also provided detailed complexity results for dl-programs under the well-founded semantics.

An experimental prototype implementation using a datalog engine and RACER [18] is available at `http://www.kr.tuwien.ac.at/staff/roman/dlwfs/`. An interesting topic for further work is to extend the presented well-founded semantics to more general dl-programs, which may, for example, allow for disjunctions, NAF-literals, and dl-atoms in the heads of dl-rules. Furthermore, employing RuleML as a versatile and expressive syntax for our formalism could provide a standardized and well-accepted interface to other applications. Finally, to further enrich description logic programs, we plan to examine the possibility of resolution mechanisms for conflicting rules, like priority relations as in courteous logic programs [16] and defeasible logic [3].

References

1. G. Alsaç and C. Baral. Reasoning in description logics using declarative logic programming. Tech. report, Computer Science and Engineering Dept., Arizona State University, 2001.
2. G. Antoniou. Nonmonotonic rule systems on top of ontology layers. In *Proc. ISWC-2002*, *LNCS* 2342, pp. 394–398, 2002.
3. G. Antoniou and G. Wagner. Rules and defeasible reasoning on the Semantic Web. In *Proc. RuleML-2003*, *LNCS* 2876, pp. 111–120, 2003.
4. F. Baader and B. Hollunder. Embedding defaults into terminological representation systems. *J. Automated Reasoning*, 14:149–180, 1995.
5. C. Baral and V. S. Subrahmanian. Dualities between alternative semantics for logic programming and nonmonotonic reasoning. *J. Automated Reasoning*, 10(3):399–420, 1993.

96   T. Eiter et al.

6. T. Berners-Lee. *Weaving the Web*. Harper, San Francisco, CA, 1999.
7. T. Berners-Lee, J. Hendler, and O. Lassila. The Semantic Web. *Scientific American*, 284(5):34–43, 2001.
8. H. Boley, S. Tabet, and G. Wagner. Design rationale for RuleML: A markup language for Semantic Web rules. In *Proc. SWWS-2001*, pp. 381–401, 2001.
9. G. Brewka. On the relationship between defeasible logic and well-founded semantics. In *Proc. LPNMR-2001, LNCS* 2713, pp. 121–132, 2001.
10. C. V. Damásio. The W^4 Project, 2002.
    `http://centria.di.fct.unl.pt/~cd/projectos/w4/index.htm`.
11. E. Dantsin, T. Eiter, G. Gottlob, and A. Voronkov. Complexity and expressive power of logic programming. *ACM Computing Surveys*, 33(3):374–425, 2001.
12. F. M. Donini, M. Lenzerini, D. Nardi, and A. Schaerf. $\mathcal{AL}$-log: Integrating datalog and description logics. *Journal of Intelligent Information Systems (JIIS)*, 10(3):227–252, 1998.
13. T. Eiter, T. Lukasiewicz, R. Schindlauer, and H. Tompits. Combining answer set programming with description logics for the Semantic Web. In *Proc. KR-2004*, pp. 141–151, 2004. Preliminary Report RR-1843-03-13, Institut für Informationssysteme, TU Wien, 2003.
14. D. Fensel, W. Wahlster, H. Lieberman, and J. Hendler, editors. *Spinning the Semantic Web: Bringing the World Wide Web to Its Full Potential*. MIT Press, 2002.
15. M. Gelfond and V. Lifschitz. Classical negation in logic programs and deductive databases. *New Generation Computing*, 17:365–387, 1991.
16. B. N. Grosof. Courteous logic programs: Prioritized conflict handling for rules. IBM Research Report RC 20836, IBM Research Division, T.J. Watson Research, 1997.
17. B. N. Grosof, I. Horrocks, R. Volz, and S. Decker. Description logic programs: Combining logic programs with description logics. In *Proc. WWW-2003*, pp. 48–57, 2003.
18. V. Haarslev and R. Möller. RACER system description. In *Proc. IJCAR-2001, LNCS* 2083, pp. 701–705, 2001.
19. I. Horrocks and P. F. Patel-Schneider. Reducing OWL entailment to description logic satisfiability. In *Proc. ISWC-2003, LNCS* 2870, pp. 17–29, 2003.
20. I. Horrocks and P. F. Patel-Schneider. A proposal for an OWL Rules Language. In *Proc. WWW-2004*, pp. 723–731, 2004.
21. I. Horrocks, P. F. Patel-Schneider, and F. van Harmelen. From $\mathcal{SHIQ}$ and RDF to OWL: The making of a web ontology language. *Journal of Web Semantics*, 1(1):7–26, 2003.
22. I. Horrocks, U. Sattler, and S. Tobies. Practical reasoning for expressive description logics. In *Proc. LPAR-1999, LNCS* 1705, pp. 161–180, 1999.
23. U. Hufstadt, B. Motik, and U. Sattler. Reasoning for description logics around $\mathcal{SHIQ}$ in a resolution framework. Technical Report 3-8-04/04, FZI Karlsruhe, 2004.
24. A. Y. Levy and M.-C. Rousset. Combining Horn rules and description logics in CARIN. *Artif. Intell.*, 104(1-2):165–209, 1998.
25. M. J. Maher and G. Governatori. A semantic decomposition of defeasible logics. In *Proc. AAAI/IAAI-1999*, pp. 299–305, 1999.
26. W. May, B. Ludäscher, and G. Lausen. Well-founded semantics for deductive object-oriented database languages. In F. Bry, R. Ramakrishnan, and K. Ramamohanarao, editors, *Proc. DOOD-1997, LNCS* 1341, pp. 320–336, 1997.
27. I. Niemelä, P. Simons, and T. Syrjänen. Smodels: A system for answer set programming. In *Proc. NMR-2000*, 2000.
28. P. Rao, K. Sagonas, T. Swift, D. S. Warren, and J. Freire. XSB: A system for efficiently computing WFS. In *Proc. LPNMR-1997, LNCS* 1265, pp. 430–440, 1997.
29. R. Rosati. Towards expressive KR systems integrating datalog and description logics: Preliminary report. In *Proc. DL-1999*, pp. 160–164, 1999.
30. T. Swift. Deduction in ontologies via ASP. In *Proc. LPNMR-2004, LNCS* 2923, pp. 275–288, 2004.

31. S. Tobies. *Complexity Results and Practical Algorithms for Logics in Knowledge Representation*. PhD thesis, RWTH Aachen, Germany, 2001.
32. K. Van Belleghem, M. Denecker, and D. De Schreye. A strong correspondence between description logics and open logic programming. In *Proc. ICLP-1997*, pp. 346–360, 1997.
33. A. Van Gelder. The alternating fixpoint of logic programs with negation. In *Proc. PODS-1989*, pp. 1–10, 1989.
34. A. Van Gelder, K. A. Ross, and J. S. Schlipf. The well-founded semantics for general logic programs. *Journal of the ACM*, 38(3):620–650, 1991.
35. W3C. OWL web ontology language overview, 2004. W3C Recommendation (10 February 2004). Available at `www.w3.org/TR/2004/REC-owl-features-20040210/`.

Defeasible Description Logics

Guido Governatori

School of Information Technology and Electrical Engineering
The University of Queensland
Brisbane, QLD 4072, Australia
guido@itee.uq.edu.au

Abstract. We propose to extend description logic with defeasible rules, and to use the inferential mechanism of defeasible logic to reason with description logic constructors.

1 Introduction

This paper examines the addition of intelligent properties to the implementation of and reasoning on ontologies, where an open world is assumed. The motivation of this work lies in a current inability to reason intuitively on ontologies with incomplete or inconsistent information. Very often it is not possible to have complete information or complete knowledge of a domain that we wish to reason on. And herein lays the problem for the logics currently employed for reasoning on knowledge bases. This problem lies in the fact that most ontologies are represented using a language based on First order logic which is inappropriate for reasoning on partial, incomplete and inconsistent knowledge. For this reason an attempt has been made, by using a language which has proven successful in the field of ontologies and combining its principles with properties of a more flexible logic, to solve in part the motivating problem driving this work. The proposed method for solving this is to integrate two established forms of logic, Description logic [8] and Defeasible logic [4,10,24]. Description logics though imparting strong and conclusive reasoning mechanisms, lack the flexibility of Defeasible logics non-monotonic reasoning mechanisms, which add flexibility to knowledge bases that have partial knowledge. The project involves specifically the addition of defeasible rules to a description logic knowledge base to achieve a flexible and decidable language on which reasoning can occur.

Though adding non-monotonicity to description logics is not entirely a new concept [19,21,7,25,26,6,28], in this paper we take a unique perspective on the problem domain and the method by which this problem could be solved.

In [6,7,25,28,26] Description logic is extended with default with and without priorities; moreover [25,26] discuss the notion of defeasible subsumption.

Another approach, discussed in [19], involves the study of the intersection between two formal logics, Description Logic Programs and Description Horn Logic, with the aim of adding a large amount of expressiveness to description logic. In [21] an extension to Description logic $\mathcal{SHOQ}$ is attempted via the

G. Antoniou and H. Boley (Eds.): RuleML 2004, LNCS 3323, pp. 98–112, 2004.
© Springer-Verlag Berlin Heidelberg 2004

addition of a preference order similar to the superiority relation in Defeasible Logic. This paper discusses the applicability of the "introduction of preferred models", in this case the preference being to "select axioms that defeat as few conclusions as possible ... or the least preferred axioms".

Finally some combinations of Defeasible logic and Description logic have been proposed. [1,5,29] propose to combine the two logics by adding a layer of rules (from Defeasible Logic) on top of ontologies in Description Logic. The language is partitioned in two disjoint classes, literals and dl-literals. In this approach dl-literals corresponds to the concepts defined in Description Logic and can appear only in the antecedents of rule, while normal literals not subject to such restriction. Thus dl-literal exhibit a monotonic behaviour while normal literals are non-monotonic. A similar approach is adopted in [13] for the integration of Description Logic knowledge bases and Logic Programs.

The paper is organised as follows: in Section 2 and 3 we introduce the two basic logic to be integrated, namely Description Logic and Defeasible Logic; then in Section 4 we discuss how the two formalisms can be combined to produce a Defeasible Description Logic, and in Section 5 we illustrate some of the added features of the new logic with the help of an example. Finally Section 6 presents a short discussion of the results and hints for future work.

2   Description Logic

Description logics are monotonic formalisms based upon first-order logic [9]. Essentially Description logics are comprised of atomic concepts and atomic roles. Atomic concepts are related to particular entities within the knowledge base, an example of this is that 'Man' may be a concept, with perhaps BILL as an instance of the concept. Atomic roles, however, are used to express binary relationships between individuals, that is wherever we may have an instance of BILL being a parent, therefore we can conclude that BILL is can be associated with the role 'hasChild', for example 'hasChild(BILL, PETER)', where hasChild is the role that binds the father, BILL, to his son, PETER. A Description logic is characterised by a set of constructors that facilitate building complex concepts and roles. Concepts are interpreted as sets of objects and roles are seen as (binary) relations between objects in the domain.

Description logic allows for the representation of concept conjunctions, concept disjunctions, and concept negations [9].

Concept conjunction relates to the ability to join one or more concepts to define a complex concept or at least its properties or characteristics. Concept conjunction can be illustrated by the following example

$$\text{Father} \sqsubseteq \text{Man} \sqcap \text{Parent}$$

Here we can see that the instances in the set of men who also appear as instances in the set of parents can be defined, as subsuming the set of instances of the concept father, which is to say all instances of the concept Father will also be instances in the set of concepts Man and Parent.

Concept disjunction relates to the ability to restrict the definition of a complex concept or at least its properties or characteristics, to appearing in the set of one concept or the other. Concept disjunction can be illustrated by the following example

$$\text{Person} \sqsubseteq \text{Man} \sqcup \text{Woman}$$

Here we can see that the instances in the set of person can appear in the set of man or in the set of woman. For this reason the set of instances of man is a subset of the set of people and furthermore the set of woman is a subset of person.

Concept negation is the construct that allows complex concepts to be defined with the negation of another concept. It is useful in situations where we want to define concepts that are disjoint to another concept as seen in the following example

$$\text{Woman} \sqsubseteq \neg\text{Man} \sqcap \text{Person}$$

In this example, the concept man is negated to denote all instances in the domain which do not appear in the set of man unioned with the concept person appears as the subset of the concept woman. Therefore all the instances in the set of Woman should appear in the set of instances for the concept Person but not in the set of Man.

Description Logic also allows value or role restriction constructs [9]. Role restriction ($\forall R.C$) is the construct that requires that all the individuals that are in a specified relationship R with the concept being described belong to the concept C. Role restriction can be illustrated using the following example

$$\forall \text{hasChild.female}$$

which returns all individuals who have only daughters and no sons.

Though description logics can offer further constructors in lower abstractions of the logic, in this paper we will focus on these four constructors. Moreover negation is applied only to atomic concepts. Therefore only the $\mathcal{ALC}^-$ subset of description logic has been extended with defeasibility (Section 4).

The semantics of Description Logic is given in terms of an interpretation, consisting of a non empty set $\Delta^{\mathcal{I}}$ and an interpretation function $\cdot^{\mathcal{I}}$, and is defined symbolically as

$$\mathcal{I} = (\Delta^{\mathcal{I}}, \cdot^{\mathcal{I}})$$

The interpretation function gives the extension of the concepts and roles, and it assigns to every atomic concept a subset of $\Delta^{\mathcal{I}}$ and every atomic role a binary relation in $\Delta^{\mathcal{I}} \times \Delta^{\mathcal{I}}$. The semantic interpretation of the operators described above is defined as follows:

Syntax	Semantics
A	$A^{\mathcal{I}} \subseteq \Delta^{\mathcal{I}}$
R	$R^{\mathcal{I}} \subseteq \Delta^{\mathcal{I}} \times \Delta^{\mathcal{I}}$
$\top$	$\Delta^{\mathcal{I}}$
$\bot$	$\emptyset$
$C \sqcap D$	$C^{\mathcal{I}} \cap D^{\mathcal{I}}$
$C \sqcup D$	$C^{\mathcal{I}} \cup D^{\mathcal{I}}$
$\neg C$	$\Delta^{\mathcal{I}} \setminus C^{\mathcal{I}}$
$\forall R.C$	$\{x \mid \forall y : (x,y) \in R^{\mathcal{I}} \to y \in C^{\mathcal{I}}\}$

Description logics knowledge bases are made up of TBoxes and ABoxes. TBoxes contain concept definitions, where concept definitions define new concepts based on preexisting concepts. An example of such a concept definition is

$$\textsf{Woman} \equiv \textsf{Person} \sqcap \textsf{Female}$$

The use of equivalence allows in this case for an instance of woman to be created where there is an instance of both person and female. Therefore in this way TBoxes in description logic knowledge bases provide definite and strict representations of the conditions required to create new concepts and in turn instances of those concepts. TBoxes however must contain only one definition for each unique concept name in the spirit of developing conflict free knowledge bases. Furthermore a definition cannot reference itself and as such must not cyclically reference itself.

ABoxes, conversely contain assertional information, they define specific roles or concepts and are known to change based on circumstances. An example of the type of information that can be present in an ABox includes

a concept instance such as $\textsf{Person}(\textsf{JILL})$

a role instance such as $\textsf{Mother}(\textsf{JILL}, \textsf{BILL})$

From this ABox we have the assertional information that JILL is an instance of the concept type Person. Furthermore the role, which binds the instances of JILL and BILL via the Mother role, is also present and it denotes that JILL is BILL's mother. As in TBoxes, unique names must be adhered to in ABoxes and as such if there exists two instances of a concept with the same instance name, these concepts are interpreted to be equivalent.

Subsumption is the basic reasoning method of description logic. Given two concepts C and D and a knowledge base Σ, the following illustrates that D subsumes C in Σ.

$$\Sigma \models C \sqsubseteq D$$

this requires that it be proved that in Σ, that D (the subsumer) is more general than C (the subsumee), or, in other terms, that the extension of C is included in the extension of D. For example

$$\textsf{Woman} \sqsubseteq \textsf{Person}$$

means that the concept of woman is considered more specialised than the concept of person. That is the set of elements belonging to the concept Woman can be found in the set of elements belonging to the concept Person, and as such the domain of Woman in a subset of the domain of Person, formally

$$\text{Woman}^{\mathcal{I}} \subseteq \text{Person}^{\mathcal{I}}$$

An extension of the above reasoning mechanism is concept equivalence. Equivalence is the reasoning mechanism whereby two concepts are checked to see if the set of instances in one concept is the same as the set of instances for the other concept. This reasoning mechanism can be represented symbolically as

$$\Sigma \models C \equiv D$$

and an example of equivalence check in description logic may involve verifying that the set of mothers is equivalent to the set of women with children

Concept satisfiability is another reasoning mechanism employed by description logics. Concept satisfiability relates to the check that is performed to ensure that there exists a semantic interpretation of the concept that does not result in the empty set. This is represented symbolically as

$$\Sigma \not\models C \equiv \bot$$

which means that the extension of C is not equivalent to the empty set (the extension of the $\bot$ concept).

3   Defeasible Logic

Defeasible Logic has been developed by Nute [24] over several years with a particular concern about computational efficiency (indeed, its efficiency is linear cf. [22]) and ease of implementation (nowadays several implementations exist [11, 23] and some of them can deal with theories consisting of over 100,000 propositional rules [23]). In [3] it was shown that Defeasible logic is flexible enough to deal with several intuitions of non-monotonic reasoning, and it has been applied to legal reasoning [2,16], automated negotiation [14,12], contracts [27], business rules [20], and multi-agent systems [18,17,15,16].

It is not possible in this short paper to give a complete formal description of the logic. However, we hope to give enough information to make the discussion intelligible. We refer the reader to [24,10,4] for more thorough treatments. As usual with non-monotonic reasoning, we have to specify 1) how to represent a knowledge base and 2) the inference mechanism.

We begin by presenting the basic ingredients of Defeasible Logic. A defeasible theory contains five different kinds of knowledge: facts, strict rules, defeasible rules, defeaters, and a superiority relation. We consider only essentially propositional rules. Rules containing free variables are interpreted as the set of their variable-free instances.

Facts are indisputable statements, for example, "Guido is a lecturer". In the logic, this might be expressed as Lecturer(GUIDO).

Strict rules are rules in the classical sense: whenever the premises are indisputable (e.g., facts) then so is the conclusion. An example of a strict rule is "Lecturers are faculty member". Written formally:

$$\text{Lecturer}(x) \rightarrow \text{FacultyMember}(x).$$

Defeasible rules are rules that can be defeated by contrary evidence. An example of such a rule is "people giving lectures are faculty members"; written formally:

$$\text{GivesLectures}(x) \Rightarrow \text{FacultyMember}(x).$$

The idea is that if we know that someone gives a lecture, then we may conclude that he/she is a faculty member, *unless there is other evidence suggesting that it may not be a faculty member.*

Defeaters are rules that cannot be used to draw any conclusions. Their only use is to prevent some conclusions. In other words, they are used to defeat some defeasible rules by producing evidence to the contrary. An example is "tutors might not be faculty members". Formally:

$$\text{Tutor}(x) \rightsquigarrow \neg\text{FacultyMember}(x).$$

The main point is that the information that somebody is a tutor is not sufficient evidence to conclude that he/she is not a faculty member. It is only evidence that the tutor *may* not be a faculty member. In other words, we do not wish to conclude ¬FacultyMember if Tutor, we simply want to prevent a conclusion FacultyMember in absence of further information.

The *superiority relation* among rules is used to define priorities among rules, that is, where one rule may override the conclusion of another rule. For example, given the defeasible rules

$$r : \quad \text{GivesLectures}(x) \Rightarrow \text{FacultyMember}(x)$$
$$r' : \text{GuestLecturer}(x) \Rightarrow \neg\text{FacultyMember}(x)$$

which contradict one another, no conclusive decision can be made about whether a guest lecturer is a faculty member. But if we introduce a superiority relation $>$ with $r' > r$, then we can indeed conclude that the guest lecturer cannot be a faculty member. The superiority relation is required to be acyclic. It turns out that we only need to define the superiority relation over rules with contradictory conclusions.

A *rule* r consists of its *antecedent* (or *body*) $A(r)$ ($A(r)$ may be omitted if it is the empty set) which is a finite set of literals, an arrow, and its *consequent* (or *head*) $C(r)$ which is a literal. Given a set R of rules, we denote the set of all strict rules in R by R_s, the set of strict and defeasible rules in R by R_{sd}, the set of defeasible rules in R by R_d, and the set of defeaters in R by R_{dft}. $R[q]$ denotes the set of rules in R with consequent q. If q is a literal, $\sim q$ denotes the complementary literal (if q is a positive literal p then $\sim q$ is $\neg p$; and if q is $\neg p$, then $\sim q$ is p).

A *defeasible theory* D is a triple $(F, R, >)$ where F is a finite set of facts, R a finite set of rules, and $>$ a superiority relation on R.

A *conclusion* of D is a tagged literal and can have one of the following four forms:

$+\Delta q$, which is intended to mean that q is definitely provable in D (i.e., using only facts and strict rules).

$-\Delta q$, which is intended to mean that we have proved that q is not definitely provable in D.

$+\partial q$, which is intended to mean that q is defeasibly provable in D.

$-\partial q$ which is intended to mean that we have proved that q is not defeasibly provable in D.

Provability is based on the concept of a *derivation* (or proof) in $D = (F, R, >)$. A derivation is a finite sequence $P = (P(1), \ldots, P(n))$ of tagged literals satisfying four conditions (which correspond to inference rules for each of the four kinds of conclusion). $P(1..i)$ denotes the initial part of the sequence P of length i

> $+\Delta$: If $P(i + 1) = +\Delta q$ then
> (1) $q \in F$ or
> (2) $\exists r \in R_s[q]$ $\forall a \in A(r) : +\Delta a \in P(1..i)$.

> $-\Delta$: If $P(i + 1) = -\Delta q$ then
> (1) $q \notin F$ and
> (2) $\forall r \in R_s[q]$ $\exists a \in A(r) : -\Delta a \in P(1..i)$.

The definition of Δ describes just forward chaining of strict rules. For a literal q to be definitely provable we need to find a strict rule with head q, of which all antecedents have been definitely proved previously. And to establish that q cannot be proven definitely we must establish that for every strict rule with head q there is at least one antecedent which has been shown to be non-provable.

> $+\partial$: If $P(i + 1) = +\partial q$ then either
> (1) $+\Delta q \in P(1..i)$ or
> (2.1) $\exists r \in R_{sd}[q]$ $\forall a \in A(r) : +\partial a \in P(1..i)$ and
> (2.2) $-\Delta \sim q \in P(1..i)$ and
> (2.3) $\forall s \in R[\sim q]$ either
> (2.3.1) $\exists a \in A(s) : -\partial a \in P(1..i)$ or
> (2.3.2) $\exists t \in R_{sd}[q]$ such that $t > s$ and
> $\qquad \forall a \in A(t) : +\partial a \in P(1..i)$

Let us work through this condition. To show that q is provable defeasibly we have two choices: (1) We show that q is already definitely provable; or (2) we need to argue using the defeasible part of D as well. In particular, we require that there must be a strict or defeasible rule with head q which can be applied (2.1). But now we need to consider possible "attacks", i.e., reasoning chains in support of $\sim q$. To be more specific: to prove q defeasibly we must show that $\sim q$ is not definitely provable (2.2). Also (2.3) we must consider the set of all rules which are not known to be inapplicable and which have head $\sim q$ (note that here we consider defeaters, too, whereas they could not be used to support the conclusion q; this is in line with the motivation of defeaters given earlier). Essentially each such rule s attacks the conclusion q. For q to be provable, each such rule s must be counterattacked by a rule t with head q with the following properties: (i) t must be applicable at this point, and (ii) t must be stronger than s. Thus each attack on the conclusion q must be counterattacked by a stronger rule. In other words, r and the rules t form a team (for q) that defeats the rules s. In an analogous manner we can define $-\partial q$ as

$-\partial$: If $P(i+1) = -\partial q$ then
(1) $-\Delta q \in P(1..i)$ and
    (2.1) $\forall r \in R_{sd}[q]\ \exists a \in A(r) : -\partial a \in P(1..i)$ or
    (2.2) $+\Delta \sim q \in P(1..i)$ or
    (2.3) $\exists s \in R[\sim q]$ such that
        (2.3.1) $\forall a \in A(s) : +\partial a \in P(1..i)$ and
        (2.3.2) $\forall t \in R_{sd}[q]$ either $t \not> s$ or
                $\exists a \in A(t) : -\partial a \in P(1..i)$

The purpose of the $-\partial$ inference rules is to establish that it is not possible to prove $+\partial$. This rule is defined in such a way that all the possibilities for proving $+\partial q$ (for example) are explored and shown to fail before $-\partial q$ can be concluded. Thus conclusions tagged with $-\partial$ are the outcome of a constructive proof that the corresponding positive conclusion cannot be obtained.

4 Defeasible Description Logics

In this section we show how to extend $\mathcal{ALC}^-$ with defeasibility. As we saw in Section 2 a knowledge base in $\mathcal{ALC}^-$ is a pair

$$(\mathcal{A}, \mathcal{T})$$

where $\mathcal{A}$, the ABox, is a set of individual assertions, and $\mathcal{T}$, the TBox, contains inclusion axioms or definitions of concepts. When we consider the relationships between a knowledge base in $\mathcal{ALC}^-$ and a defeasible theory we have that the ABox corresponds to the set of facts, while the TBox corresponds to the monotonic part of the rules in a defeasible theory. Given the syntactic limitations of $\mathcal{ALC}^-$, we can give a more precise characterisation of the TBox in terms of strict rules (see also [5]). In particular given an inclusion axiom

$$\sqcap_{i=1}^{n} C_i \sqsubseteq \sqcap_{j=1}^{m} D_j$$

the inclusion axiom is equivalent to the following set of strict rules (the set of rules induced by $\mathcal{T}$)

$$C_1, \ldots, C_n \to D_1$$

$$\vdots$$

$$C_1, \ldots, C_n \to D_m$$

In case $n = m = 1$ and C_i, D_j are atomic concepts (i.e., concepts not defined in terms of other concepts), we also have to include the contrapositive of the inclusion axiom, namely

$$\neg D_j \to \neg C_i$$

This means that we can use either structural subsumption of $\mathcal{ALC}^-$ or strict derivability of defeasible logic to deal with the monotonic part of a defeasible description logic knowledge base. To add non-monotonicity we introduce defeasible logic rules, and defeasible logic proof theory to a knowledge base in $\mathcal{ALC}^-$. Hence a defeasible description logic theory is a structure

$$(\mathcal{A}, \mathcal{T}, R, >)$$

where, as before $\mathcal{A}$ is the ABox, $\mathcal{T}$ is the TBox, R is a set of rules (strict rules, defeasible rules and defeaters), and $>$ –the superiority relation– is a binary relation defined over the rules in R plus the strict rules induced by the inclusion axioms in $\mathcal{T}$, according to the construction given above.

We can now give the conditions to derive new role restrictions, but before we have to determine the domain of the theory. The domain of the theory corresponds to the Herbrand universe of the ABox of the theory, that is, the set of all individuals occurring in the assertions in $\mathcal{A}$; we will use Δ_T to denote it.

$+\Delta\forall R.C$: If $P(i+1) = +\Delta\forall R.C(a)$ then
$\quad \forall b \in \Delta_T$ either
$\quad (1)\ -\Delta R(a,b)$ or
$\quad (2)\ +\Delta C(b)$

$-\Delta\forall R.C$: If $P(i+1) = -\Delta\forall R.C(a)$ then
$\quad \exists b \in \Delta_T$ such that
$\quad (1)\ +\Delta R(a,b)$ and
$\quad (2)\ -\Delta C(b)$

Similarly the conditions to derive role restriction in a defeasible way are

$+\partial\forall R.C$: If $P(i+1) = +\partial\forall R.C(a)$ then
$\quad \forall b \in \Delta_T$ either
$\quad (1)\ -\partial R(a,b)$ or
$\quad (2)\ +\partial C(b)$

To prove a positive defeasible role restriction $-\partial \alpha R.C(a)$ we have to prove that for all the elements b in the domain of the knowledge base either we cannot prove that b is not related via R with a, or we can show that b is a instance of the concept C.

Given the syntactic limitation of the language, it is not possible to have rules for $\neg \forall R.C$: negation is limited to atomic concept. Therefore the argument for proving a positive defeasible role restriction cannot be rebutted by another argument, but only undercut by arguments undermining the arguments used to prove the two parts of the argument for it.

$-\partial \forall R.C$: If $P(i+1) = -\partial \forall R.C(a)$ then
$\quad \exists b \in \Delta_T$ such that
$\quad (1) +\partial R(a, b)$ and
$\quad (2) -\partial C(b)$

To prove $-\partial \forall R.C(a)$ then there must exist an element b in the domain of the knowledge base such that it is defeasibly provable that b is in the role R with the concept instance a from the role restriction statement and it must be defeasibly not provable that b is an instance of the concept C.

It is immediate to verify that the condition for $-\partial \forall R.C$ corresponds to the semantic condition that evaluates $\forall R.C$ as false. Then according to the principle of strong negation advanced in [3] as tool to define derivation conditions in defeasible logic[1], we obtain the current clause for $+\partial \forall R.C$. Again it is easy to see that, intuitively, it matches the cases when $\forall R.C$ is true. Let us consider the following alternative condition

$+\partial \forall R.C$: If $P(i+1) = +\partial \forall R.C(a)$ then
$\quad \forall b \in \Delta_T$ if $+\partial \neg C(b)$ then $-\partial R(a, b)$

This definition is based on the idea that, given an interpretation of a description logic knowledge base, every element of the domain is either in the extension of a concept or in its complement. Thus if b does not satisfy C, it satisfies $\neg C$[2]. Then a must not be related to b, if a belongs to the interpretation of $\forall R.C$. However this condition leads to (possibly) counterintuitive results. For example, given the following theory,

$$\Rightarrow \neg C(b)$$
$$\Rightarrow C(b)$$
$$R(a, b)$$

we derive $+\partial \forall R.C(a)$ simply because we fail to prove that $\neg C(b)$ is (defeasibly) the case, but on the other hand we do not have undisputed evidence of the truth of $C(b)$. While this may be appropriate in some interpretations, we believe that this is not the correct result in many other interpretations.

---

[1] The strong negation of a formula is closely related to the function that simplifies a formula by moving all negations to an innermost position in the resulting formula and replaces the positive tags with the respective negative tags and vice-versa.

[2] Here we have another complication with this definition, since in general $\neg C$ might not be defined in the language.

5 An Example

The following is an example of a Defeasible Description Logic knowledge base. It includes a list of concepts and the instances of those concepts as well as a list of roles and their instances. Furthermore three defeasible rules are specified each containing a role restriction constructor.

ABox

Faculty(ITEE)	Faculty(ARTS)
Faculty(LAW)	IteeCourse(INFS4201)
IteeCourse(COMP4600)	ArtsCourse(PSCY1020)
LawCourse(LAWS3010)	Student(DANIELLA)
DualDegree(ADRIAN)	Student(ROBIN)
Supervisor(GUIDO)	Supervisor(PENNY)
takes(DANIELLA, INFS4201)	takes(DANIELLA, COMP4600)
takes(ROBIN, PSCY1020)	takes(ADRIAN, COMP4600)
takes(ROBIN, COMP4600)	takes(ADRIAN, LAWS3010)
supervises(GUIDO, DANIELLA)	supervises(PENNY, ROBIN)
supervises(GUIDO, ADRIAN)	supervises(PENNY, ADRIAN)

TBox

$$IteeStudent(x) \sqsubseteq Student(x)$$
$$DualDegree(x) \sqsubseteq IteeStudent(x)$$

Rules

$$\forall supervises.IteeStudent(x) \Rightarrow facultyMember(x, ITEE)$$
$$Student(x), \forall takes.IteeCourse(x) \Rightarrow IteeStudent(x)$$
$$Student(x), \forall takes.ArtsCourse(x) \Rightarrow \neg IteeStudent(x)$$

Finally the superiority relation is empty.

The ABox describes entries in a university database, while the TBox and the rules provide integrity constraints on possible legal records. For example the first rule says that ITEE faculty members usually can only supervise ITEE students; the second rules establish that non ITEE students have to take courses outside ITEE. Finally the last rule states that in normal circumstances students taking only arts courses are not enrolled in ITEE.

From the above Defeasible Description Logic knowledge base we can derive additional information other than that which is explicitly asserted. The method by which we can derive this information includes using a combination of subsumption and role restriction reasoning methods.

An example of the information that can be derived is, via subsumption, that the dual degree student Adrian can be classified as an ITEE student also (strict positive derivation $+\Delta$). Via the strict rule

$$\text{DualDegree(ADRIAN)} \rightarrow \text{IteeStudent(ADRIAN)}$$

Daniella can be classed as an ITEE student (positive defeasible derivation $+\partial$), this is due to the fact that Daniella is a student and every course taken by Daniella is an ITEE course ($+\partial \forall \text{takes.IteeCourse(Daniella)}$). To prove this we have to notice that there are no rules with head $\text{takes}(x, \text{Daniella})$, thus for every element y in the domain such that $\text{takes}(x, \text{Daniella})$ is not given in the ABox we can prove $-\partial \text{takes}(x, \text{Daniella})$. For the remaining elements of the domain, namely INFS4201 and COMP4600, we have to prove that $+\partial \text{IteeCourse(INFS4201)}$ and $+\partial \text{IteeCourse(COMP4600)}$. Both follow immediately since they are in the ABox, and hence are facts of the given theory.

Furthermore as Guido is a supervisor and he supervises Daniella and Adrian who are both ITEE students we can deduce via

$$\forall \text{supervises.IteeStudent(GUIDO)} \Rightarrow \text{facultyMember(GUIDO, ITEE)}$$

that it is defeasibly provable that Guido is an ITEE faculty member (positive defeasible derivation $+\partial$). Deriving information in this way using a combination of role restriction and structural subsumption is, we believe, unique to Defeasible Description logic, and there would be no natural way to express this information in other current formalisms used for reasoning on ontological knowledge bases.

Furthermore given the challenge of discovering if Penny is a member of the ITEE faculty we are left with some decisions to make. Here we can see that Penny supervises two students. Adrian is the first student and we have already concluded that Adrian is an ITEE student due to the fact that he is classified as a dual degree student. The other student that Penny supervises is Robin. Robin is given as a student in the knowledge base. We can observe in the knowledge base that Robin takes one Arts course (PSCY1020) and one ITEE course (COMP4600). When we try to show that Robin is an ITEE student via the rule

$$\text{Student(ROBIN)}, \forall \text{takes.IteeCourse(ROBIN)} \Rightarrow \text{IteeStudent(ROBIN)}$$

we can show that $-\partial \text{IteeStudent(Robin)}$. The reason for this is that we cannot show that the role restriction in this rule is defeasibly provable, in fact we can demonstrate the converse. $-\partial \text{takes.IteeCourse(Robin)}$ due to the presence of the fact Arts(PSCY1020) and the role $\text{takes(ROBIN, PSCY1020)}$, this concept and role is conducive to the conditions demonstrate the behaviour of negative role restriction.

Furthermore as Robin is defeasibly not an ITEE student we defeasibly cannot conclude that Penny is a member of the ITEE faculty. Given the rule

$$\forall \text{supervises.IteeStudent(PENNY)} \Rightarrow \text{facultyMember(PENNY, ITEE)}$$

we can show that the role restriction for this rule fails and is defeasibly not provable due to the fact that we are given the information that Penny supervises

Robin and that we can derive that Robin is defeasibly not an ITEE student (this is derived in the same way we derived that Robin is not an ITEE student). As the role restriction is defeasibly not provable then we cannot defeasibly imply that Penny is a faculty member of ITEE.

6   Conclusion

In cases where we have conflicts in a knowledge base Description logic has historically proved useless at reasoning and collapses whereas Defeasible logic can be used to derive some meaningful solutions in the presence of these conflicts, via non-monotonic reasoning. Defeasible logic reasoning however is not as strong or conclusive as the reasoning in Description logic and for this reason Defeasible logic has not been considered appropriate for the reasoning on the knowledge bases of ontologies. From the inherent unsuitability of both formalisms for reasoning on partial or incomplete knowledge bases in a decidable way the aims for this paper was developed. We believe that the combination of defeasible rules with a Description logic knowledge base to derive Defeasible derivability is significant to current reasoning methods employed on ontologies.

Essentially what the addition of defeasible assertions adds to description logic is the ability to reason on knowledge bases where conflicting information is present. In this situation description logic alone will fail but through Defeasible Description Logic we are able to at least defeasibly derive some useful information. Our ability to derive these defeasible conclusions in such a decidable way means that description logic is extended via the two new strengths of derivability making reasoning on conflicting or incomplete knowledge bases conducive to deriving some useful information. Furthermore defeasible logic is extended through the reasoning mechanism of subsumption and the role restriction constructor.

Future work based on this work could include adding further description logic constructors to Defeasible Description logic and studying the strengths of derivation further. In the future this intuition could significantly be extended by adding additional constructors from Description logic at a lower level of abstraction, with a view to completely mapping the constructors in Description logic to a Defeasible Description logic. Furthermore the strengths of derivation could be studied more closely and even extended to produce new derivation types. A more in depth test of the viability of this logic could also be possible future work, carried out by implementing a knowledge base using Defeasible Description logic and doing comparative tests of the formalism against a knowledge base implemented with Description logic

References

1. Grigoris Antoniou. Nonmonotonic rule system on top of ontology layer. In I. Horrocks and J. Hendler, editors, *ISWC 2002*, number 2432 in LNCS, pages 394–398, Berlin, 2002.

2. Grigoris Antoniou, David Billington, Guido Governatori, and Michael J. Maher. On the modeling and analysis of regulations. In *Proceedings of the Australian Conference Information Systems*, pages 20–29, 1999.
3. Grigoris Antoniou, David Billington, Guido Governatori, and Michael J. Maher. A flexible framework for defeasible logics. In *Proc. American National Conference on Artificial Intelligence (AAAI-2000)*, pages 401–405, Menlo Park, CA, 2000. AAAI/MIT Press.
4. Grigoris Antoniou, David Billington, Guido Governatori, and Michael J. Maher. Representation results for defeasible logic. *ACM Transactions on Computational Logic*, 2(2):255–287, 2001.
5. Grigoris Antoniou and Gerd Wagner. Rules and defeasible reasoning on the semantic web. In M. Schroeder and G. Wagner, editors, *RuleML 2003*, number 2876 in LNCS, pages 111–120, Berlin, 2003.
6. F. Baader and B. Hollunder. Embedding defaults into terminological knowledge representation formalism. *Journal of Automated Reasoning*, 14:149–180, 1995.
7. F. Baader and B. Hollunder. Priorities on defaults with prerequisites and their application in treating specificity in terminological default logic. *Journal of Automated Reasoning*, 14:41–68, 1995.
8. Franz Baader, Diego Calvanes, Deborah McGuinnes, Daniele Nardi, and Peter Patel-Schneider, editors. *The Description Logics Handbook*. Cambridge University Press, Cambridge, 2003.
9. Franz Baader and Werner Nutt. Basic description logics. In Baader et al. [8], chapter 2, pages 43–95.
10. David Billington. Defeasible logic is stable. *Journal of Logic and Computation*, 3:370–400, 1993.
11. Michael Covington, Donald Nute, and A. Vellino. *Prolog Programming in Depth*. Prentice Hall, 1997.
12. Marlon Dumas, Guido Governatori, Arthur H. M. ter Hofstede, and Phillipa Oaks. A formal approach to negotiating agents development. *Electronic Commerce Research and Applications*, 1(2):193–207, 2002.
13. T. Eiter, T. Lukasiewicz, R. Schindlauer, and H. Tompits. Combining answer set programming with description logics for the semantic web. In *In Proceedings of the 9th International Conference on Principles of Knowledge Representation and Reasoning*, pages 141–151, 2004.
14. Guido Governatori, Marlon Dumas, Arthur H.M. ter Hofstede, and Phillipa Oaks. A formal approach to protocols and strategies for (legal) negotiation. In Henry Prakken, editor, *Procedings of the 8th International Conference on Artificial Intelligence and Law*, pages 168–177. IAAIL, ACM Press, 2001.
15. Guido Governatori and Vineet Padmanabhan. A defeasible logic of policy-based intention. In Tamás D. Gedeon and Lance Chun Che Fung, editors, *AI 2003: Advances in Artificial Intelligence*, volume 2903 of *LNAI*, pages 414–426, Berlin, 3-5 December 2003.
16. Guido Governatori and Antonino Rotolo. A computational framework for non-monotonic agency, institutionalised power and multi-agent systems. In Daniéle Bourcier, editor, *Legal Knowledge and Inforamtion Systems*, volume 106 of *Frontieres in Artificial Intelligence and Applications*, pages 151–152, Amsterdam, 2003. IOS Press.
17. Guido Governatori and Antonino Rotolo. Defeasible logic: Agency and obligation. In Alessio Lomuscio and Donald Nute, editors, *Deontic Logic in Computer Science*, number 3065 in LNAI, pages 114–128, Berlin, 2004.

18. Guido Governatori, Antonino Rotolo, and Shazia Sadiq. A model of dynamic resource allocation in workflow systems. In Klaus-Dieter Schewe and Hugh E. Williams, editors, *Database Technology 2004*, number 27 in Conference Research and Practice of Information Technology, pages 197–206. Australian Computer Science Association, ACS, 19-21 January 2004.
19. B.N. Grosof, I. Horrocks, R Volz, and S. Decker. Description logic programs: combining logic programs with description logic. In *Proceedings of the twelfth international conference on World Wide Web*, pages 48–57. ACM Press, 2003.
20. B.N. Grosof, Y. Labrou, and H.Y. Chan. A declarative approach to business rules in contracts: Courteous logic programs in XML. In *Proceedings of the 1st ACM Conference on Electronic Commerce (EC-99)*. ACM Press, 1999.
21. S. Heymans and D. Vermeir. A defeasible ontology language. In R. Meersman and Z. Tari, editors, *Confederated International Conferences: CoopIS, DOA and ODBASE 2002*, number 2519 in LNCS, pages 1033–1046, Berlin, 2002. Springer-Verlag.
22. Michael Maher. Propositional defeasible logic has linear complexity. *Theory and Practice of Logic Programming*, 1(6):691–711, November 2001.
23. Maher. M.J., A. Rock, G. Antoniou, D. Billignton, and T. Miller. Efficient defeasible reasoning systems. *International Journal of Artificial Intelligence Tools*, 10(4):483–501, 2001.
24. Donald Nute. Defeasible logic. In *Handbook of Logic in Artificial Intelligence and Logic Programming*, volume 3, pages 353–395. Oxford University Press, 1987.
25. L. Padgham and T. Zhang. A terminological logic with defaults: A definition and an application. In *Proc. IJCAI'93*, pages 662–668, Los Altos, 1993. Morgan Kaufmann.
26. J. Quantz and V. Royer. A preference semantics for defaults in terminological logics. In *Proc KR'92*, pages 294–305, Los Altos, 1992. Morgan Kaufmann.
27. D.M. Reeves, B.N. Grosof, M.P. Wellman, and H.Y. Chan. Towards a declarative language for negotiating executable contracts. In *Proceedings of the AAAI-99 Workshop on Artificial Intelligence in Electronic Commerce (AIEC-99)*. AAAI Press / MIT Press, 1999.
28. U. Straccia. Default inheritance reasoning in hybrid KL-ONE-style logics. In *Proc. IJCAI'93*, pages 676–681, Los Altos, 1993. Morgan Kaufmann.
29. Kewen Wang, David Billington, Jeff Blee, and Grigoris Antoniou. Combining description logic and defeasible logic for the semantic web. In Grigoris Antoniou and Harlod Boley, editors, *RuleML 2004*, LNCS, Berlin, 2004. Springer-Verlag.

Semantic Web Reasoning with Conceptual Logic Programs

Stijn Heymans, Davy Van Nieuwenborgh*, and Dirk Vermeir**

Dept. of Computer Science
Vrije Universiteit Brussel, VUB
Pleinlaan 2, B1050 Brussels, Belgium
{sheymans,dvnieuwe,dvermeir}@vub.ac.be

Abstract. We extend Answer Set Programming with, possibly infinite, open domains. Since this leads, in general, to undecidable reasoning, we restrict the syntax of programs, while carefully guarding useful knowledge representation mechanisms such as negation as failure and inequalities. Reasoning with the resulting Conceptual Logic Programs can be reduced to finite, normal Answer Set Programming, for which reasoners are available.

We argue that Conceptual Logic Programming is a useful tool for uniformly representing and reasoning with both ontologies and rules on the Semantic Web, as they can capture a large fragment of the OWL DL ontology language, while extending it in various aspects.

1 Introduction

Ontology languages such as OWL and OWL DL[5] are set to play a vital role on the future Semantic Web, as they are designed to represent a wide range of knowledge on the Web and to ensure decidable reasoning with it. Decidability of such languages often results from the decidability of the underlying Description Logic (DL)[4] that defines its formal semantics, e.g., the DL $\mathcal{SHOIQ}(\mathbf{D})$ is the DL corresponding to OWL DL.

Another well-established knowledge representation formalism is Answer Set Programming (ASP)[11], a Logic Programming (LP) paradigm that captures knowledge by programs whose answer sets express the intended meaning of this knowledge. The answer set semantics presumes that all relevant domain elements are present in the program. Such a closed domain assumption is, however, problematic if one wishes to use ASP for ontological reasoning since ontologies describe knowledge in terms of concepts and interrelationships between them, and are thus mostly independent of constants.

E.g., consider the knowledge that managers drive big cars, that one is either a manager or not, and that Felix is definitely not a manager. This is represented by the program P_1:

$$bigCar(X) \leftarrow Manager(X)$$
$$Manager(X) \vee not\ Manager(X) \leftarrow$$
$$\neg Manager(felix) \leftarrow$$

* Supported by the FWO.
** This work was partially funded by the Information Society Technologies programme of the European Commission, Future and Emerging Technologies under the IST-2001-37004 WASP project.

G. Antoniou and H. Boley (Eds.): RuleML 2004, LNCS 3323, pp. 113–127, 2004.
© Springer-Verlag Berlin Heidelberg 2004

Using traditional ASP, grounding would yield the program

$$bigCar(felix) \leftarrow Manager(felix)$$
$$Manager(felix) \vee not\ Manager(felix) \leftarrow$$
$$\neg Manager(felix) \leftarrow$$

which has a single answer set $\{\neg Manager(felix)\}$ such that one would wrongfully conclude that there are never managers or persons that drive big cars.

We resolve this by introducing, possibly infinite, *open domains*. Under the *open answer set semantics* the example has an answer set ($\mathcal{H} = \{felix, heather\}$, $M = \{\neg Manager(felix), Manager(heather), bigCar(heather)\}$) where $\mathcal{H}$ is a *universe* for P_1 that extends the constants present in P_1 and M is an answer set of P_1 grounded with $\mathcal{H}$. One would rightfully conclude that it is possible that there are persons that are managers and thus drive big cars. Note the use of disjunction and negation as failure in the head of $Manager(X) \vee not\ Manager(X) \leftarrow$. Such rules will be referred to as *free rules* since they allow for the free introduction of literals; answer sets are, consequently, not subset minimal.

The catch is that reasoning, i.e. satisfiability checking of a predicate, with *open domains* is, in general, undecidable. In order to regain decidability, we restrict the syntax of programs while retaining useful knowledge representation tools such as negation as failure and inequality. Moreover, the result, *(local) Conceptual Logic Programs (CLPs)*, ensures a reduction of reasoning to finite, closed, ASP, making CLPs amenable for reasoning with existing answer set solvers.

As opposed to the CLPs in [16,15], we support constants in this paper. Constants in a CLP have the effect that the tree-model property, a decidability indicator, is replaced by the more general forest-model property. Furthermore, [16,15] characterized reasoning with CLPs by checking non-emptiness of two-way alternating tree-automata[31]. Although such automata are elegant theoretical tools, they are of little practical use, hence the importance of an identification of CLPs that can be reduced to traditional ASP.

Conceptual logic programs prove to be suitable for Semantic Web reasoning, for we can simulate an expressive DL closely related to the ontology language OWL DL. Since CLPs, as a LP paradigm, are also a natural framework for representing rule-based knowledge, they present a unifying framework for reasoning with ontologies and rules. Some additional benefits of CLPs, compared with OWL DL, are their ability to close the domain at will and to succinctly represent knowledge that is not trivially expressible using OWL DL. Finally, several query problems, in the context of databases satisfying ontologies, can be stated as satisfiability problems w.r.t. CLPs and are consequently decidable.

The remainder of the paper is organized as follows. In Section 2, we extend ASP with open domains, and in Section 3, we define (local) CLPs and reduce reasoning to normal ASP. In Section 4, we show the simulation of an expressive class of DLs and discuss benefits of using CLPs for Semantic Web reasoning. Section 5 relates other work to our approach. Finally, Section 6 contains conclusions and directions for further research. Due to space restrictions, proofs have been omitted; they can be found in [14].

2   Answer Set Programming with Open Domains

Terms are *constants* or *variables*, denoted as lowercase or uppercase characters respectively. An *atom* is either a unary $q(s)$ or a binary $f(s,t)$ for predicates q and f, and terms s and t. A *literal* is an atom or an atom preceded by the classical negation symbol $\neg$. We assume $\neg\neg a = a$ for an atom a; for a set of literals α, $\neg\alpha = \{\neg l | l \in \alpha\}$, and α is *consistent* if $\alpha \cap \neg\alpha = \emptyset$. An *extended literal* is a literal l or a literal preceded by the *negation as failure* (naf) symbol *not*. A set of unary literals ranging over a common term s may be denoted as $\alpha(s)$, e.g., $\{a(s), not\ b(s)\} = \{a, not\ b\}(s)$. Similarly, a set of binary literals over (s,t) can be denoted as $\alpha(s,t)$. The *positive part* of a set of extended literals α is $\alpha^+ = \{l | l \in \alpha, l\ literal\}$, while the *negative part* of α is $\alpha^- = \{l | not\ l \in \alpha\}$, e.g., $\{a, not\ b\}^+ = \{a\}$ and $\{a, not\ b\}^- = \{b\}$.

A *disjunctive logic program* (DLP) is a set of rules $\alpha \leftarrow \beta$ where α, the *head*, and β, the *body*, are sets of extended literals and $|\alpha^+| \leq 1$, i.e. the head contains at most one ordinary literal[1]. Atoms, (extended) literals, rules, and programs are *ground* if they do not contain variables. The constants appearing in a DLP P are denoted by $\mathcal{H}_P$, the unary predicates (possibly negated)[2] in P are $upreds(P) = \{l | l(x)\ in\ P\}$, $bpreds(P)$ are the binary predicates, and $preds(P) = upreds(P) \cup bpreds(P)$. A *universe* $\mathcal{H}$ for a DLP P is any non-empty extension of $\mathcal{H}_P$, i.e. $\mathcal{H}_P \subseteq \mathcal{H}$. The *grounded* version $P_\mathcal{H}$ of a DLP P w.r.t. a universe $\mathcal{H}$ for P is the program P with all variables replaced by all possible elements from $\mathcal{H}$. $P_\mathcal{H}$ may be infinite if $\mathcal{H}$ is; we assume, however, that a grounded version $P_\mathcal{H}$ originates from a finite P.

E.g., the program P_2: $sel(I,S) \vee not\ sel(I,S) \leftarrow$; $av(i) \leftarrow$; $av(I) \leftarrow sel(I,S)$; expresses that an item is sold by a seller or not, an item is available if it has a seller, and we have a particular available item i. The constants in P_2 are $\mathcal{H}_P = \{i\}$; some of the universes for P_2 are $\mathcal{H}_1 = \{i, s\}$ or an infinite $\mathcal{H}_2 = \{i, x_1, x_2, \dots\}$.

For a grounded P, let $\mathcal{L}_P$ be the set of literals that can be formed from P. A consistent subset of $\mathcal{L}_P$ is an *interpretation* of P. An interpretation I *satisfies* a literal l, denoted $I \models l$, if $l \in I$; an extended literal *not* l is satisfied by I if $l \notin I$, and I satisfies a set α of extended literals, denoted $I \models \alpha$ iff I satisfies every element of α. A rule $r : \alpha \leftarrow \beta$, $\alpha \neq \emptyset$, in a grounded P is satisfied by I, denoted $I \models r$, if $I \models l$ for some $l \in \alpha$ whenever $I \models \beta$. If $\alpha = \emptyset$, i.e. the rule is a *constraint*, $I \models r$ iff $I \not\models \beta$. An interpretation I is a model of a grounded P if I satisfies every rule in P. For a *simple* grounded program P, i.e. not containing naf, an *answer set* of P is a subset minimal model of P. If P is not simple, we first reduce it for a particular interpretation I of P, with the *Gelfond-Lifschitz transformation*[22], to the simple *GL-reduct* $P^I = \{\alpha^+ \leftarrow \beta^+ \mid \alpha \leftarrow \beta \in P, \beta^- \cap I = \emptyset, \alpha^- \subseteq I\}$. An interpretation M of a grounded P is an *answer set* of P if M is an answer set of P^M.

For a DLP P, not grounded, an *open interpretation* is a pair $(\mathcal{H}, I)$ where $\mathcal{H}$ is a universe for P and I is an interpretation of $P_\mathcal{H}$. An *open answer set* of P is an open interpretation $(\mathcal{H}, M)$ such that M is an answer set of $P_\mathcal{H}$. In the following, we usually omit the "open" qualifier. A $p \in upreds(P)$ is *satisfiable* w.r.t. P iff there exists an answer set $(\mathcal{H}, M)$ of P and some $x \in \mathcal{H}$ such that $p(x) \in M$, in which case we

---

[1] This restriction, which makes the GL-reduct disjunction-free, is not imposed by classical DLPs.

[2] In the future, we silently assume the "(possibly negated)" phrase.

also say that $(\mathcal{H}, M)$ satisfies p. A program P is *consistent* if it has an answer set. The associated reasoning tasks are *satisfiability checking* and *consistency checking*, where the latter can be reduced to the former by introducing a new predicate p, e.g., with a rule $p(X) \vee not\ p(X) \leftarrow$.

With a universe $\mathcal{H} = \{i, s, x\}$ for P_2 both $(\mathcal{H}, M_1 = \{av(i), sel(x, s), av(x)\})$ and $(\mathcal{H}, M_2 = \{av(i)\})$ are answer sets of P_2. Since M_1 contains $sel(x, s)$, the GL-reduct $P_{2\mathcal{H}}^{M_1}$ will contain $sel(x, s) \leftarrow$, which in turn motivates the presence of $sel(x, s)$ in M_1. On the other hand, since $sel(x, s) \notin M_2$, the rule $sel(x, s) \vee not\ sell(x, s) \leftarrow$ is automatically satisfied and will not be considered for inclusion in the GL-reduct. Intuitively, $sel(I, S) \vee not\ sel(I, S) \leftarrow$ can be used to freely introduce sel-literals, provided no other rules prohibit this, e.g., a constraint $\leftarrow sel(x, s)$ makes sure no answer set contains $sel(x, s)$. We will call a predicate f *free* if $f(X, Y) \vee not\ f(X, Y) \leftarrow$ or $f(X) \vee not\ f(X) \leftarrow$ is in the program, or is silently assumed to be in it, for a binary or unary f respectively. Similarly, a ground literal l is free if we have $l \vee not\ l \leftarrow$.

Open answer sets are a generalization of the k-belief sets in [12]. A k-belief set of a program P is a pair $\langle k, B \rangle$ where k is a nonnegative integer and B is an answer set of P_k, which is the grounding of P with its own constants and k new ones. Obviously, every k-belief set is an open answer set; the opposite is false as we may have infinite universes and, consequently, infinite open answer sets while k-belief sets are finite. Since reasoning, e.g., satisfiability checking, is undecidable under the k-belief semantics[25], reasoning under the open answer set semantics is too.

3   Conceptual Logic Programs

Since *Open Answer Set Programming* is, in general, undecidable, we seek to restrict the structure of DLPs to regain decidability while retaining enough expressiveness for solving practical problems. An important indication of decidability is the *tree-model property*, e.g., in modal logics[30], or its generalization, the *forest-model property*, as in DLs with individuals[18].

A program P has the forest-model property if the following holds: if P has an answer set that satisfies a unary predicate p, then P has an answer set with a forest shape that satisfies p in a root of a tree in this forest. E.g., consider the program P_3 representing the knowledge that a company can be trusted for doing business with if it has the ISO 9000 quality certificate and at least two different trustworthy companies are doing business with it:

$$trust(C) \leftarrow t\_bus(C, C_1), t\_bus(C, C_2), C_1 \neq C_2, qual(C, iso9000)$$
$$\leftarrow t\_bus(C, D), not\ trust(D)$$

with t_bus and $qual$ free predicates, and $iso9000$ a constant. An answer set[3] of P_3, e.g., $M = \{trust(x_1), t\_bus(x_1, x_2), t\_bus(x_1, x_3), qual(x_1, iso9000), trust(x_2), \ldots\}$, is such that for every trusted company x_i in M, i.e. $trust(x_i) \in M$, there must be $t\_bus(x_i, x_j)$, $t\_bus(x_i, x_k)$ and $trust(x_j)$, $trust(x_k)$ with $x_j \neq x_k$; additionally, every trusted company has the $iso9000$ quality label. This particular answer set has a forest shape, as can be seen from Figure 1: we call it a *forest-model*. The forest in

---

[3] The universe $\mathcal{H}$ can be deduced from this answer set.

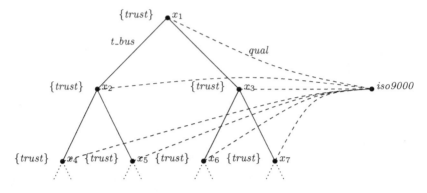

Fig. 1. Forest-Model

Figure 1 consists of two trees, one with root x_1 and one, a single node tree, with root $iso9000$. The labels of a node x in a tree, e.g., $\{trust\}$ for x_2, encode which literals are in the corresponding answer set, e.g. $trust(x_2) \in M$, while the labeled edges indicate relations between domain elements. The dashed arrows, describing relations between anonymous domain elements $x \in \mathcal{H} \setminus \mathcal{H}_P$, and constants, appear to be violating the forest structure; their labels can, however, be stored in the label of the starting node, e.g., $qual(x_2, iso9000)$ can be kept in the label of x_2 as $qual^{iso9000}$. Since there are only a finite number of constants, the number of different labels in a forest would still be finite. It is clear that M satisfies the predicate $trust$ in the root of a tree.

A particular class of programs with this forest-model property are *Conceptual Logic Programs* (CLPs).

Definition 1. *A CLP is a DLP such that a rule is of one of the following types:*

- *free rules $l \lor not\ l \leftarrow$ for a literal l, which allow for the free addition of the literal l, if not prohibited by other rules,*
- *unary rules[4] $a(s) \leftarrow \beta(s), \cup_m \gamma_m(s, t_m), \cup_m \delta_m(t_m), \cup_{i \neq j} t_i \neq t_j$, such that, if $\gamma_m \neq \emptyset$ then $\gamma_m^+ \neq \emptyset$, and, in case t_m is a variable: if $\delta_m \neq \emptyset$ then $\gamma_m \neq \emptyset$,*
- *binary rules $f(s, t) \leftarrow \beta(s), \gamma(s, t), \delta(t)$ with $\gamma^+ \neq \emptyset$ if t is a variable,*
- *constraints $\leftarrow a(s)$.*

where i and j are within the range of m.

P_1, P_2, and P_3 are examples of CLPs. CLPs are designed to ensure the forest-model property. E.g., a rule $q(X) \leftarrow not\ f(X, Y), \neg q(Y)$ is not a CLP rule since, if $\neg q$ is free, $\{q(x), \neg q(y)\}$ is an answer set that cannot be transformed into a tree due to the lack of a connection between nodes x and y. The same argument applies to rules of the form $q(X) \leftarrow \neg q(Y)$. One may have, however, a rule $q(X) \leftarrow \neg q(a)$ for a constant a, since an answer set $\{q(x), \neg q(a)\}$ consists of two trees, with roots x and a respectively.

---

[4] We will write unary rules, for compactness, as $a(s) \leftarrow \beta(s), \gamma_m(s, t_m), \delta_m(t_m), t_i \neq t_j$, with variables assumed to be pairwise different.

A rule $f(X, Y) \leftarrow v(X)$ is not allowed since it may enforce f-connections that break the tree-structure. On the other hand, $f(X, a) \leftarrow v(X)$ is allowed, as it only connects nodes x and the constant a. Note that more general rules than the ones in Definition 1 can be easily obtained by unfolding atoms in the bodies, resulting in rules with a tree structure. A complicated constraint $\leftarrow \beta$ is equivalent to the unary rule $a(s) \leftarrow \beta$ and the simple constraint $\leftarrow a(s)$. The idea of ensuring such connectedness of models in order to have desirable properties, like decidability, is similar to the motivation behind the *guarded fragment* of predicate logic[3].

Theorem 1. *Conceptual logic programs have the forest-model property.*

Forest-models of a CLP consist of at most $c + 1$ trees, with c the number of constants in the program. Each constant is the root of a tree, and an extra tree may be needed if a predicate can only be satisfied by an anonymous element, which will be the root of this tree.

Those trees may be infinite, but have bounded branching. For every label of a node x containing a predicate p, we have that $p(x)$ is in the forest-model, such that there must be some rule $p(x) \leftarrow \beta^+(x), \gamma_m^+(x, y_m), \delta_m^+(y_m)$ with a true body (if there were no such rule there would be no reason to include $p(x)$ in the forest-model, violating the minimality of answer sets). Thus, intuitively, in order to make p true in x, one needs to introduce at most $|\{y_m\}|$ successor nodes[5]. Since the size of the label at x is, roughly, bounded by the number of predicates in the program, this introduction of new successors of x only needs to occur a bounded number of times, resulting in the bounded branching.

In [15], decidability of satisfiability checking was shown by a reduction to two-way alternating tree-automata[31]. Since the CLPs in this paper also contain constants the automata reduction is not directly applicable. Moreover, while automata provide an elegant characterization, few implementations are available.

We slightly restrict CLPs, resulting in *local CLPs*, such that satisfiability checking can be reduced to normal, finite ASP, and, consequently, performed by existing answer set solvers such as DLV[21] and Smodels[27].

We first indicate how infinite forest-models can be turned into finite answer sets: cut every path in the forest from the moment there are duplicate labels and copy the connections of the first node in such a duplicate pair to the second node of the pair. Intuitively, when we reach a node that is in a state we already encountered, we proceed as that previous state, instead of going further down the tree. This cutting is similar to the blocking technique for DL tableaux[4], but the minimality of answer sets makes it non-trivial and only valid for local CLPs, as we indicate below. Considering the forest-model in Figure 1, we can cut everything below x_2 and x_3 since they have the same label as x_1. Furthermore, since $t\_bus(x_1, x_2)$, $t\_bus(x_1, x_3)$, and $qual(x_1, iso9000)$, we have $t\_bus(x_i, x_2)$, $t\_bus(x_i, x_3)$, and $qual(x_i, iso9000)$ for $i = 2$ and $i = 3$, resulting in the answer set depicted in Figure 2.

This *cutting* is not possible for arbitrary CLPs. E.g., $a(X) \leftarrow f(X, Y), a(Y)$ and $a(X) \leftarrow b(X)$ with b and f free predicates. A possible forest-model of this small program is $\{a(x), f(x, y), a(y), f(y, z), b(z), a(z)\}$ with a tree $\{x \to y \to z\}$. Since

---

[5] This bound can be easily tightened, e.g., if y_m is a constant there is no need for a successor y_m, since constants are treated as roots of their own tree.

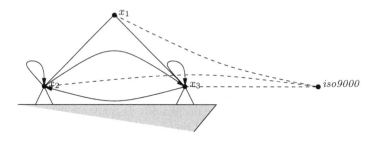

Fig. 2. Bounded Finite Model

x and y have the same label we cut at y, however, in the resulting answer set $a(x)$ is not motivated, as $b(z)$ is no longer present. The result of cutting is thus not minimal. Local CLPs solve this by making sure that a literal $a(x)$ is always motivated by x itself, successors y of x, or constants, such that, upon cutting, no motivating literals for literals higher up in the tree are cut away. Formally, local[6] CLPs are CLPs where rules $a(s) \leftarrow \alpha(s), \gamma_m(s, t_m), \beta_m(t_m), t_i \neq t_j$ and $f(s,t) \leftarrow \alpha(s), \gamma(s,t), \beta(t)$ are such that for every $b \in \beta^+_{(m)}$, either $b(t_{(m)}) \vee not\ b(t_{(m)}) \leftarrow\in P$ or for all rules $r : b(s) \leftarrow \mathrm{body}(r), \mathrm{body}(r)^+ = \emptyset$. The programs P_1, P_2, and P_3 are local CLPs.

Every infinite forest-model of a local CLP can thus be made into a finite answer set, and moreover, we can put a bound, depending only on the program, on the number of domain elements that are needed for the finite version. Since there are only a finite number of labels m, every path of length longer than m will contain a duplicate label. The branching of every tree in a forest-model is also bounded, say by n, and there is a bounded number of trees in the forest-model ($c + 1$ for c the number of constants in the program), such that the number of nodes in an answer set that resulted from cutting is bounded by some k_P for a local CLP P. We can then reduce satisfiability checking w.r.t. a local CLP P to normal ASP by introducing at least k_P constants.

Theorem 2. *Let P be a local CLP. $p \in \mathit{upreds}(P)$ is satisfiable w.r.t. P iff there is an answer set M of $\psi(P)$ containing a $p(x_i)$, $1 \leq i \leq k_P$, where $\psi(P) = P \cup \{cte(x_i) \leftarrow \mid 1 \leq i \leq k_P\}$.*

In the non-trivial "only if" direction, a forest-model will be transformed into an answer set containing less than k_P domain elements by the cutting technique described above, which in turn will be mapped to the constants of $\psi(P)$.

4   Semantic Web Reasoning with Conceptual Logic Programs

Description Logics[4] play an important role in the deployment of the Semantic Web, as they provide the formal semantics of (part of) ontology languages such as OWL[5]. Using

---

[6] The conditions for local are too strict, as is shown in [14], in the sense that there are CLPs that are not local but for which the infinite answer sets can still be made finite. However, since local CLPs are a syntactical restriction of CLPs, locality is a sufficient condition that is easy to check.

concept and *role names* as basic building blocks, *terminological* and *role axioms* in such DLs define subset relations between complex *concept* and *role expressions* respectively.

The semantics of DLs is given by interpretations $\mathcal{I} = (\Delta^{\mathcal{I}}, \cdot^{\mathcal{I}})$ where $\Delta^{\mathcal{I}}$ is a non-empty domain and $\cdot^{\mathcal{I}}$ is an interpretation function. $\mathcal{ALCHOQ}(\sqcup, \sqcap)^7$ is a particular DL with syntax and semantics as in Table 1; concept names A and individuals $\{o\}$ are the base concept expressions, P is a role name, establishing the base role expression, D and E are arbitrary concept expressions, and R and S are arbitrary role expressions.

Table 1. Syntax and Semantics $\mathcal{ALCHOQ}(\sqcup, \sqcap)$

concept names	$A^{\mathcal{I}} \subseteq \Delta^{\mathcal{I}}$
role names	$P^{\mathcal{I}} \subseteq \Delta^{\mathcal{I}} \times \Delta^{\mathcal{I}}$
individuals	$\{o\}^{\mathcal{I}} \subseteq \Delta^{\mathcal{I}}, |\{o\}^{\mathcal{I}}| = 1$
conjunction of concepts	$(D \sqcap E)^{\mathcal{I}} = D^{\mathcal{I}} \cap E^{\mathcal{I}}$
disjunction of concepts	$(D \sqcup E)^{\mathcal{I}} = D^{\mathcal{I}} \cup E^{\mathcal{I}}$
conjunction of roles	$(R \sqcap S)^{\mathcal{I}} = R^{\mathcal{I}} \cap S^{\mathcal{I}}$
disjunction of roles	$(R \sqcup S)^{\mathcal{I}} = R^{\mathcal{I}} \cup S^{\mathcal{I}}$
existential restriction	$(\exists R.D)^{\mathcal{I}} = \{x | \exists y : (x, y) \in R^{\mathcal{I}} \wedge y \in D^{\mathcal{I}}\}$
universal restriction	$(\forall R.D)^{\mathcal{I}} = \{x | \forall y : (x, y) \in R^{\mathcal{I}} \Rightarrow y \in D^{\mathcal{I}}\}$
qualified number restriction	$(\leq n\ R.D)^{\mathcal{I}} = \{x | \#\{y | (x, y) \in R^{\mathcal{I}} \wedge y \in D^{\mathcal{I}}\} \leq n\}$
	$(\geq n\ R.D)^{\mathcal{I}} = \{x | \#\{y | (x, y) \in R^{\mathcal{I}} \wedge y \in D^{\mathcal{I}}\} \geq n\}$

The *unique name assumption* - if $\{o_1\} \neq \{o_2\}$ then $\{o_1\}^{\mathcal{I}} \neq \{o_2\}^{\mathcal{I}}$ - ensures that different individuals are interpreted as different domain elements[8]. For concept expressions D and E, *terminological axioms* $D \sqsubseteq E$ are satisfied by an interpretation $\mathcal{I}$ if $D^{\mathcal{I}} \subseteq E^{\mathcal{I}}$. Role axioms $R \sqsubseteq S$ are interpreted similarly. An axiom $X \equiv Y$ stands for $X \sqsubseteq Y$ and $Y \sqsubseteq X$. A *knowledge base* Σ is a set of terminological and role axioms; $\mathcal{I}$ is a *model* of Σ if $\mathcal{I}$ satisfies every axiom in Σ. A concept expression C is *satisfiable* w.r.t. Σ if there exists a model $\mathcal{I}$ of Σ such that $C^{\mathcal{I}} \neq \emptyset$.

As an example, the human resources department may have an ontology specifying the company's structure: (a) *Personnel* consists of *Management*, *Workers* and *john*, (b) *john* is the boss of some manager, and (c) managers only take orders from other managers and are the boss of at least three *Workers*. This corresponds to the following $\mathcal{ALCHOQ}(\sqcup, \sqcap)$ knowledge base Σ_1:

$$Personnel \equiv Management \sqcup Workers \sqcup \{john\}$$
$$\{john\} \sqsubseteq \exists boss.Management$$
$$Management \sqsubseteq (\forall t\_orders.Management) \sqcap (\geq 3\ boss.Workers)$$

---

[7] DLs are named according to their constructs: $\mathcal{AL}$ is the basic DL[26], and $\mathcal{ALCHOQ}(\sqcup, \sqcap)$ adds negation of concept expressions ($\mathcal{C}$), role hierarchies ($\mathcal{H}$), individuals (or nominals) ($\mathcal{O}$), qualified number restrictions ($\mathcal{Q}$), and conjunction ($\sqcap$) and disjunction ($\sqcup$) of roles.

[8] Note that OWL does not make the unique name assumption, but one may enforce it using the *AllDifferent* construct.

A model of this knowledge base is $\mathcal{I} = (\{j, w_1, w_2, w_3, m\}, \cdot^{\mathcal{I}})$, with $\cdot^{\mathcal{I}}$ defined by $Workers^{\mathcal{I}} = \{w_1, w_2, w_3\}$, $Management^{\mathcal{I}} = \{m\}$, $\{john\}^{\mathcal{I}} = \{j\}$, $Personnel^{\mathcal{I}} = \{j, w_1, w_2, w_3, m\}$, $boss^{\mathcal{I}} = \{(j, m), (m, w_1), (m, w_2), (m, w_3)\}$, and $t\_orders^{\mathcal{I}} = \emptyset$.

We can rewrite Σ_1 as an equivalent CLP P_4. The axioms in Σ_1 correspond to the constraints

$\leftarrow Personnel(X), not\ (Management \sqcup Workers \sqcup \{john\})(X)$
$\leftarrow (Management \sqcup Workers \sqcup \{john\})(X), not\ Personnel(X)$
$\leftarrow \{john\}(X), not\ (\exists boss.Management)(X)$
$\leftarrow Management(X), not\ ((\forall t\_orders.Management) \sqcap (\geq 3\ boss.Workers))(X)$

in P_4, where the concept expressions are used as predicates, and indicating, in case of the first constraint, that if the answer set contains some $Personnel(x)$ then it must also contain $(Management \sqcup Workers \sqcup \{john\})(x)$. Those constraints are the kernel of the translation; we still need, however, to simulate the DLs semantics by rules that define the different DL constructs.

The predicate $(Management \sqcup Workers \sqcup \{john\})$ is defined by rules

$(Management \sqcup Workers \sqcup \{john\})(X) \leftarrow Management(X)$
$(Management \sqcup Workers \sqcup \{john\})(X) \leftarrow Workers(X)$
$(Management \sqcup Workers \sqcup \{john\})(X) \leftarrow \{john\}(X)$

and thus, by minimality of answer sets, if $(Management \sqcup Workers \sqcup \{john\})(x)$, there must either be a $Management(x)$, a $Workers(x)$, or a $\{john\}(x)$. The other way around, if one has a $Management(x)$, a $Workers(x)$, or a $\{john\}(x)$, one must have, since answer sets are models, $(Management \sqcup Workers \sqcup \{john\})(x)$. This behavior is exactly what is required by the $\sqcup$-construct.

The predicate $(\exists boss.Management)$ is defined by $(\exists boss.Management)(X) \leftarrow boss(X, Y), Management(Y)$, such that, if $(\exists boss.Management)(x)$ is in the answer set, there must be, by minimality, a y such that $boss(x, y)$ and $Management(y)$ are in the answer set and vice versa.

The conjunction predicate $((\forall t\_orders.Management) \sqcap (\geq 3\ boss.Workers))$ is defined by

$$((\forall t\_orders.Management) \sqcap (\geq 3\ boss.Workers))(X) \leftarrow$$
$$(\forall t\_orders.Management)(X), (\geq 3\ boss.Workers)(X)$$

and the body predicates by the rules

$$(\forall t\_orders.Management)(X) \leftarrow not\ \exists t\_orders.\neg Management(X)$$
$$(\geq 3\ boss.Workers)(X) \leftarrow boss(X, Y_1), boss(X, Y_2), boss(X, Y_3),$$
$$Workers(Y_1), Workers(Y_2), Workers(Y_3),$$
$$Y_1 \neq Y_2, Y_2 \neq Y_3, Y_1 \neq Y_3$$

and

$$\exists t\_orders.\neg Management(X) \leftarrow t\_orders(X, Y), (\neg Management)(Y)$$
$$(\neg Management)(X) \leftarrow not\ Management(X)$$

Finally, we need to introduce free rules for all concept and role names. Intuitively, concept names and roles names are types and thus contain some instances or not.

$$Workers(X) \vee not\ Workers(X) \leftarrow$$
$$Personnel(X) \vee not\ Personnel(X) \leftarrow$$
$$Management(X) \vee not\ Management(X) \leftarrow$$
$$boss(X, Y) \vee not\ boss(X, Y) \leftarrow$$
$$t\_orders(X, Y) \vee not\ t\_orders(X, Y) \leftarrow$$

The individual $\{john\}$ is taken care of by introducing a constant $john$ in the program with the rule $\{john\}(john) \leftarrow$. The only possible value of X in a $\{john\}(X)$ is then $john$.

The DL model $\mathcal{I}$ corresponds to the open answer set $(\mathcal{H}, M)$ with $\mathcal{H} = (\Delta^{\mathcal{I}} \setminus \{j\}) \cup \{john\}$ and $M = \{C(x) \mid C \in upreds(P_4), x \in C^{\mathcal{I}}\} \cup \{R(x, y) \mid R \in bpreds(P_4), (x, y) \in R^{\mathcal{I}}\}$, with a slight abuse of notation, i.e. using C and R as predicates and DL expressions. Formally, we define the *closure* $clos(C, \Sigma)$ of a concept expression C and a knowledge base Σ as the smallest set satisfying the following conditions:

- for every concept (role) expression D (R) in $\{C\} \cup \Sigma$ we have $D(R) \in clos(C, \Sigma)$,
- for every D in $clos(C, \Sigma)$, we distinguish the following cases:

$$D = \neg D_1 \qquad \Rightarrow D_1 \in clos(C, \Sigma)$$
$$D = D_1 \sqcup D_2 \quad \Rightarrow \{D_1, D_2\} \subseteq clos(C, \Sigma)$$
$$D = D_1 \sqcap D_2 \quad \Rightarrow \{D_1, D_2\} \subseteq clos(C, \Sigma)$$
$$D = \exists R.D_1 \quad \Rightarrow \{R, D_1\} \subseteq clos(C, \Sigma)$$
$$D = \forall R.D_1 \quad \Rightarrow \{D_1, \exists R.\neg D_1\} \subseteq clos(C, \Sigma)$$
$$D = (\leq n\ Q.D_1) \Rightarrow \{(\geq n+1\ Q.D_1)\} \subseteq clos(C, \Sigma)$$
$$D = (\geq n\ Q.D_1) \Rightarrow \{Q, D_1\} \subseteq clos(C, \Sigma)$$

- for $R \sqcup S \in clos(C, \Sigma)$, $\{R, S\} \subseteq clos(C, \Sigma)$,
- for $R \sqcap S \in clos(C, \Sigma)$, $\{R, S\} \subseteq clos(C, \Sigma)$.

The CLP $\Phi(C, \Sigma)$ that simulates satisfiability checking of C w.r.t. Σ is then constructed by introducing for concept names A, role names P, and individuals $\{o\}$ in $clos(C, \Sigma)$, rules $A(X) \vee not\ A(X) \leftarrow$, $P(X, Y) \vee not\ P(X, Y) \leftarrow$, and facts $\{o\}(o) \leftarrow$. For every other construct $B \in clos(C, \Sigma)$, we introduce, depending on the particular construct, a rule with B in the head as in Table 2.

Table 2. CLP Translation $\Phi(C, \Sigma)$

$\neg D(X) \leftarrow not\ D(X)$	$D \sqcap E(X) \leftarrow D(X), E(X)$
$D \sqcup E(X) \leftarrow D(X)$	$D \sqcup E(X) \leftarrow E(X)$
$\exists R.D(X) \leftarrow R(X, Y), D(Y)$	$\forall R.D(X) \leftarrow not\ \exists R.\neg D(X)$
$R \sqcup S(X, Y) \leftarrow R(X, Y)$	$R \sqcap S(X, Y) \leftarrow R(X, Y), S(X, Y)$
$R \sqcup S(X, Y) \leftarrow S(X, Y)$	$(\leq n\ R.D)(X) \leftarrow not\ (\geq n+1\ R.D)(X)$
$(\geq n\ R.D)(X) \leftarrow R(X, Y_1), \ldots, R(X, Y_n), D(Y_1), \ldots, D(Y_n), Y_1 \neq Y_2, \ldots$	

This completes the simulation of $\mathcal{ALCHOQ}(\sqcup, \sqcap)$ using CLP.

Theorem 3. *An $\mathcal{ALCHOQ}(\sqcup, \sqcap)$ concept expression C is satisfiable w.r.t. a knowledge base Σ iff C is satisfiable w.r.t. $\Phi(C, \Sigma)$.*

Proof Sketch. For the "only if" direction, take C satisfiable w.r.t. Σ, i.e. there exists a model $\mathcal{I} = (\Delta^{\mathcal{I}}, \cdot^{\mathcal{I}})$ with $C^{\mathcal{I}} \neq \emptyset$. We rename the element $x \in \{o\}^{\mathcal{I}}$ from $\Delta^{\mathcal{I}}$ by o, which is possible by the unique name assumption. We then construct the answer set $(\mathcal{H}, M)$ with $\mathcal{H} = \Delta^{\mathcal{I}}$ and $M = \{C(x) \mid x \in C^{\mathcal{I}}, C \in clos(C, \Sigma)\} \cup \{R(x, y) \mid (x, y) \in R^{\mathcal{I}}, R \in clos(C, \Sigma)\}$. One can show that $(\mathcal{H}, M)$ is an answer set of $\Phi(C, \Sigma)$.

For the "if" direction, we have an open answer set $(\mathcal{H}, M)$ that satisfies C, i.e. $C(x) \in M$ for some $x \in \mathcal{H}$. Define an interpretation $(\Delta^{\mathcal{I}}, \cdot^{\mathcal{I}})$, with $\Delta^{\mathcal{I}} = \mathcal{H}$, and $A^{\mathcal{I}} = \{y \mid A(y) \in M\}$, for concept names A, $P^{\mathcal{I}} = \{(y, z) \mid P(y, z) \in M\}$, for role names P, and $\{o\}^{\mathcal{I}} = \{o\}$, for $o \in \mathcal{H}_{\Phi(C, \Sigma)}$. $\mathcal{I}$ is defined on concept expressions and role expressions as in Table 1, and we can show that $\mathcal{I}$ is a model of Σ such that $C^{\mathcal{I}} \neq \emptyset$.   □

Note that, in general, the resulting CLP $\Phi(C, \Sigma)$ is not local, e.g., a DL expression $\exists R.(A \sqcap B)$ is translated as the rules $\exists R.(A \sqcap B)(X) \leftarrow R(X, Y), A \sqcap B(Y)$ and $A \sqcap B(X) \leftarrow A(X), B(X)$, such that there is a positive $A \sqcap B$ atom that is not free in a body and there is a rule with $A \sqcap B$ in the head and a body that has a non-empty positive part. $\Phi(C, \Sigma)$ has, however, the convenient property that it is *positively acyclic*, i.e. recursion only occurs through negative (with naf) literals; for more details, see [14]. It is sufficient to note that the body of a rule in $\Phi(C, \Sigma)$ is structurally "smaller" than the head, e.g., $A \sqcap B$ is smaller than $\exists R.A \sqcap B$. This permits us to replace the rule with $\exists R.A \sqcap B$ in the head by the two rules $\exists R.(A \sqcap B)(X) \leftarrow R(X, Y), not \, (A \sqcap B)'(Y)$; $(A \sqcap B)'(X) \leftarrow not \, (A \sqcap B)(X)$; i.e. we negate $A \sqcap B(Y)$ twice. The resulting CLP is now local.

Such a procedure does not work for arbitrary CLPs, e.g., we have that $(\{x\}, \{l(x)\})$ is not an open answer set of the rule $l(X) \leftarrow l(X)$, since, although it is a model of $l(x) \leftarrow l(x)$, it is not a minimal model - the empty set is. Transforming the rule, however, by doubly negating the body yields $l(X) \leftarrow not \, l'(X)$ and $l'(X) \leftarrow not \, l(X)$, which does have $(\{x\}, \{l(x)\}$ as an answer set since the GL-reduct contains only the rule $l(x) \leftarrow .$

The $\mathcal{ALCHOQ}(\sqcup, \sqcap)$ simulation shows the feasibility of Semantic Web reasoning with CLPs, as $\mathcal{ALCHOQ}(\sqcup, \sqcap)$ is an expressive DL closely related to the DL $\mathcal{SHOIQ}(\mathbf{D})$, i.e. $\mathcal{SHOQ}(\mathbf{D})$[18] with support for inverted roles, and $\mathcal{SHOIQ}(\mathbf{D})$ is the DL corresponding to the ontology language OWL DL[5]. $\mathcal{ALCHOQ}(\sqcup, \sqcap)$ differs from the DL $\mathcal{SHOIQ}(\mathbf{D})$ by its lack of inverted roles, data types $(\mathbf{D})$ and transitivity of roles (which distinguish $\mathcal{S}$ from $\mathcal{ALC}$); it adds the role constructs $\sqcup$ and $\sqcap$ though.

Since CLP, as a logic programming paradigm, is a natural framework for expressing rules, it can be used to represent and reason with both ontological and rule-based knowledge. Additionally, CLP enables nonmonotonic reasoning on the Semantic Web, identified in [7] as one of the requirements on a logic for reasoning on the Web.

Translating existing DL ontologies to CLP or devising new ontologies that need only DL-like constructs with CLP is not always a good idea. As one sees from the above simulation, the CLP version of a DL ontology produces a lot of overhead rules, specifying the implicit DL semantics. As a result, the translated CLP is likely to be less compact than the original DL knowledge base. However, two remarks are in order here. Firstly, CLPs could nevertheless prove useful as an underlying implementation mechanism for uniform reasoning with both DL ontologies and CLP rules: they ensure a decidable environment for making inferences. Secondly, not all common knowledge can be elegantly represented by DLs; some useful constructs cannot be represented at all. We highlight three advantages of using CLPs for representing knowledge:

Closed Domain Reasoning. Using CLPs, we can explicitly close the domain, i.e. only allow reasoning with constants. Indeed, one can, as in [12], simply add the rules $H(a) \leftarrow$ for every constant a, and a constraint $\leftarrow not\ H(X)$ such that all domain elements must be constants. A similar intervention, restricting the reasoning to individuals, is impossible within standard DLs[9] and was one of the arguments to extend DLs with nonmonotonic tools[9].

Generalized Number Restrictions. The translation of DL ontologies tend to produce some overhead, however, CLPs are more articulate than DLs in other aspects. E.g., representing the knowledge that a team must at least consist of a technical expert, a secretary, and a team leader, where the leader and the technical expert are not the same, can be done by $team(X) \leftarrow member(X, Y_1), tech(Y_1), member(X, Y_2), secret(Y_2),$ $leader(X, Y_3), Y_1 \neq Y_3$. Note that this definition of a team does not exclude non-listed members to be part of the team. Moreover, in the presence of other rules with $team$ in the head, a team may be qualified by one of those rules. E.g., including a fact $team(007)$, would qualify 007 as a team, regardless of its members. Representing such *generalized number restrictions* using DLs would be significantly harder while arguably less succinct.

Query Containment, Consistency, and Disjointness. Those three query problems were identified in [4] as important for ontology reasoning. Query containment is the problem of deciding whether for every database D satisfying an ontology, the result of a query Q_1 to D is contained in the result of Q_2 to D. Instead of the usual conjunctive Datalog queries, we can use CLPs to represent both queries and ontology. E.g., a query $Q_1(X) \leftarrow Management(X)$ retrieves the managers and $Q_2(X) \leftarrow boss(X, Y_1), boss(X, Y_2), Y_1 \neq Y_2$ retrieves the persons that supervise more than two persons. Clearly, Q_1 is contained in Q_2 w.r.t. the ontology P_4 since, according to P_4, managers must supervise at least three workers.

Moreover, all three query problems can be reduced to satisfiability checking w.r.t. a CLP; intuitively, in the query containment case, one extends the ontology with a rule $r(X) \leftarrow Q_1(X), not\ Q_2(X)$, against which unsatisfiability of r is checked. More detail can be found in [14].

5   Related Work

There are basically two lines of research that try to reconcile Description Logics with Logic Programming. The approaches in [6,13,23,2,20,28] simulate DLs with LP, possibly with a detour to FOL, while [8,24,10] attempt to unite the strengths of DLs and LP by letting them coexist and interact.

---

[9] One could enforce closed domain reasoning in DLs by working internally with CLPs.

In [6], the simulation of a DL with acyclic axioms in *open logic programming* is shown. An open logic program is a program with possibly undefined predicates and a FOL-theory; the semantics is the completion semantics, which is only complete for a restrictive set of programs. The open-nes lies in the use of undefined predicates, which are comparable to free predicates with the difference that free predicates can be expressed within the CLP framework. More specifically, open logic programming simulates reasoning in the DL $\mathcal{ALCN}$, $\mathcal{N}$ indicating the use of unqualified number restrictions, where terminological axioms consist of non-recursive concept definitions; $\mathcal{ALCN}$ is a subclass of $\mathcal{ALCHOQ}(\sqcup, \sqcap)$.

[13] imposes restrictions on the occurrence of DL constructs in terminological axioms to enable a simulation using Horn clauses. E.g., axioms containing disjunction on the right hand side, as in $D \sqsubseteq C \sqcup D$, universal restriction on the left hand side, or existential restriction on the right hand side are prohibited since Horn clauses cannot represent them. Moreover, neither negation of concept expressions nor number restrictions can be represented. So-called *Description Logic Programs* are thus incapable of handling expressive DLs; however, [13]'s forte lies in the identification of a subclass of DLs that make efficient reasoning through LPs possible. [23] extends the work in [13], for it simulates non-recursive $\mathcal{ALC}$ ontologies with disjunctive deductive databases. Compared with, possibly recursive, $\mathcal{ALCHOQ}(\sqcup, \sqcap)$, those are still rather inexpressive.

In [2], the DL $\mathcal{ALCQI}$ is successfully translated into a DLP. However, to take into account infinite interpretations [2] presumes, for technical reasons, the existence of function symbols, which leads, in general, to undecidability of reasoning.

[20] and [28] simulate reasoning in DLs with a LP formalism by using an intermediate translation to first-order clauses. In [20], $\mathcal{SHIQ}^-$ knowledge bases, i.e. $\mathcal{SHIQ}$ knowledge bases with the requirement that roles S in $(\leq nS.C)$ have no subroles, are reduced to first-order formulas, on which basic superposition calculus is then applied. The result is transformed into a function-free version which is translated to a disjunctive Datalog program.

[28] translates $\mathcal{ALCQI}$ concepts to first-order formulate, grounds them with a finite number of constants, and transforms the result to a logic program. One can use a finite number of constants by the finite-model property for $\mathcal{ALCQI}$-concept expressions; in the presence of terminological axioms this is no longer possible. The resulting program is, however, not declarative anymore such that its main contribution is that it provides an alternative reasoner for DLs, whereas CLPs can be used both for reasoning with DLs and for a direct and elegant expression of knowledge. Furthermore, CLPs are also interesting from a pure LP viewpoint since they constitute a decidable class of DLPs under the open answer set semantics.

Along the second line of research, an $\mathcal{AL}$-log[8] system consists of two subsystems: a DL knowledge base and a Datalog program, where in the latter variables may range over DL concept instances, thus obtaining a flow of information from the structural DL part to the relational Datalog part. This is extended in [24] for disjunctive Datalog and the $\mathcal{ALC}$ DL. A further generalization is attained in [10] where the particular DL can be the expressive $\mathcal{SHIF}(\mathbf{D})$, $\mathcal{F}$ stands for functional restrictions, or $\mathcal{SHOIN}(\mathbf{D})$. Moreover, the flow of information can go both ways.

Finally, a notable approach, which cannot be categorized in one of the two lines of research described above[10], is the SWRL[19] initiative. SWRL is a *Semantic Web Rule Language* and extends the syntax and semantics of OWL DL with unary/binary Datalog RuleML[1], i.e. Horn-like rules. This extension is undecidable[17] but lacks, nevertheless, interesting knowledge representation mechanisms such as negation as failure.

A reduction from query problems to (un)satisfiability problems for DLs may be found in [29].

6   Conclusions and Directions for Further Research

We extended ASP with open domains, defined CLPs to regain decidability, and reduced reasoning with CLPs to finite, closed, ASP. The simulation of an expressive fragment of the OWL DL ontology language, as well as additional LP mechanisms such as negation as failure and closed world reasoning, illustrates the relevance of CLPs for Semantic Web reasoning. We concluded with a description of related work.

We plan to further relax the restrictions on CLPs by working towards a graph-model property. A prototype implementation, using heuristics, is also envisaged.

References

1. The Rule Markup Initiative. http://www.ruleml.org.
2. G. Alsaç and C. Baral. Reasoning in Description Logics using Declarative Logic Programming. http://www.public.asu.edu/~guray/dlreasoning.pdf, 2002.
3. H. Andréka, I. Németi, and J. Van Benthem. Modal languages and bounded fragments of predicate logic. *J. of Philosophical Logic*, 27(3):217–274, 1998.
4. F. Baader, D. Calvanese, D. McGuinness, D. Nardi, and P. Patel-Schneider. *The Description Logic Handbook*. Cambridge University Press, 2003.
5. S. Bechhofer, F. van Harmelen, J. Hendler, I. Horrocks, D. L. McGuinness, P. F. Patel-Schneider, and L. A. Stein. OWL Web Ontology Language Reference, 2004.
6. K. Van Belleghem, M. Denecker, and D. De Schreye. A Strong Correspondence between DLs and Open Logic Programming. In *Proc. of ICLP'97*, pages 346–360, 1997.
7. F. Bry and S. Schaffert. An Entailment Relation for Reasoning on the Web. In *Proc. of Rules and Rule Markup Languages for the Semantic Web*, LNCS, pages 17–34. Springer, 2003.
8. F. M. Donini, M. Lenzerini, D. Nardi, and A. Schaerf. AL-log: Integrating Datalog and Description Logics. *J. of Intell. and Cooperative Information Systems*, 10:227–252, 1998.
9. F. M. Donini, D. Nardi, and R. Rosati. Description Logics of Minimal Knowledge and Negation as Failure. *ACM Trans. Comput. Logic*, 3(2):177–225, 2002.
10. T. Eiter, T. Lukasiewicz, R. Schindlauer, and H. Tompits. Combining Answer Set Programming with DLs for the Semantic Web. In *Proc. of KR 2004*, pages 141–151, 2004.
11. M. Gelfond and V. Lifschitz. The Stable Model Semantics for Logic Programming. In *Proc. of ICLP'88*, pages 1070–1080, Cambridge, Massachusetts, 1988. MIT Press.
12. M. Gelfond and H. Przymusinska. Reasoning in Open Domains. In *Logic Programming and Non-Monotonic Reasoning*, pages 397–413. MIT Press, 1993.
13. B. N. Grosof, I. Horrocks, R. Volz, and S. Decker. Description Logic Programs: Combining Logic Programs with Description Logic. In *Proc. of WWW 2003*, pages 48–57, 2003.

---

[10] Although it tends towards the coexisting approach.

14. S. Heymans, D. Van Nieuwenborgh, and D. Vermeir. Decidable Open Answer Set Programming. Technical report, Vrije Universiteit Brussel, Dept. of Computer Science, 2004.
15. S. Heymans and D. Vermeir. Integrating Description Logics and Answer Set Programming. In *Proc. of PPSWR 2003*, number 2901 in LNCS, pages 146–159. Springer, 2003.
16. S. Heymans and D. Vermeir. Integrating Ontology Languages and Answer set Programming. In *Proc. of WebS'03*, pages 584–588. IEEE Computer Society, 2003.
17. I. Horrocks and P. F. Patel-Schneider. A Proposal for an OWL Rules Language. In *Proc. of the Thirteenth International World Wide Web Conference (WWW 2004)*. ACM, 2004.
18. I. Horrocks and U. Sattler. Ontology Reasoning in the $\mathcal{SHOQ}(\mathbf{D})$ Description Logic. In *Proc. of IJCAI'01*, pages 199–204. Morgan Kaufmann, 2001.
19. I. Horrocks, P. F. Schneider, H. Boley, S. Tabet, B. Grosof, and M. Dean. SWRL: A Semantic Web Rule language Combining OWL and RuleML, May 2004.
20. U. Hustadt, B. Motik, and U. Sattler. Reducing $\mathcal{SHIQ}^-$ Description Logic to Disjunctive Datalog Programs. FZI-Report 1-8-11/03, Forschungszentrum Informatik (FZI), 2003.
21. N. Leone, W. Faber, and G. Pfeifer. DLV homepage. http://www.dbai.tuwien.ac.at/proj/dlv/.
22. V. Lifschitz. Answer Set Programming and Plan Generation. *AI*, 138(1-2):39–54, 2002.
23. B. Motik, R. Volz, and A. Maedche. Optimizing Query Answering in Description Logics using disjunctive deductive databases. In *Proc. of KRDB'03*, pages 39–50, 2003.
24. R. Rosati. Towards Expressive KR Systems Integrating Datalog and Description Logics: Preliminary Report. In *Proc. of DL'99*, pages 160–164, 1999.
25. J. Schlipf. Some Remarks on Computability and Open Domain Semantics. In *Proc. of the Worksh. on Struct. Complexity and Recursion-Theoretic Methods in Log. Prog.*, 1993.
26. M. Schmidt-Schaub and G. Smolka. Attributive Concept Descriptions with Complements. *Artif. Intell.*, 48(1):1–26, 1991.
27. P. Simons. Smodels homepage. http://www.tcs.hut.fi/Software/smodels/.
28. T. Swift. Deduction in Ontologies via Answer Set Programming. In Vladimir Lifschitz and Ilkka Niemelä, editors, *LPNMR*, volume 2923 of *LNCS*, pages 275–288. Springer, 2004.
29. S. Tessaris. Querying expressive DLs. In *Proc. of DL-2001*, 2001.
30. M. Y. Vardi. Why is Modal Logic so Robustly Decidable? Technical report, 1997.
31. M. Y. Vardi. Reasoning about the Past with Two-Way Automata. In *Proc. of ICALP '98*, pages 628–641. Springer, 1998.

Bossam: An Extended Rule Engine for OWL Inferencing

Minsu Jang and Joo-Chan Sohn

Intelligent Robot Division, Electronics & Telecommunications Research Institute,
Gajeong-dong 161, Yuseong-gu, Daejeon-si, 305-350, South Korea
{minsu, jcsohn}@etri.re.kr

Abstract. In this paper, we describe our effort to build an inference engine for OWL reasoning based on the rule engine paradigm. Rule engines are very practical and effective for their representational simplicity and optimized performance, but their limited expressiveness and web unfriendliness restrict their usability for OWL reasoning. We enumerate and succinctly describe extended features implemented in our rule engine, Bossam, and show that these features are necessary to promote the effectiveness of any ordinary rule engine's OWL reasoning capability. URI referencing and URI-based procedural attachment enhance web-friendliness. OWL importing, support for classical negation and relieved range restrictedness help correctly capture the semantics of OWL. Remote binding enables collaborated reasoning among multiple Bossam engines, which enhances the engine's usability on the distributed semantic web environment. By applying our engine to the W3C's OWL test cases, we got a plausible 70% average success rate for the three OWL species. Our contribution with this paper is to suggest a set of extended features that can enhance the reasoning capabilities of ordinary rule engines on the semantic web.

1 Introduction

The semantic web is an extension of the current web in which information is given well-defined meaning [1], by representing data formally and explicitly in a sharable way. According to the semantic web stack, ontology and rules are the two key components for formal and explicit data representation. To interpret data represented in ontology and rules and derive new information, an appropriate inference mechanism is necessary.

There are a number of reasoning mechanisms for the semantic web, but each of them has its own pros and cons. Dedicated description logic reasoning engines like FaCT[2] and Pellet[3] are great for their firm theoretical soundness, but they are not very useful for practical problems as they strictly stick to open-world assumption and logical perfection. We believe that practical solutions need to provide flexible reasoning ability that can deal with dynamic and very conflicting knowledge space. Another class of tools such as Hoolet [4] and Surnia [5] are based on automatic theorem provers and share the similar low practicality problem with description logic reasoning engines. These reasoning tools cannot deal with ECA rules and do not allow ref-

G. Antoniou and H. Boley (Eds.): RuleML 2004, LNCS 3323, pp. 128–138, 2004.

erencing external objects in the rules. OWL reasoning engines like Jena [6], F-OWL [7], and [8] are based on logic programming or production rule system. With effective reasoning algorithms, they can process rules quite effectively. But [6] does not yet support negation in its rule language, and JESS-based tools like [8] support only negation-as-failure so they cannot correctly capture the semantics of OWL which is based on classical monotonic logic. On the other hand, [7] supports both negation-as-failure and classical negation, but it does not support procedural attachment. As procedural attachment is a necessary feature for practical applications, lacking the feature imposes many problems to utilize the tool in the real setting. Also, these tools put strict range-restrictedness on the head of rules. Range restrictedness dictates that every variable in the consequent part should also be present in the antecedent. But to properly implement entailments imposing OWL comprehension principle, it's necessary to introduce new variables in the consequent part.

We were motivated by the situation that there's no reasoning engine that provides sufficient expressiveness and extra-logical features we identified as required for effective OWL reasoning. We started to build Bossam as a typical rule engine and then added to it a set of extended feature elements to promote effectiveness of the engine's OWL reasoning capability.

Bossam is a RETE-based forward chaining engine, which is equipped with extended representational and extra-logical features:

- Support for both negation-as-failure and classical negation
- Relieved range-restrictedness in the rule heads
- Remote binding for cooperative inferencing among multiple rule engines

In the following two sections, we generally characterize Bossam by presenting its expressiveness and web-friendliness enhancements. In section 4 and 5, we describe Bossam's extended expressiveness elements and remote binding feature.

2 Bossam's Expressiveness

Fig.1 illustrates the expressiveness of Bossam. The outermost rectangle is the boundary of first-order logic's expressiveness. Description logic and horn logic form two overlapping fragments inside FOL. Logic programming is largely a part of FOL, but it contains extra-logical features, such as negation-as-failure, procedural attachment, conflict resolution etc, which are not characterized inside FOL. The extra-logical features are essential even though they defile the clarity of a logic system's formal characterization. Because, in most real-life applications, interaction with external objects, rapid decision making etc are key requirements, which are possible only through employing aforementioned extra-logical features.

As explained in Fig.1, Bossam is based on LP, with two added expressiveness fragments: (4) and (6). Fragment (4) provides syntactic convenience useful for concise rule writing. Bossam breaks down the rules containing elements of (4) into several horn rules according to Lloyd-Topor transformation [9]. With fragment (4), it's easy to write OWL inference rules that create an RDF graph with multiple nodes as an entailment from a premise document, which is not easy with horn rules. In Bossam, every atom contained in the conjunction at the consequent is derived into a fact in case of the rule firing. As for the fragment (6), we give detailed description in section 4.

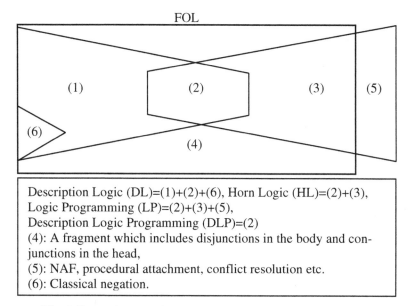

Description Logic (DL)=(1)+(2)+(6), Horn Logic (HL)=(2)+(3),
Logic Programming (LP)=(2)+(3)+(5),
Description Logic Programming (DLP)=(2)
(4): A fragment which includes disjunctions in the body and conjunctions in the head,
(5): NAF, procedural attachment, conflict resolution etc.
(6): Classical negation.

Fig. 1. Expressiveness of Bossam corresponds to (2)+(3)+(4)+(5)+(6).

3   Web Friendliness Enhancements

Any web rules language should make it easy to write rules with URIs. Bossam offers some simple enhancements with its rule language and its interpreter so that URIs can be used intuitively in its rule-bases.

3.1   Seamless URI Integration

Bossam facilitates web friendliness by adding URI as its native symbol type. Actually, all the symbols – except variable symbols – in Bossam's rule-base are URIs. The following example shows a rule and a fact, which are written in Bossam rule language.

```
prefix family = http://family.com/Family#;
namespace = http://family.com/Johns#;
rule r1 is
    if
        family:isFatherOf(?x,?y)
        and family:isBrotherOf(?z,?x)
```

```
then
   family:isUncleOf(?z,?y);
fact f1 is
   family:isFatherOf(John,Bob);
```

In the example above, `family:isFatherOf` and `family:isBrotherOf` may be the terms defined in a remote OWL ontology. Bossam can import remote OWL documents into its internal working memory and perform reasoning on them. The keyword `namespace` is used to define the base namespace of the rule-base. In the above example, the constant `John` specified in the fact `f1` is expanded to a full URI: http://family.com/Johns#John. As shown, it's easy in Bossam's rule language to specify and refer to namespaces and URIs. For a rule language to be used on the web, it should offer syntactic medium to seamlessly and intuitively integrate web resources into its rules.

3.2 OWL Importing

Many a web resource referred in Bossam rules are OWL vocabularies. For OWL reasoning, we wrote a set of OWL inference rules in Bossam rule language. Bossam imports and translates OWL ontology into a list of Bossam facts and then applies the OWL inference rules on them.

There're two approaches to OWL translation. The first is to translate OWL documents into a collection of RDF triples and then each triple into a plain fact with three terms [10] [11]. The second is to translate OWL documents into a set of sentences of the target logic system [4] [12]. The first approach is very simple and general, but some basic logical meanings contained in the original documents are not preserved in the translated result. That is, even the elementary logic constructs are axiomatized such that the implied logical relations in the original OWL constructs are not preserved in the translated result [15]. The second approach does guarantee semantics-preserving translation, but the translatability is limited by the target language's expressiveness.

Table 1. OWL ontology translation examples

OWL statements	Bossam facts
`<owl:Class rdf:ID="Person"/>` `<Person rdf:about="#Sam"/>`	`owl:Class(Person);` `Person(Sam);`

`<owl:Individual rdf:about="#John">`
`<person:father rdf:resource="#Sam"/>`
`</owl:Individual>`
	`person:father(John,Sam);`

`<owl:Class rdf:about="#Human">`
`<owl:unionOf`
`rdf:parseType="Collection">`
`<owl:Class rdf:about="#Woman"/>`
`<owl:Class rdf:about="#Man" />`
`</owl:intersectionOf>`
`</owl:Class>`
	`owl:unionOf(Human, <Woman, Man>);`

With Bossam, we chose the first approach in favor of its simplicity. Bossam translates RDF triples involved in declaring OWL classes and restrictions into 1-ary predicates, and the triples declaring property values into 2-ary predicates. And RDF collections are translated into Bossam's built-in list constants. Table 1 shows three basic examples of Bossam's OWL translation strategy.

3.3 Web-Friendly Procedural Attachment Mechanism

Even though web ontology is appropriate for expressing and sharing static knowledge, it's not adequate for denoting rapidly changing knowledge such as the values of sensors, stock quotes, etc. This kind of knowledge can be made readily accessible by calling external objects. Also, the ability to alter the status of external objects has been the common requirement for rule applications, which might be the same for rule applications on the web. Reading from and writing values onto external objects can be realized by procedural attachment mechanism.

In Bossam, we implemented a web-friendly procedural attachment mechanism, which can be extended to call any object exposed on the web. We defined a special URI structure for denoting calls to external java objects. Here's an example.

```
java://org.etri.sensor/Temperature#get(?x,?loc,?t)
```

The URI scheme, `java`, indicates that the URI is denoting a resource different from usual web resources; in this case, a java object. The path part denotes the package name and the class name. Then, the fragment ID, `get`, denotes the method name. Every external object in the reasoning context is checked for its type and bound to `?x` if it is of the type `org.etri.sensor.Temperature`. `?loc` is the input parameter to the method. The returned value or object from calling the method `get(?loc)` on `?x` is then bound to `?t`.

Extending URI structure in this way is an intuitive way of incorporating external data or objects on the web into reasoning, as it can easily be extended to denote web services, database tables, CORBA objects etc.

4 Extended Expressiveness

We describe in this section two extended expressiveness elements that are not supported in typical rule engines. The introduced expressiveness elements help correctly capture the semantics of OWL.

4.1 Support for Classical Negation, as Well as NAF

OWL semantics is based on open-world assumption, so classical negation should be available for correct representation of OWL semantics. For example, a disjoint class relation, $C1 = \neg C2$, can be written as two rules, {if C1(?x) then neg C2(?x); if C2(?x) then neg C1(?x)}, where neg represents a classical negation. Ordinary rule engines are based on closed-world assumption and they cannot properly represent and process classical negation.

Bossam includes two symbols for denoting negations: `not` for NAF and `neg` for classical negation. Bossam can natively perform de Morgan's law on classical negation, and declares inconsistency by detecting the presence of both positive and negative facts inside its knowledge base.

In [13] and [14], some interesting examples of showing the usefulness of using both NAF and classical-negation on the web are introduced. One representative example involving both NAF and classical-negation is the *coherence principle*, which is the basis of common-sense reasoning [14]. The principle can be expressed in Bossam rule language as follows.

```
rule cp11 is if neg ?p(?x) then not ?p(?x);
rule cp12 is if neg ?p(?x,?y) then not ?p(?x,?y);
rule cp21 is if ?p(?x) then not neg ?p(?x);
rule cp22 is if ?p(?x, ?y) then not neg ?p(?x,?y);
```

`cp11` and `cp21` are for 1-ary predicates, and `cp12` and `cp22` are for 2-ary predicates. For some interesting examples and implications of the principle, the reader is referred to [14].

We conjecture that there're two kinds of knowledge that will be circulating on the semantic web. The first is the static knowledge such as genealogy, monetary system, membership representation schema etc that contains general truths that do not change often. And the second is the dynamic knowledge such as membership management rules, payment strategies, business contract rules etc that contains strategic and business-centric truths and policies that do change often according to the business and strategic needs. Monotonic reasoning based on open-world assumption is appropriate for processing static knowledge to guarantee correct and safe propagation of truths. But for dynamic knowledge, flexible and context-sensitive non-monotonic reasoning is more appropriate to efficiently draw practical conclusions. We think it should become a common requirement for an inference mechanism on the semantic web that it has to effectively deal with a mixed set of static and dynamic knowledge. To satisfy the requirement, an inference mechanism should be able to correctly represent and perform reasoning with knowledge involving both negation-as-failure and classical-negation.

4.2 Relieved Range Restrictedness

Most rule engines put a strict restriction on the rules: every variable in the consequent part should appear in the antecedent part. This is called range restrictedness [9]. Range restrictedness guarantees the safeness of rules.

But some OWL entailments require creation of new RDF resources in the consequent part of rules. OWL *comprehension principle* is the representative example. As a sample, consider a cardinality restriction with a cardinality value 1. This OWL restriction entails a pair of a minimum and a maximum cardinality restriction both with a cardinality value 1. That is, *restriction(p, cardinality(1))* entails {*restriction(p, minCardinality(1)) and restriction(p, maxCardinality(1))*}. This entailment requires two new restrictions be created as a conclusion. To express this in a production rule, two new variables should be introduced at the consequent, which is not possible with typical rule engines. Bossam supports this by relieving range-restrictedness.

We extended typical production algorithm so that range restrictedness can be alleviated in a specific case. In Bossam, you can introduce new variables in *type-declaring 1-ary predicates* in the consequent part. The introduced variables can be referenced in subsequent predicates in the same consequent. The following is a simple Bossam rule that implements the aforementioned comprehension principle regarding cardinality restriction.

```
rule CardinalityEntailment001 is
  if
    owl:Restriction(?r) and owl:onProperty(?r,?p)
    and owl:cardinality(?r,?n)
  then
    owl:Restriction(?r1) and owl:onProperty(?r1,?p)
    and owl:minCardinality(?r1,?n)
    and owl:Restriction(?r2) and owl:onProperty(?r2,?p)
    and owl:maxCardinality(?r2,?n);
```

In the consequent part of the rule above, two new variables, `r1` and `r2`, are introduced for the predicate `owl:Restriction`. Upon encountering predicates of the form like this, Bossam internally creates new anonymous resources and binds each of them to the corresponding new variable.

5 Remote Binding for Distributed Reasoning

Remote binding is a simple mechanism to enable cooperative reasoning among multiple Bossam engines. On the semantic web, knowledge bases, whether they are specified in ontology or rules, are distributed and managed independently. To perform reasoning on them, it is necessary to collect and combine knowledge from various sources. One direct way to accomplish this is to read all the required ontologies and rule-bases from remote hosts and combine them into one big local knowledge base. This approach is easy to implement, but it should be noted that as the size of knowledge base gets bigger, the performance of reasoning mechanisms downgrades very quickly. It's important to keep the size of a knowledge base reasonable.

Distributed (or collaborated) reasoning, when implemented in a proper way, enables sharing knowledge between inference engines and each of them can be free from knowledge saturation. Bossam provides a collaboration mechanism that enables a simple form of distributed reasoning. Every instance of Bossam engine maintains a *knowledge catalog* that maps namespaces to engines. When a Bossam engine encounters a vocabulary it does not maintain locally, it looks up the catalog to find a list of relevant engines based on the namespace of the vocabulary. Upon finishing the lookup, the engine issues a query to each relevant engine one by one until a satisfactory answer is achieved.

Fig 2 shows the overall structure of remote binding mechanism. The knowledge catalog contains a map of namespaces to physical URIs. Each URI refers to the point of contact to send queries about the corresponding namespace. In the current version of Bossam, knowledge catalogs should be specified and provided by the user.

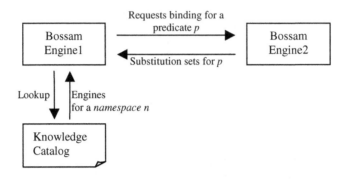

Fig. 2. Overall structure of remote binding

In remote binding, the content of a query is the request for substitution set for a predicate p. The answer to the query is a set of bindings, which in turn is fed by the asking engine into its ongoing process of producing further implied models.

In RETE network, unification is performed at alpha nodes. In Bossam, when a RETE network is built, an alpha node capable of remote binding is created whenever a predicate with a predicate symbol that has a foreign namespace is encountered. The remote-binding alpha nodes always contact remote inference engines to perform unification.

6   OWL Inference Test Results

In this section, we present Bossam's OWL inference test results. We tested Bossam against OWL test cases defined by W3C [17], in part, to validate the effectiveness of our approach. Out of the 10 categories of OWL tests, we applied our engine only to positive entailment tests that are more relevant to the inferencing capability.

6.1   On Processing Positive Entailment Tests

Each OWL positive entailment test is composed of two OWL documents: one premise document and one conclusion document. OWL reasoning engine should be able to entail the conclusion document when given with the premise document as an input. For each positive entailment test, we executed an inference session on Bossam with the given test's premise document and then queried the engine with the conclusion document to find out if the conclusion document holds in the models Bossam produced from the premise document. To do this, we converted each conclusion document into a Bossam query, which is then transformed into a Bossam rule for further processing.

The following is an example that illustrates the basic approach of the conversion. This example document was depicted from the OWL test case at http://www.w3.org/2002/03owlt/FunctionalProperty/Manifest005#test. The namespace prefix eg corresponds to http://www.example.org/, and foo corresponds to http://www.example.org/foo#.

(d1) Original conclusion document in N3 [16]:

```
eg:foo#object rdf:type owl:Thing.
_:a rdf:type owl:Restriction.
eg:foo#prop rdf:type owl:FunctionalProperty.
_:a owl:onProperty eg:foo#prop.
_:a owl:maxCardinality "1"^^xsd:nonNegativeInteger.
eg:foo#object rdf:type _:a.
```

(d2) Bossam query generated from (d1):

```
(((((?a(foo:object) and   owl:Restriction(?a)
    ) and owl:onProperty(?a,foo:prop)
   ) and owl:FunctionalProperty(foo:prop)
  ) and owl:Thing(foo:object)
 ) and owl:maxCardinality(?a,1)
)
```

(d3) Bossam rule transformed from (d2):

```
rule q is
  if
     ?a(foo:object) and owl:Restriction(?a)
     and owl:onProperty(?a,foo:prop)
     and owl:FunctionalProperty(foo:prop)
     and owl:Thing(foo:object)
     and owl:maxCardinality(?a,1)
  then
     Result(?a);
```

As can be seen, anonymous RDF nodes in the conclusion document are converted into Bossam variables. Bossam tries to answer the query by finding some successful bindings to the variables. If a conclusion document does not contain anonymous RDF nodes, it's converted into a query composed of only ground predicates. As Bossam is a forward-chaining engine that is data-driven, it internally converts queries into rules and applies the rules to the forward-chaining process to see if the rules fire with successful bindings. If any rule fires, then the corresponding query is declared to be true.

6.2 Test Results

Table.2 summarizes the success rates of Bossam and other OWL inference engines. The number of tests for each species of OWL is 23 for OWL Lite, 29 for OWL DL, and 41 for OWL Full [17]. The success rate of Bossam marked middle to high among representative OWL inference engines.

Table 2. OWL Test Results (data excerpted from W3C site, as of Dec. 2003)

Engine Species	Bossam	Hoolet	Cerebra	Pellet	Euler	FOWL	FaCT	Surnia	Jena2
OWL Lite	95%	82%	73%	82%	100%	65%	4%	26%	69%
OWL DL	51%	62%	51%	89%	100%	6%	10%	3%	17%
OWL Full	68%	N/A	12%	82%	100%	48%	N/A	41%	68%

One thing to be noted is that other engines listed in Table 2 do not offer the practical features that Bossam do offer. For example, there's no engine except Bossam in Table 2 that supports procedural attachment, two negations and remote binding. Also, it needs to be commented that description logic based engines like Pellet, FaCT and Cerebra are not capable of dealing with rules.

As the semantic web technology development progresses further into the higher layer of the semantic web stack, rule-processing capability will be much required from reasoning engines. And, as the semantic web technology gets wide acceptance by the business fields, practical – extra-logical – reasoning features will become the deciding factor for choosing the solutions for web reasoning.

7 Concluding Remarks

If a reasoning tool were to be utilized pervasively in the real world settings, it should provide rich practical features. The strength of successful reasoning mechanisms, especially rule engines, is related to their highly efficient reasoning performance and rich extra-logical features. On the semantic web, we believe that the reasoning tools inheriting the pros of (currently commercial) rule engines will survive as the most viable reasoning mechanism.

In this paper, we described Bossam, a rule engine extended with various features to improve web friendliness, OWL reasoning capability, and usability on the web. We plan to extend and refine reasoning capability of Bossam to make it a more reliable and competitive reasoning tool for the semantic web, and to investigate the possibility of applying it to some real semantic web applications. Especially, we're trying to extend Bossam's remote binding mechanism so that knowledge catalog can be automatically created and maintained.

References

1. Berners-Lee, T., Hendler, J., Lassila, O.: The Semantic Web. Scientific American (2001)
2. Horrocks, I.: The FaCT System. LNAI, Vol. 1397. Springer-Verlag, Berlin (1998) 307-312
3. Maryland Information and Network Dynamics Lab.: Pellet OWL Reasoner. (2003) http://www.mindswap.org/2003/pellet/index.shtml
4. Bechhofer, S.: Hoolet OWL Reasoner (2003) http://owl.man.ac.uk/hoolet/
5. Hawke, S.: Surnia (2003) http://www.w3.org/2003/08/surnia/
6. Hewlett-Packard: Jena Semantic Web Framework (2003) http://jena.sourceforge.net/
7. UMBC: F-OWL: An OWL Inference Engine in Flora-2 http://fowl.sourceforge.net/
8. Gandon, F. L., Sadeh, N.: OWL inference engine using XSLT and JESS. http://mycampus.sadehlab.cs.cmu.edu/public_pages/OWLEngine.html
9. Grosof, B., Gandhe, M., Finin, T.: SweetJess: Inferencing in Situated Courteous RuleML via Translation to and from Jess Rules. (2003) http://ebusiness.mit.edu/bgrosof/paps/sweetjess-wp-050203.pdf
10. Kopena, J., Regli, W.: DAMLJessKB: A Tool for Reasoning with the Semantic Web, LNCS, Vol. 2870. Springer-Verlag, Berlin Heidelberg New York (2003) 628-643
11. Fikes, R., Frank, G., Jenkins, J.: JTP: A Query Answering System For Knowledge Represented in DAML. (2002)
12. Grosof, B., Horrocks, I., Volz, R., Decker, S.: Description logic programs: Combining logic programs with description logic. In Proceedings of WWW2003. (2003) 48
13. Wagner, G.: Web Rules Need Two Kinds of Negation. LNCS, Vol. 2901. Springer-Verlag, Berlin Heidelberg New York (2003) 33-50
14. Alferes, J., Damicio, C., Pereira, L.: Semantic Web Logic Programming Tools. LNCS 2901 (2003) 16-32
15. Horrocks, I., Volz, R.: Rule Language. A Deliverable from IST Project 2001-33052 WonderWeb. (2003)
16. Berners-Lee, T.: Primer: Getting into RDF and Semantic Web using N3. (2004) http://www.w3.org/2000/10/swap/Primer.html
17. Jeremy J. Carroll, Jos De Roo: OWL Web Ontology Language Test Cases. W3C Recommendation 10 February 2004 (2004) http://www.w3.org/TR/owl-test/

Extending SWRL to Express Fully-Quantified Constraints

Craig McKenzie, Peter Gray, and Alun Preece

University of Aberdeen, Department of Computing Science
Aberdeen AB24 3UE, UK
{cmckenzie,pgray,apreece}@csd.abdn.ac.uk
http://www.csd.abdn.ac.uk/research/akt/cif

Abstract. Drawing on experience gained over a series of distributed knowledge base and database projects, we argue for the utility of an expressive quantified constraint language for the Semantic Web logic layer. Our Constraint Interchange Format (CIF) is based on classical range-restricted FOL. CIF allows the expression of invariant conditions in Semantic Web data models, but the choice of how to implement the constraints is left to local reasoners.

We develop the quantified constraint representation as an extension of the current proposal for a Semantic Web Rule Language (SWRL). An RDF syntax for our extended CIF/SWRL is given in this paper. While our approach differs from SWRL in that existential quantifiers are handled explicitly rather than using OWL-DL constructs, we believe our proposal is still fully compatible with the use of the various OWL species as well as RDFS.

We demonstrate the use of the CIF/SWRL representation in the context of a practical Semantic Web reasoning application, based on the CS AK-Tive Space demonstrator (the 2003 Semantic Web Challenge winner). We indicate where in our application it makes sense to use the existing SWRL directly, and where our CIF/SWRL allows more complex constraints to be expressed in a natural manner.

1 Introduction and Motivation

Over the course of several projects, we have developed an approach to knowledge fusion in open, distributed environments [2,10,11]. The central idea in our approach is, in response to some user's request, to gather pertinent data from multiple network sources, along with constraints on how the data can be used. These data and constraints are then fused by mediator software into a dynamically-composed constraint satisfaction problem (CSP), which is then dispatched to a solver on the network. The solutions (if any) are then relayed back to the user. The data and constraints are expressed against a semantic data model/ontology because it may be necessary to transform them at run-time; for example, entities/classes in the data model may need to be mapped (rewritten) from a local schema/ontology to a common interchange schema/ontology. Constraints

G. Antoniou and H. Boley (Eds.): RuleML 2004, LNCS 3323, pp. 139–154, 2004.

in our approach are represented using an expressive quantified constraint language — the Constraint Interchange Format (CIF) — based on classical range-restricted first-order logic, and derived from the Colan/Daplex constraint/query languages [1].

This approach has been applied chiefly to e-commerce problems, where some package goods need to be assembled and configured to meet some requirement, and each component of the package puts constraints on the other components. For example, in configuring a personal computer system for a user, the choice of operating system may constrain the choice of peripherals; or, in configuring a package holiday, the choice of excursions may constrain the timing of the trip.

In recent work we have applied this approach to the Semantic Web [6,12]. In many ways, this "new generation" Web is an ideal environment for the kind of problem-solving activity we envisaged in our earlier work, as it fits the W3C's vision of a task-oriented Web "better enabling people and computers to work in cooperation"[1]. The lower layers of the Semantic Web architecture (RDF/RDFS) fit our minimal requirements for data to be expressed against a semantic data model, while the ontology layer (OWL) allows far richer modelling, and also supports some elements of ontology mapping (for example, *equivalentClass*).

The current leading proposal for a representation at the Semantic Web logic layer is the Semantic Web Rule Language (SWRL)[2]. While we embrace this proposal, we will argue in this paper that it is not sufficiently expressive for our own needs, and we therefore propose an extension to SWRL that allows the representation of the kinds of fully-quantified constraints used in our earlier versions of CIF. In doing this, we bring forward some aspects of an earlier RDF-compatible encoding of CIF [12] and align this with the constructs of SWRL, to create a layered CIF/SWRL representation (with an accompanying RDF syntax). We will make arguments for allowing forms of logic more expressive than current SWRL on the open Semantic Web, and also discuss how a representation based on range-restricted FOL (which takes a closed-world assumption) does not in practice contradict the vision of an open-world Web.

To illustrate our approach situated in the Semantic Web context, later sections of the paper introduce a new application which builds on the CS AKTive Space demonstrator (winner of the 2003 Semantic Web Challenge) [13]. The CS AKTive Space is a large-scale repository of semantic metadata on computing science activities in the UK; our application — AKTive Workgroup Builder — uses constraints to select individuals from the CS AKTive Space to form working groups that satisfy particular requirements. This could be used, for example, to form "expert panels", suggest partners for collaborative projects, or organise workshops. We will show how "vanilla SWRL" and CIF/SWRL are both useful for the AKTive Workgroup Builder.

The paper is organised as follows: Section 2 discusses various forms of rule used in database and knowledge-based systems, and compares these forms with the kind of fully-quantified constraints used in our approach. Section 3 introduces

---

[1] http://www.w3.org/2001/sw/

[2] http://www.w3.org/Submission/SWRL/

the proposed CIF/SWRL representation, including its abstract and RDF syntaxes, aligned with those of SWRL. Section 4 presents our illustrative AKTive Workgroup Builder application, and highlights examples of the use of SWRL and CIF/SWRL in this demonstrator. Section 5 discusses issues arising from our approach, and Section 6 concludes with some pointers to ongoing and future work.

2   Rules and Constraints: How They Differ

People use the word "rules" rather freely. In fact there are a variety of different kinds which need to be distinguished. We discuss these below, with examples from SWRL and from our own work using Colan and Daplex [1]: derivation rules, rewrite rules, event-condition-action (ECA) rules, and quantified constraints.

Derivation Rules. Derivation rules are the simplest form. They are essentially a rule for calculating a derived value on-the-fly, often by some kind of table lookup in a database, They are a technology often used to provide *views* of stored data in databases. For example, we have a rule for a person's uncle (adapted from the SWRL proposal, and using the informal SWRL syntax where ?x denotes a variable, and adding explicit universal quantifiers):

$(\forall \text{?x,?p,?s,?g})$ hasParent(?x,?p) $\wedge$ hasSibling(?p,?s) $\wedge$
    hasSex(?s,?g) $\wedge$ (?g='male') $\Rightarrow$ hasUncle(?x,?s)

In our Daplex language, originally used to define integration schemas for heterogeneous distributed databases on the Multibase project, we would define the relationship functionally thus:

```
define hasUncle(P in Person) ->> Person
Sb in hasSibling(hasParent(P)) such that hasSex(Sb) = 'male'
```

Here a predicate rel(X,Y) is replaced by Y in relfunc(X), where relfunc is a function whose values may be stored or computed. In this example it computes the set of those siblings of the parent of P who are male. The set is computed by the function hasUncle, and it may, of course, be empty for some individuals. The functional form helps to make clear the functional dependency of the derived information.

Rewrite Rules. These rules are useful in query optimisation, for replacing one expression by an equivalent expression, usually involving less database access. For example in our Antibody Protein database [8] we have:

```
with common C in chain, i in integer
rewrite r in residues(C) such that pos(r) = i
into absolutepos(C,i)
```

This replaces a sequential search down a protein chain for the ith residue in sequence by a direct lookup of the residue using a precomputed table-driven function absolutepos. In FOL we could write this as:

$(\forall?c,?r,?i)$ Chain(?c) $\wedge$ hasResidue(?c,?r) $\wedge$ hasPos(?r,?i)
$\Rightarrow$ hasAbsolutePos(?c,?i,?r)

It looks the same as a derivation rule but it is used differently. The implication should really be replaced by $\Leftrightarrow$ (*is logically equivalent to*). This means that we can substitute an occurrence of the body, which has particular expressions denoting values for ?c, ?i and ?r, by the head having used the same expressions in place of ?c, ?i and ?r. Having done this substitution, we can then do algebraic simplification and further substitutions. Consequently the final formula may look very different from the original one. Thus we do not execute a chain of rules at runtime, instead we execute them at compile time and compile away various unneeded computations, which is a very powerful query optimisation technique.

Event-Condition-Action (ECA) Rules. The rewrite rule used above relies on the correctness of a stored table, relating residue to position in a protein chain. Fortunately, such relationships do not change, except slowly by evolution, and then we would be referring to a different chain. If we were referring to something more dynamic, like pre-booked seats in a passenger aircraft, then we would need a mechanism to update our stored relationship and keep it in correspondence with changes in passenger bookings for a given flight. This can be done by ECA rules (sometimes called triggered rules). For example:

```
ON Death of Passenger P
WHERE P isBookedOnFlight F and (Other Conditions...)
DO RemoveBooking(P,F).
```

As is well known, combinations of ECA rules can interact in unpredictable ways through side-effects in their state changing actions. A neat way of overcoming this is to code-generate the rules so that they satisfy *invariant constraints* that must be maintained under update [3]. This allows us to keep the declarative stance of pure logic, despite using rules with state changing actions. We shall now review such constraints.

Quantified Constraints. A quantified constraint [4] is not just an isolated condition. It is a formula of FOL, where all the free variables have universal or existential (or maybe numerical) quantifiers. Such formulae are very suitable for expressing domain-specific semantics for collections of stored data. For example, suppose it is a rule that all tutors with "research" status in some department only supervise students with computing grades above 60. In FOL this is expressible as:

$(\forall?t,?s,?g)$ Tutor(?t) $\wedge$ hasStatus(?t,'research') $\wedge$
supervises(?t,?s) $\wedge$ hasSubjectGrade(?s,'Computing',?g) $\Rightarrow$ (?g>60)

This is easily representable in SWRL, since it is a conjunctive DataLog query. However, the interesting question is how it is interpreted pragmatically. It is not really worth using it to infer an inequality about the value of ?g when using a database, since we can just ask the database for the actual value of ?g directly! Instead, it is more about keeping consistency of groups of values stored in a database, so that we can compile away certain checks that would otherwise be made at runtime.

In order to maintain the validity of the constraint efficiently, we code generate a number of ECA rules which are triggered by changes in supervisors' status, or creation of new supervisees, and which make only those checks that are necessary for data to be valid for the given incremental change. The creation of these rules can be done systematically from a knowledge of the constraints and the schema, as explained in [3], following original ideas in [9]. Better still, if new constraints are added, or old ones retracted, then the ECA rules can be updated accordingly — an example of automatic maintenance which is far superior to that of relying on collections of hand-coded checks and triggers installed over time by a mix of different programmers.

Thus the lesson for the Semantic Web is that quantified constraints may have alternative implementations. It should be possible to send a constraint across the Web, and to allow the remote site to process or implement the constraint as it thinks best. If it is an equational constraint the site's processing engine might enforce it by a derivation rule which always calculates the derived property value according to the constraint equation. If the derived property depends on accessing many other stored data values (a large "join", in database terms) then it may be better to cache the derived value and use triggered ECA rules to keep it up to date. There is much literature on how to do this efficiently. We feel that this approach is in keeping with the spirit of the Web, by granting the local site autonomy to choose *how* to implement the constraint, while the constraint itself guarantees *what* is being held invariant.

Using Mixed Quantifiers in Quantified Constraints. Quantified Constraints need not be pure DataLog; they may wish to conclude the existence of some fact or the truth of some relationship(association). In the example above we established that research tutors should only supervise bright students, with grades above 60. However, the constraint leaves open the possibility that a research tutor supervises no students. To make a stronger statement we need an existential quantifier on the right-hand side, in the conclusion, as below:

```
(∀?t) Tutor(?t) ∧ hasStatus(?t,'research') ⇒
    (∃?s,?g) supervises(?t,?s) ∧ hasSubjectGrade(?s,'Computing',?g) ∧
        (?g>60)
```

This is a straightforward piece of range-restricted FOL, but it is not DataLog. The existential quantifier is represented by a Skolem function of the enclosing quantified variable ?t, and thus the formula in conjunctive normal form is no longer function free; it includes terms like supervises(?t,Student(?t)) which are not allowed in DataLog.

In our experience with using the Colan data sublanguage [1,4], in a number of projects [3,6,11], we have found the need to express constraints of the form:

$$(\forall?x,?y) \ P1(?x) \ \wedge \ q1(?x,?y) \ \wedge \ \ldots \ \Rightarrow$$
$$(\forall?r,?s) \ P2(?r) \ \wedge \ q2(?x,?s) \ \wedge \ \ldots \ \Rightarrow$$
$$(\exists?u,?v) \ Pn(?u) \ \wedge \ qn(?y,?v) \ \wedge \ \ldots$$

Thus there are some universally quantified implications, followed by a conjunction of predicates, possibly existentially quantified. There is a special case with no universal quantifiers followed just by existential quantifiers, asserting a minimum cardinality for some entity type or relationship type. We have not found the need for further universal quantifiers inside the existential quantifiers. Our constraint syntax is recursive, and allows for this possibility, but we have not found the need for it.

Constraint Interchange Format (CIF). Following our experience with Colan in the KRAFT and Conoise projects, we proposed [12] a constraint interchange format that was based purely on RDF and RDFS, which was expressive enough to encode constraints of the form above. It was based purely on range-restricted FOL with the usual connectives (and, or, not). The intention was that constraints could be passed to a constraint logic solver or theorem prover, or Prolog solver for Horn clauses with function symbols. We could have included Description Logic, but found that the data model provided by RDFS was perfectly adequate for our uses. This is because we were basically doing A-Box reasoning, relying on the presence of assertions and instances, rather than T-Box reasoning without them.

We defined constraint types recursively by the following BNF[3]:

```
<Constraint>       ::=  <ImpliesConstraint> | <ExistsConstraint> | <unQuantifiedBody>
<ImpliesConstraint> ::= Each <Var> in <Entity> [SuchThat <BoolExp>] <Constraint>
<ExistsConstraint>  ::= Some <Var> in <Entity> [SuchThat <BoolExp>] <Constraint>
<unQuantifiedBody>  ::= <BoolExp>
```

Here <BoolExp> expands to any well-formed formula using only variables that have been quantified in an outer construct. The Predicates in the formulae may refer to membership of a specific collection of entities or stored relationships, or may be evaluable predicates (as in Prolog). The entities and relationships have RDFS declarations. This syntax is serialisable in RDF/XML.

Compared to SWRL, this form of RDF had the virtue that it treated universal and existential quantifiers on a similar footing and was easy to parse. By contrast, we feel that SWRL has got into difficulties by trying to combine RuleML, based on DataLog which does not allow existential quantifiers in the consequent [5], with OWL which allows existential quantifiers in T-Box fashion as a *someValuesFrom* construct in an OWL DL expression. This means that existential quantifiers become a restricted special case which is much harder to parse, analyse and transform.

Our vision is in accordance with that of Section 7 of the May 2004 SWRL proposal[4], in that we want to see a Semantic Web logic language that can be

---

[3] http://www.csd.abdn.ac.uk/research/akt/cif/

[4] http://www.w3.org/Submission/2004/SUBM-SWRL-20040521/

used with a variety of reasoners. In particular, we have a vision of constraints expressed against one ontology that can be transformed, by simple homomorphism, to apply to data stored in another ontology, or a shared ontology, in which the constraints can then be combined with constraints similarly transformed from other ontologies.

3   Extending SWRL to CIF/SWRL

In designing a re-formulation of CIF we undertook to incorporate SWRL constructs where possible, while also striving to simplify the original CIF syntax. Constraints are essentially defined as quantified implications, so we re-use the implication structure from SWRL, but allow for nested quantified implications within the consequent of an implication. The innermost-nested implication will have an empty body as it is always of the form "*true* $\Rightarrow$ ...". In line with the presentation of SWRL, we first introduce an informal, human-readable syntax, then present the formal abstract syntax and finally the RDF serialisation.

The human-readable syntax is straightforward, as it simply adds the quantifiers and supports nested implications, where the innermost has an empty body:

```
(∀?x∈X, ?y∈Y) p(?x,?y) ∧ Q(?x) ⇒
    (∀?z∈Z) q(?x,?z) ∧ R(?z) ⇒
        (∃?v∈V) s(?y,?v)
```

Abstract Syntax. Here we focus on the extensions to the abstract syntax given in SWRL and OWL documentation, using the same EBNF syntax. A `constraint` structure retains the `URIreference` and `annotation` features from OWL/SWRL so as to allow statements to be made about the constraints themselves (see Section 5). Note that nesting is handled by extending the original SWRL grammar, allowing a `constraint` to appear recursively inside a `consequent`. The definition of `antecedent` is unchanged from SWRL and appears here only for completeness. As defined by the SWRL EBNF, an `atom` may be a unary (class) predicate (for example, `P(I-variable(x))`) or a binary (property) predicate (for example, `q(I-variable(y) I-variable(z))`). The only other significant new piece of syntax is the `quantifiers` structure, a list of individual quantifier expressions, each of which contains a reference to a SWRL `I-variable` and an OWL/RDFS class. So, in the informal expression "?x ∈ X" x is an `I-variable` and X is an OWL/RDFS class identifier.

We have simplified the original CIF syntax to have just one generic form of constraint, which may have a mixture of quanitifiers in any order desired. In practice this greatly flattens the nested structures.

```
constraint  ::= 'Implies(' [ URIreference ] { annotation }
                quantifiers antecedent consequent ')'
antecedent  ::= 'Antecedent(' { atom } ')'
```

```
consequent   ::= 'Consequent(' constraint | { atom } ')'
quantifiers  ::= 'Quantifiers(' { q-atom } ')'
q-atom       ::= quantifier '(' q-var q-set ')'
quantifier   ::= 'forall' | 'exists'
q-var        ::= I-variable
q-set        ::= classID
```

Here is the informal example re-cast into the abstract syntax. Note the empty antecedent in the innermost-nested implication.

```
Implies(
    Quantifiers(forall(I-variable(x) X) forall(I-variable(y) Y))
    Antecedent(p(I-variable(x) I-variable(y)) Q(I-variable(x)))
    Consequent(
        Implies(
            Quantifiers(forall(I-variable(z) Z))
            Antecedent(q(I-variable(x) I-variable(z)) R(I-variable(z)))
            Consequent(
                Implies(
                    Quantifiers(exists(I-variable(v) V))
                    Antecedent()
                    Consequent(s(I-variable(y) I-variable(v)))))))))
```

RDFS Syntax (Sketch). Rather than present the full, verbose RDFS XML definitions for our additional CIF syntax, here we merely sketch the necessary extensions to the SWRL RDF syntax:[5]

- We define a new `rdfs:Class` `cif:Constraint`, with two attached properties `cif:hasQuantifiers` and `cif:hasImplication`. The range of the former is an RDF list (of quantifier structures in practice) and the range of the latter is a `ruleml:Imp`.
- We define the parent class `cif:Quantifier` with two sub-classes: `cif:Forall` and `cif:Exists`. Two properties `cif:var` and `cif:set` complete the implementation of the `q-atom` from the abstract syntax. The range of both is an RDF resource: in the case of `cif:var` this will be a URIref to a SWRL variable, while for `cif:set` it will identify an OWL/RDFS class.
- Note that the SWRL RDF syntax allows the `body` of an implication to be any RDF list, so it already allows the nested inclusion of a `cif:Constraint`.

Example CIF/SWRL constraints in RDF syntax are shown in the next section.

4   Illustrative Application: AKTive Workgroup Builder

As a test-bed for our reformulated CIF we sought a Semantic Web application that was practical, used real-world RDF data, and in which realistic constraints

---

[5] Definition of an XML syntax for CIF/SWRL, extending the SWRL/RuleML XML syntax, would be trivial. We do not cover this here, preferring the pure-RDF approach to Semantic Web structure encoding.

could be expressed. The AKT project (of which the CIF work is a part) had already developed the CS AKTive Space application (winner of the 2003 Semantic Web Challenge) [13]. The CAS includes a very large repository of RDF data covering computing science research in the UK. We therefore decided that the task of dynamically composing "workgroups" from the pool of available computing science academic staff suited our criteria for a test-bed application.

The process of constructing a workgroup involves several steps:

- Defining constraints about the nature of the workgroup; for example, defining the minimum and maximum group size, the focus of the workgroup, etc.
- Gathering the RDF data about the pool of people to be considered.
- Understanding and reasoning against the data to determine eligibility; for example, is a person available to participate, do they have the relevant skills/interests, etc.
- Finally, using a constraint satisfaction problem solver to compose workgroups that satisfy the constraints.

Our AKTive Workgroup Builder (AWB) could be used, for example, to form "expert panels", suggest partners for collaborative projects, or organise workshops.

In its current form, the AWB does not directly import its data from the CAS for several reasons. Most fundamentally, the data in the CAS repository is expressed against the AKT Portal Ontology[6], which is OWL Full. The lack of reasoning support for OWL Full led us to produce a restricted reformulation of the core of the AKT Portal Ontology in OWL Lite, allowing us to use the software included in HPs Jena toolkit[7] to perform ontological inference and reasoning. The other problems in directly using the CAS data related to scalability and data provenance. The sheer size of the full repository (currently over 10 million RDF statements covering over 2000 people and their related projects, publications and other activities) made direct use of this data in developing the AWB very difficult. Because the data is harvested from the open Web/Semantic Web, it inevitably contains contradictions, errors, duplications, incompleteness, and other provenance issues. These problems of scale and trust, while being interesting and exciting problems in their own right, were tangential to our current scope of work.

For the initial version of the AWB, then, we elected to focus on data relating to the members of the five partner groups in the AKT project: Aberdeen, Edinburgh, Open University, Sheffield and Southampton. Essentially, this cut-down AWB would allow us to compose working groups for our own activities. So, the data in the current AWB repository can best be regarded as a locally-cached subset of the full CAS data store, expressed against an OWL Lite cut-down version of the AKT Portal Ontology. The instance data is almost identical to the original, while the ontology definitions are mostly just weakenings of the OWL Full original.

---

[6] http://www.aktors.org/ontology/portal
[7] http://jena.sourceforge.net

The AWB is implemented as a J2EE application with Jena managing the RDF processing, and MySQL as the back-end DBMS. Since the reasoning usually takes longer than a user is prepared to wait with a Web application (even with the cut-down dataset), the AWB uses a messaging mechanism in order to "call back" the user when the results are ready for inspection.

Reasoning in the AWB: SWRL. The entailments generated by the Jena Owl Reasoner used by the AWB are all class or property based derivations. For example, a `Professor-In-Academia` is a sub-class of `Person`, therefore all instances of `Professor-In-Academia` are also `Person`s. Similarly, a `Person` with the property `has-supervisor` must be the more specific sub-class of `PhD-Student` as dictated by the domain of this property (only the `PhD-Student` class has the `has-supervisor` property).

For our reasoning to cover realistic situations we needed more expressivity. For example, if someone has published a paper on Machine Learning, this implies that they have an interest in this area, even if they have not explicitly stated it in their research interests. The fact cannot be derived from a class or property hierarchy. While the Jena reasoner API has its own internal form for inference rules, it was important to us to state these derivation rules on the Semantic Web using SWRL. To illustrate, suppose we are interested in deriving the ontology property `has-base-location` for a person, from the rule: "if a person has an affiliation with an organisation, and that organisation has a postal address with a city then this implies that the person has a base location of the same city". In FOL:

```
(∀?p,?u,?a,?c) Person(?p) ∧ Organisation(?u) ∧
   has-affiliation(?p,?u) ∧ has-postal-address(?u,?a) ∧
      address-city(?a,?c) ⇒ has-base-location(?p,?c)
```

In SWRL RDF syntax this looks as shown in Figure 1. Note that the ontology URI is represented by the entity "&akt;" all classes in this reduced version of the AKT Portal Ontology are OWL classes, defined only with OWL Lite constructs.

Reasoning in the AWB: CIF. The above example works well because it uses ontology properties of an individual to derive further ontological information about that same individual and uses only the universal quantifier. However, trying to express an existentially quantified sentence (from which we wish to form a constraint) in SWRL is more awkward. For example, if we wanted to say, "every workgroup must contain at least 1 member who is a Professor":

```
(∀?g∈Workgroup)(∃?p∈Professor-In-Academia) has-member(?g,?p)
```

In the SWRL document it is shown how this kind of existentially-quantified statement can be expressed implicitly using the OWL DL `someValuesFrom` construct as part of a class restriction on the `Workgroup` class. As we argued in Section 2, we prefer to express all the quantifiers uniformly and explicitly, and leave the reasoner the option of transforming the constraint expressions to a

```
<swrl:Imp>
 <swrl:body rdf:parseType="Collection">
  <swrl:ClassAtom>
   <swrl:classPredicate rdf:resource="&akt;#Person"/>
   <swrl:argument1 rdf:resource="#p"/>
  </swrl:ClassAtom>
  <swrl:ClassAtom>
   <swrl:classPredicate rdf:resource="&akt;#Organization"/>
   <swrl:argument1 rdf:resource="#u"/>
  </swrl:ClassAtom>
  <swrl:IndividualPropertyAtom>
   <swrl:propertyPredicate rdf:resource="&akt;#has-affiliation"/>
   <swrl:argument1 rdf:resource="#p"/>
   <swrl:argument2 rdf:resource="#u"/>
  </swrl:IndividualPropertyAtom>
  <swrl:IndividualPropertyAtom>
   <swrl:propertyPredicate rdf:resource="&akt;#has-postal-address"/>
   <swrl:argument1 rdf:resource="#u"/>
   <swrl:argument2 rdf:resource="#a"/>
  </swrl:IndividualPropertyAtom>
  <swrl:IndividualPropertyAtom>
   <swrl:propertyPredicate rdf:resource="&akt;#address-city"/>
   <swrl:argument1 rdf:resource="#a"/>
   <swrl:argument2 rdf:resource="#c"/>
  </swrl:IndividualPropertyAtom>
 </swrl:body>
 <swrl:head rdf:parseType="Collection">
  <swrl:IndividualPropertyAtom>
   <swrl:propertyPredicate rdf:resource="&akt;#has-base-location"/>
   <swrl:argument1 rdf:resource="#p"/>
   <swrl:argument2 rdf:resource="#c"/>
  </swrl:IndividualPropertyAtom>
 </swrl:head>
</swrl:Imp>
```

Fig. 1. SWRL RDF/XML for the rule: "if a person has an affiliation with an organisation, and that organisation has a postal address with a city then this implies that the person has a base location of the same city".

suitable implementation form (for example, a rewriting of the constraint to use an OWL DL reasoner would be possible in this case). So CIF/SWRL makes it possible to represent both the quantifiers in a uniform and explicit way. The CIF/SWRL for this constraint in RDF syntax is shown in Figure 2. Note the empty body.

We will now examine a more complex constraint, that would be far more cumbersome and unintuitive to capture in SWRL/OWL DL alone, and also illustrates how solving in CIF can interplay with rule-based reasoning in SWRL. Consider the constraint, "any workgroup with at least 5 members must contain people from different sites". For this we use the derived property has-base-location from our SWRL example to indicate a persons "site". The FOL is:

$$(\forall ?g \in \text{Workgroup}) \ \text{has-size}(?g, ?s) \land (?g \geq 5) \Rightarrow$$
$$(\exists ?p1, ?p2 \in \text{Person}) \ \text{has-member}(?g, ?p1) \land \text{has-base-location}(?p1, ?b1) \land$$
$$\text{has-member}(?g, ?p2) \land \text{bas-base-location}(?p2, ?b2) \land (?b1 \neq ?b2)$$

```
<cif:Constraint>
 <cif:hasQuantifiers rdf:parseType="Collection">
  <cif:Forall>
   <cif:var rdf:resource="#g"/>
   <cif:set rdf:resource="&akt;#Workgroup"/>
  </cif:Forall>
  <cif:Exists>
   <cif:var rdf:resource="#p"/>
   <cif:set rdf:resource="&akt;#Professor-In-Academia"/>
  </cif:Exists>
 </cif:hasQuantifiers>
 <cif:hasImplication>
  <swrl:Imp>
   <swrl:body rdf:parseType="Collection"/>
   <swrl:head rdf:parseType="Collection">
    <swrl:IndividualPropertyAtom>
     <swrl:classPredicate rdf:resource="&akt;#has-member"/>
     <swrl:argument1 rdf:resource="#g"/>
     <swrl:argument2 rdf:resource="#p"/>
    </swrl:IndividualPropertyAtom>
   </swrl:head>
  </swrl:Imp>
 </cif:hasImplication>
</cif:Constraint>
```

Fig. 2. RDF/XML for the constraint, "every workgroup must contain at least 1 member who is a Professor".

What makes this example interesting is that ordering and positioning of the quantifiers can be retained and the meaning does not need to be compromised to be able to write this in CIF/SWRL. The RDF/XML for this example is shown in Figure 3; note the nested implication where the recursive nesting of Constraint structures terminates with an implication where the body is empty.

5   Discussion

In our previous work, we have shown how the solving of CIF constraints can be implemented by dynamically composing the constraints and available data instances into a constraint satisfaction problem, code-generated for use with a particular finite domain solver [7,6][8]. This approach works well with the CIF constraints, which are range-restricted FOL. Of course we are making a closed world assumption here, at the time the finite domain CSP is composed, and this might seem contradictory to the general vision of an open world Semantic Web (and specifically the open world assumption underpinning OWL DL). In practice, there is no contradiction: a finite number of candidate instances are always available at run-time, whether gathered from a local cache (as in the current AWB) or acquired through some wider search (which is always "best-effort" on the Web). As explained in Section 2, this is because we are essentially

---

[8] Solvers used to date include ECLiPSe (http://www.icparc.ic.ac.uk/eclipse/) and the Sicstus Prolog FD library (http://www.sics.se/isl/sicstus/)

```
<cif:Constraint>
 <cif:hasQuantifiers rdf:parseType="Collection">
  <cif:Forall>
   <cif:var rdf:resource="#g"/>
   <cif:set rdf:resource="&akt;#Workgroup"/>
  </cif:Forall>
 </cif:hasQuantifiers>
 <cif:hasImplication>
  <swrl:Imp>
   <swrl:body rdf:parseType="Collection">
    <swrl:IndividualPropertyAtom>
     <swrl:classPredicate rdf:resource="&akt;#has-size"/>
     <swrl:argument1 rdf:resource="#g"/>
     <swrl:argument2 rdf:resource="#s"/>
    </swrl:IndividualPropertyAtom>
    <swrl:DatavaluedPropertyAtom>
     <swrl:propertyPredicate rdf:resource="&swrlb;#greaterThanOrEqual"/>
     <swrl:argument1 rdf:resource="#s"/>
     <swrl:argument2 rdf:datatype="&xsd;#int">5</swrl:argument2>
    </swrl:DatavaluedPropertyAtom>
   </swrl:body>
   <swrl:head rdf:parseType="Collection">
    <cif:Constraint>
     <cif:hasQuantifiers rdf:parseType="Collection">
      <cif:Exists>
       <cif:var rdf:resource="#p1"/>
       <cif:set rdf:resource="&akt;#Person"/>
      </cif:Exists>
      <cif:Exists>
       <cif:var rdf:resource="#p2"/>
       <cif:set rdf:resource="&akt;#Person"/>
      </cif:Exists>
     </cif:hasQuantifiers>
     <cif:hasImplication>
      <swrl:Imp>
       <swrl:body rdf:parseType="Collection"/>
       <swrl:head rdf:parseType="Collection">
        ...details of body omitted: simply a list of </swrl:IndividualPropertyAtom>s ...
       </swrl:head>
      </swrl:Imp>
     </cif:hasImplication>
    </cif:Constraint>
   </swrl:head>
  </swrl:Imp>
 </cif:hasImplication>
</cif:Constraint>
```

Fig. 3. RDF/XML for the constraint, "any workgroup with at least 5 members must contain people from different sites".

doing A-Box reasoning, relying on the presence of assertions and instances, rather than T-Box reasoning without them.

As we said before, our approach is not incompatible with the use of other reasoning mechanisms (in fact, part of our motivation for doing this work is to explore the interplay of multiple reasoners — see Section 6). For example, OWL DL class restrictions can usefully be employed in CIF expressions to specify the domains of variables, both in the quantifier expressions (as the value of a `cif:var` property) and within the heads and bodies of the implications (allowed by the abstract syntax in Section 3 as unary-predicate `atoms`). We have yet to properly explore the computational complexities arising from this usage, however, or to come to a point where we can recommend "best practice".

However, an important point about the original design of CIF, which is retained in the reformulation presented here, is that it is perfectly feasible to use CIF with only RDFS data models. This is true of SWRL as well, although of course SWRL has no way to handle existential quantification without OWL DL constructs — not a problem for CIF. Given the relatively much wider use of RDFS than OWL on the current Semantic Web (Dublin Core, RSS, vCards, and FOAF[9] are among the most widely-instantiated Semantic Web schemas) we feel this makes CIF immediately useful for practical applications.

One part of the proposed CIF syntax that we have not explored in this paper, chiefly for reasons of space, is the representation of disjunction and negation. These are allowed in CIF implication heads and bodies, although we are still experimenting with various forms to avoid over-complexity in the RDF/XML syntax. Again, we also aim ultimately to move to a point where we can recommend "best practice" in the use of these more elaborate forms of constraint; we believe more research is needed generally in this area.

As a final point, it is worth noting that the URIreference and annotation features from OWL/SWRL allow statements to be made about constraints. This supports the usual authorship and provenance information to be attached to constraints, which is always useful, but also allows other kinds of metadata specific to the usage of constraints. For example, we may attach properties indicating the "strength" of the constraint — is it *hard* or *soft* (that is, can it be relaxed?), or are there particular exceptional conditions under which it may become hard or soft? In general, we have an interest in using constraint reification in the solving process [2], where it becomes useful to reason about which constraints are currently satisfied and which are not, and to use techniques such as negotiation and argumentation to relax (or in some cases harden) constraints. We hope that the the URIreference and annotation features will be a useful mechanism in constraint reification.

6   Conclusion and Future Directions

In this paper, we have proposed a representation for fully-quantified constraints at the Semantic Web logic layer, in the form of an extension to the implication constructs available in the SWRL proposal. We illustrated the use of the CIF/SWRL constraints alongside SWRL derivation rules in a practical application: the AKTive Workgroup Builder. Work on the AWB is ongoing; currently we are employing three forms of reasoning:

---

[9] Technically FOAF (Friend-of-a-Friend) is an OWL Full ontology; however, there is only very limited use of OWL constructs in FOAF term definitions, chiefly to indicate which properties can be used a unique identifiers for instances. Users of FOAF need little or no real understanding of OWL to use it, which perhaps explains its rapid uptake; see, for example: http://www.plink.org

- Jena is used to perform OWL Lite reasoning at the ontology level, as part of the task of assembling candidate instances for the solving process.
- We are experimenting with the use of Hoolet[10] to implement the SWRL derivation rules.
- Through a PrologBeans interface we are harnessing the SICStus Prolog finite domain constraint solver.

Looking ahead, our interest lies in combining these various mechanisms into a practical hybrid reasoning suite, and in exploring complexity and scalability trade-offs.

Related work within the AKT project at Aberdeen covers other constraint-solving approaches and support tools. For example, we are applying constraint-satisfaction to configuration design, and are developing a constraint editor to allow end-users to express CIF constraints.[11]

Acknowledgements. This work is supported under the Advanced Knowledge Technologies (AKT) Interdisciplinary Research Collaboration (IRC), which is sponsored by the UK Engineering and Physical Sciences Research Council (EPSRC) under grant number GR/N15764/01. The AKT IRC comprises the Universities of Aberdeen, Edinburgh, Sheffield, Southampton, and the Open University. For further information see http://www.aktors.org. The constraint fusion services were developed in the context of the KRAFT and CONOISE projects, funded by the EPSRC and British Telecom.

References

1. N. Bassiliades and P.M.D Gray. CoLan: a Functional Constraint Language and Its Implementation. *Data and Knowledge Engineering*, 14:203–249, 1994.
2. S. Chalmers, A. D. Preece, T. J. Norman, and P. Gray. Commitment management through constraint reification. In *3rd International Joint Conference on Autonomous Agents and Multi Agent Systems (AAMAS 2004)*, 2004.
3. S.M. Embury and P.M.D. Gray. Compiling a Declarative, High-Level Language for Semantic Integrity Constraints. In R. Meersman and L. Mark, editors, *Database Application Semantics: Proceedings of 6th IFIP TC-2 Working Conference on Data Semantics*, pages 188–226, Atlanta, USA, May 1995. Chapman and Hall.
4. P. M. D. Gray, S. M. Embury, K. Hui, and G. J. L. Kemp. The evolving role of constraints in the functional data model. *Journal of Intelligent Information Systems*, 12:113–137, 1999.
5. B. Grosof, I. Horrocks, R. Volz, and S. Decker. Description logic programs: Combining logic programs with description logic. In *Proceedings of the Twelfth International World Wide Web Conference*, pages 48–57. ACM, 2003.
6. K. Hui, S. Chalmers, P. Gray, and A. Preece. Experience in using RDF in agent-mediated knowledge architectures. In L. van Elst, V. Dignum, and A. Abecker, editors, *Agent-Mediated Knowledge Management (LNAI 2926)*, pages 177–192. Springer-Verlag, 2004.

---

[10] http://owl.man.ac.uk/hoolet/
[11] Details are available at: http://www.csd.abdn.ac.uk/research/akt/

7. K. Hui, P. Gray, G. Kemp, and A. Preece. Constraints as mobile specifications in e-commerce applications. In R. Meersman, K. Aberer, and T. Dillon, editors, *Semantic Issues in e-Commerce Systems*, pages 327–341. Kluwer, 2003.
8. G. Kemp, P. Gray, and A. Sjöstedt. Rewrite rules for quantified subqueries in a federated database. In L. Kerschberg and M. Kafatos, editors, *Proceedings of the Thirteenth International Conference on Scientific and Statistical Database Management*, pages 134–143. IEEE Computer Society Press, 2001.
9. J.-M. Nicolas. Logic for Improving Integrity Checking in Relational Databases. *Acta Informatica*, 18:227–253, 1982.
10. T. J. Norman, A. D. Preece, S. Chalmers, N. R. Jennings, M. M. Luck, V. D. Dang, T. D. Nguyen, V. Deora, J. Shao, W. A. Gray, and N. J. Fiddian. CONOISE: Agent-based formation of virtual organisations. In *Research and Development in Intelligent Systems XX*, pages 353–366. Springer-Verlag, 2003.
11. A. Preece, K. Hui, A. Gray, P. Marti, T. Bench-Capon, Z. Cui, and D. Jones. KRAFT: An agent architecture for knowledge fusion. *Inernational Journal of Cooperative Information Systems*, 10(1 & 2):171–195, 2001.
12. A. Preece, K. Hui, and P. Gray. An FDM-based constraint language for semantic web applications. In P. Gray, L. Kerschberg, P. King, and A. Poulovassilis, editors, *Agent-Mediated Knowledge Management (LNAI 2926)*, pages 417–434. Springer-Verlag, 2004.
13. N. Shadbolt, N. Gibbins, H. Glaser, S. Harris, and m. c. schraefel. CS AKTive Space, or how we learned to stop worrying and love the semantic web. *IEEE Intelligent Systems*, pages 41–47, May/June 2004.

An Extension to OWL with General Rules*

Jing Mei, Shengping Liu, Anbu Yue, and Zuoquan Lin

Department of Information Science, Peking University, Beijing 100871, China
{mayyam,lsp,yueanbu,lz}@is.pku.edu.cn

Abstract. In Semantic Web, using rules to add more expressive power has drawn considerable attention. Recently ORL (OWL Rules Language) has been presented where OWL is extended with Horn clause rules. In this paper we propose an extension to OWL with more general rules involving not only atoms but also literals with classical negation and negation as failure. We present first the abstract syntax for our OWL extension and then its semantics via the Answer Set Programming(ASP). Furthermore, we discuss the iterative procedures for reasoning between OWL axioms and ASP rules.

1   Introduction

With the development of Semantic Web, both RDF and OWL have become W3C recommendations, and adding rule languages on top of the ontology layer is currently an active area of research.

Recently, I. Horrocks and P. Patel-Schneider proposed the OWL Rules Language called ORL [10], in which OWL is extended with Horn clause rules in a syntactically and semantically coherent manner. As we all knew that Horn clause rule is of the form "head←body" where both head and body consist of atoms, including neither classical negation (denoted as ¬) nor default negation (i.e., negation as failure, denoted as *not*). However it was suggested that two kinds of negation could be useful [7,8]: the classical negation is required to express negative information and the default negation is required to model incomplete information and exceptions in Web content. For example, if it does not rain (in the sense of classical negation), then we will go out on a picnic; but if we do not know whether it will rain or not (in the sense of default negation), then we had better stay at home. It is considered as a requirement of representing much more information on Semantic Web to extend OWL with general rules involving the two kinds of negation.

Answer Set Programming(ASP)[14] provides the expressiveness of general rules. In ASP, a rule is of the same form as Horn clause rule, but both body and head consist of *literal* and *not(literal)* where *literal* is an *atom p* or its negation ¬*p*. ASP is a well-established logic programming language based on answer sets(or stable model) semantics [15,21]. ASP allows declarative problem-solving based on the application of negation as failure, i.e., one concludes, from a failure to

---

* This work was supported by the National Natural Science Foundation of China under grant numbers 60373002 and 60496323.

G. Antoniou and H. Boley (Eds.): RuleML 2004, LNCS 3323, pp. 155–169, 2004.
© Springer-Verlag Berlin Heidelberg 2004

prove a proposition, that the proposition is false. Nowadays, there are rather efficient solvers that can compute the answer sets of programs defining thousands of atoms within few seconds [4].

To extend OWL with general rules in ASP, a key challenge is the semantic discrepancy between OWL and ASP. OWL is based on a conventional model theory and is designed to be monotonic, whereas ASP is based on stable model semantics and has non-monotonic features. To address the challenge, hybrid approach is taken into account. The basic idea of hybrid approach is to combine the semantic and computational strengths of the two systems [20], where the description logic engine (such as FaCT and RACER) can be employed for OWL segment and the answer set engine (such as SMODELS and DLV) for ASP segment.

Our proposal for extending OWL with ASP rules is based on a hybrid reasoning framework. The OWL ontology[1] with general rules is called *extended ontology*. At the beginning, OWL axioms and facts are handled as usual, and then, with the information obtained from OWL, ASP programs and rules are parsed and interpreted to compute the answer set, which is a minimal model of ASP program. Considering that conclusions in ASP answer set can be viewed as new OWL assertions, OWL inference mechanism should be triggered again and such iterative inferences would proceed until no change is reached.

The remainder of the paper is organized as follows. In Section 2 we give a brief introduction to ASP. Next, we introduce the syntax of extended ontology in Section 3 and present the semantics for extended ontology based on the idea of ASP in Section 4. In Section 5 we discuss local closed world information in extended ontology, as well as the iterative procedures for reasoning between OWL axioms and ASP rules. Finally, we close with related works in Section 6 and planned future work in Section 7.

2 Brief Introduction to ASP

Answer Set Programming (ASP) (a.k.a. Stable Logic Programming or A-Prolog) is the realization of many theoretical works in non-monotonic reasoning and AI applications of logic programming(LP) in the last 12 years [14]. The following are some basic definitions about ASP and its stable model semantics.

An ASP program is a finite set of rules $Head \leftarrow Body$ where $Head$ and $Body$ are each a finite set of extended literals.

$Head = \{HL_1, \cdots, HL_l;\ not\ HL_{l+1}, \cdots, not\ HL_m\}$

$Body = \{BL_1, \cdots, BL_k;\ not\ BL_{k+1}, \cdots, not\ BL_n\}$

where $HL_i, BL_j (1 \le i \le m, 1 \le j \le n)$ are literals, '*not*' is a logical connective called negation as failure (naf) or default negation which should be distinguished from the classical '*neg*' denoted as $\neg$. By the epistemic interpretation of logic programs, '$\neg p$' can be interpreted as "believe that p is false" while '*not p*' as "there is no reason to believe in p" [14].

Note that it is disjunctive if there are multiple literals in $Head$, while it is conjunctive if there are multiple literals in $Body$.

---

[1] we mainly consider OWL DL, here OWL refers to OWL DL throughout this paper.

An extended literal is an expression of the form L or not L where L is a literal. A literal is an expression of the form A or $\neg A$ where A is an atom. An atom is a n-ary predicate, and according to the OWL specification, it can be of the form $C(x)$, $P(x,y)$, $Q(x,z)$, $sameAs(x,y)$, $differentFrom(x,y)$ where x,y,z are variables or constants and C, P, Q, sameAs, differentFrom are predicate symbols.

A $ground$ atom is an atom without variables, and a $ground$ literal or a $ground$ extended literal likewise. For a set X of literals, $\neg X = \{\neg l|\ l \in X\}$ where we define $\neg\neg a$ as a. A set of ground literals X is $consistent$ if $X \cap \neg X = \emptyset$.

Given a program P and its $Herbrand$ $universe$ $\mathcal{H}(P)$ (noting there is no function in either ASP or OWL, so in our discussion $\mathcal{H}(P)$ is just the set of all constants appearing in P), we call $P_{\mathcal{H}(P)}$ the $grounded$ $program$ obtained from P by substituting every variable in P with every possible constant in $\mathcal{H}(P)$. The $base$ of a grounded program $P_{\mathcal{H}(P)}$ is the set $B_{\mathcal{H}(P)}$ of ground atoms that can be constructed using the predicates in $P_{\mathcal{H}(P)}$ with the constants in $\mathcal{H}(P)$ [19].

An $interpretation$ I of a grounded program P is any consistent set of literals that is a subset of $B_{\mathcal{H}(P)} \cup \neg B_{\mathcal{H}(P)}$.

Let P be a grounded program whose rules do not contain negation as failure, and such rule is of the form below:

$$HL_1\ or\ \cdots\ or\ HL_l \leftarrow BL_1,\ \cdots,\ BL_k \qquad\qquad \text{- - -(1)}$$

An interpretation I of a grounded program P without naf $satisfies$ a rule in P with form(1) if, $\{HL_1,\ \cdots,\ HL_l\} \cap I \neq \emptyset$ whenever $\{BL_1,\ \cdots,\ BL_k\} \subseteq I$. An interpretation I is a $model$ of P without naf if I satisfies every rule in P.

For an arbitrary grounded program P and an interpretation I, the Gelfond-Lifschitz transformation [15][21][19] is the program P_I, obtained by deleting in P:

- each rule that has $not(BL)$ in its $Body$ with $BL \in I$
- each rule that has $not(HL)$ in its $Head$ with $HL \notin I$
- all $not(L)$ in its $Body$ and $Head$ of the remaining rules

An interpretation I is an $answer$ set of P if I coincides with a minimal model of P_I (relative to set inclusion).

3   Abstract Syntax

The basic idea of our extension to OWL is similar to that of ORL [10] to some extent, but general rules involve not only atoms but also literals with classical negation and negation as failure. Our goal is to integrate OWL ontology and ASP programs, while maintaining maximum backwards compatibility with OWL's existing syntax and semantics, as well as employing the idea of ASP to present the new definitions of interpretation and model. Hence, the syntactic choices for extended ontology are important.

3.1   Abstract Syntax for Extended Ontology

The abstract syntax for extended ontology is conformed to the OWL DL Abstract Syntax[17], while adding a new kind of directive (namely Program) in the ontology and a new kind of axiom (namely Rule) to OWL abstract syntax.

A program consists of rules and a rule has an ordered pair $< Head, Body >$. Since the stable model semantics has different strategies between programs with naf and programs without naf, both *Head* and *Body* will be divided into two parts, one is a (possibly empty) set of *"programLiteral"* and the other is a (possibly empty) set of *"not(programLiteral)"*. A programLiteral[2] is an *"atom"* or *"neg(atom)"*, and atoms are defined as being of the form C(x), P(x, y), Q(x, z), sameAs(x, y), differentFrom(x, y) where C is an OWL DL class description, P is an OWL DL individualvaluedProperty and Q is datavaluedProperty, x, y is either a variable or an OWL individual, and z is either a variable or an OWL DL data value [10].

Now, we present extended ontology abstract syntax based on OWL[17] and ORL[10], with some new built-in terms like "rule", "head", "body", "programLiteral", "atom" etc., while retaining terms of OWL ontology unchanged such as "axiom", "fact", "description", "individual" etc.

```
ontology   ::= 'Ontology(' [ontologyID] {directive} ')'
directive  ::= 'Program(' programID {rule} ')' | axiom | fact
rule       ::= 'Rule(' ruleID ['Deprecated'] [head] [body] ')'
head ::= 'Head(' {programLiteral} {'not('programLiteral')'} ')'
body ::= 'Body(' {programLiteral} {'not('programLiteral')'} ')'
programLiteral ::= atom | 'neg('atom')'
atom ::=  description '(' i-object ')'
       | individualvaluedPropertyID '(' i-object i-object ')'
       | datavaluedPropertyID '(' i-object d-object ')'
       | 'sameAs(' i-object i-object ')'
       | 'differentFrom(' i-object i-object ')'
i-object   ::= i-variable | individualID
d-object   ::= d-variable | dataLiteral
i-variable ::= 'I-variable(' URIreference ')'
d-variable ::= 'D-variable(' URIreference ')'
```

Extended ontology incorporate information about classes, properties, individuals for OWL, as well as programs, rules, variables for ASP, each of which can have an identifier which is a URI reference. Different from ORL [10] where no identifier is specified for rule in a rule axiom, programID and ruleID are required in our proposal due to the straightforward semantics.

Informally, an atom C(x) holds if x is an instance of the class description or data range C, an atom P(x,y) holds if x is related to y by property P, an atom sameAs(x,y) holds if x is interpreted as the same object as y, an atom differentFrom(x,y) holds if x and y are interpreted as different objects [12].

3.2   Example

Consider a well-known example in non-monotonic reasoning: in general, most birds can fly, but being a subclass of Bird, penguins do not fly. Writing with DL

---

[2] To distinguish from the term "literal" in RDF and OWL, we rename the term "literal" in Logic Programming as "programLiteral".

(Description Logic, the logical foundation of OWL), the axioms are Bird⊑Flying and Penguin⊑Bird. If Guimo is an instance of Penguin, namely Penguin(Guimo), it can be easily concluded that Bird(Guimo) and Flying(Guimo). This wrong conclusion that Guimo can fly is due to the monotonic semantics of OWL.[3]

However, integrating OWL and ASP, the correct result will be obtained. We add two ASP rules, while retaining the subclass relationship between Penguin and Bird unchanged, namely: (1) Penguin⊑Bird; (2) neg(Flying(x))←Penguin(x); (3) Flying(x)←Bird(x), not(neg(Flying(x))). The first rule states if an individual is a penguin then it can not fly, while the second rule states if an individual is a bird and there is no assertion to state it can not fly, then it is a flying one.

Example 1. An extended ontology in abstract syntax

```
Ontology(ex:caseOntology
    Class(ex:Flying)
    Class(ex:Penguin)
    Class(ex:Bird)
    SubClassOf(ex:Penguin ex:Bird)
    Individual(ex:Guimo type(ex:Penguin))
    I-variable(ex:x)
    Program(ex:caseProgram
        Rule(ex:firstRule
            Head(neg(ex:Flying(ex:x)))
            Body(ex:Penguin(ex:x) ) )
        Rule(ex:secondRule
            Head(ex:Flying(ex:x))
            Body(ex:Bird(ex:x)
                not(neg(ex:Flying(ex:x))))))))
```

Before the formal semantics introduced, we consider informally its implicit reasoning. Firstly, in Logic Programming, a *fact* is a rule with empty *Body*. In our proposal, all OWL facts are ASP facts, so "Penguin(Guimo)← ." is an underlying ASP rule. Furthermore, new information inferred from OWL should also be viewed as ASP facts. For example, we have Bird(Guimo) from the SubClassOf axiom in OWL, thus there is another underlying ASP rule: "Bird(Guimo)← ."

And then, from the two predefined ASP rules and from the Gelfond-Lifschitz transformation introduced in Section 2, we will get ¬Flying(Guimo) from ex: firstRule, and delete ex: secondRule because of the effect of "*not*". Consequently, the solution is {Penguin(Guimo), Bird(Guimo), ¬Flying(Guimo)}, which is in accordance with commonsense.

4   Semantics

Based on the direct model-theoretic semantics for OWL[17], we extend the definitions of interpretation and model via the idea of ASP, then we also provide an interpretation of the previous Example 1 which is exactly its model.

---

[3] Obviously we can not simply state Bird⊓¬Penguin⊑Flying to solve this nonmonotonic reasoning, considering that ostrich cannot fly and birds whose wings are broken cannot fly etc., so enumerations are inefficient.

4.1   Interpretation

The semantics here starts with the notion of vocabulary. OWL DL vocabulary[17] is included, as well as some new terms such as program, rule, variable and atom.

Definition 1 (Extended ontology vocabulary). *An extended ontology vocabulary V consists of :*

V_0 : *the OWL DL vocabulary $V_0 = \langle V_C, V_D, V_I, V_{DP}, V_{IP}, V_{AP}, V_O, V_L \rangle$,*
     where the former seven sets of URI references in turn are the class names, the datatype names, the individual names, the data-valued property names, the individual-valued property names, the annotation property names, the ontology names of a vocabulary, and the last one is a set of literals;
V_A : *a set of atoms;*
V_P : *the program names of a vocabulary;*
V_R : *the rule names of a vocabulary;*
V_{IV} : *the individual variable names of a vocabulary;*
V_{DV} : *the data literal variable names of a vocabulary.*

In addition to abstract OWL interpretation [17], a set PL and a series of mappings PI, RI, AI, LI are all involved in the extended ontology interpretation.

Definition 2 (Extended ontology interpretation). *An extended ontology interpretation I with an extended ontology vocabulary V is a tuple:*
$I = \langle I_0, R, L, S, PL, PI, RI, AI, LI \rangle$ *where,*

I_0 : *the abstract OWL interpretation with OWL DL vocabulary V_0,*
     $I_0 = \langle R_0, EC, ER, LV, L_0, S_0 \rangle$ where R_0 is the resources of I_0, EC and ER respectively provides meaning for URI references that are used as OWL classes/datatypes and OWL properties, and LV is the literal values of I_0, there $LV \subseteq R_0$ disjoint from $O = EC(owl : Thing) \subseteq R_0$
R : *the resources of I, an extension of R_0, $R_0 \subseteq R$*
L : *$TL \cup V_{DV} \to LV$, an extension of L_0, TL is the set of typed literals in V_L*
S : *$V_I \cup V_{IV} \to O$, an extension of S_0*
$PL \subseteq R$: *the ground programLiterals of I being of form $C(a)$, $P(a,b)$, $Q(a,c)$, $\neg C(a), \neg P(a,b), \neg Q(a,c)$, where $a, b \in O$, $c \in LV$, and $C \in V_C$, $P \in V_{IP}$, $Q \in V_{DP}$*
PI : *$V_P \to 2^{PL}$ where 2^{PL} means the powerset of a set PL*
RI : *$V_R \to < headlit, headnot, bodylit, bodynot >$,*
     where the four elements in the tuple are each a subset of PL
AI : *$V_A \to 2^{PL}$ where 2^{PL} means the powerset of a set PL*
LI : *$LI(pl) \in PL$, where pl is of form "atom" or "neg(atom)" and atom $\in V_A$*

Given an abstract OWL interpretation I_0, we extend I_0 such that S maps i-variables to elements of $O = EC(owl : Thing)$ and L maps d-variables to elements of LV, just as ORL's binding did [10]. Furthermore, PI provides meaning for URI references that used as ASP programs. RI assign URI reference that used as ASP rule to a tuple in which each element is a subset of PL. AI provides meaning for ASP atoms. LI assign "*atom*" or "*neg(atom)*" to a ground programLiteral in PL where atom $\in V_A$. About PL, the prefix symbol "$\neg$" is used for distinguishing negative atoms from atoms, noting that all ground programLiterals are listed one by one in PL.

We have ignored another two atoms *sameAs(x,y)* and *differentFrom(x,y)*, because it was pointed out that the two forms can be seen as "syntactic sugar": they are convenient, but do not increase the expressive power of the language, i.e., such (in)equalities can already be expressed using the combined power of OWL and rules without explicit (in)equality atoms [12].

4.2 Model

In the following, we will present a model for an extended ontology step by step. First, the mapping AI is listed, indicating that the range of AI is involved wholly in PL. Second, the mapping LI is shown by every possible binding in a rule. Third, on the basis of LI, the mapping RI divide a rule into four parts. Fourth, there are some special rules constructed from OWL inference results, and these newly-built rules should be handled with RI in the same way. Finally, the four parts of $RI(r)$ will play an important role in $PI(p)$, especially when an interpretation I is a model.

Recalling ASP stable model semantics in Section 2, $O=EC(owl:Thing) \subseteq R$ plus $LV \subseteq R$ in OWL are just the *Herbrand universe* $\mathcal{H}(p)$ of a ASP program $p \in V_P$. Consequently, $p_{\mathcal{H}(p)}$ will be a grounded program via every possible binding $S(iv)$ and $L(dv)$, i.e., $p_{\mathcal{H}(p)}$ is obtained from p by substituting every variable $iv \in V_{IV}$ with every possible individual $S(iv) \in O$ and every variable $dv \in V_{DV}$ with every possible literal value $L(dv) \in LV$.

At Table 1, based on the Herbrand universe $\mathcal{H}(p)$ of p, we map every atom $A \in V_A$ to a set of ground atoms by the mapping AI. Notice if $x \in V_I$ (i.e. x is a constant) then $S(x)$ is a given element in O, else $x \in V_{IV}$ (i.e. x is a variable) and it is possible for $S(x)$ to be assigned to an arbitrary element in O. Similarly, $L(z)$ has only one value in LV if $z \in TL$ (i.e. z is a constant), else $z \in V_{DV}$ (i.e. z is a variable) and $L(z)$ traverses every possible element in LV.

Table 1. Mapping of atom $A \in V_A$

A	$AI(A)=$
$C(x)$	$\{C(S(x))\mid x \in V_I\} \bigcup$
$C \in V_C$	$\{C(S(a))\mid x \in V_{IV}, \forall a \in V_I\}$
$P(x,y)$	$\{P(S(x),S(y))\mid x \in V_I, y \in V_I\} \bigcup$
$P \in V_{IP}$	$\{P(S(a),S(y))\mid x \in V_{IV}, y \in V_I, \forall a \in V_I\} \bigcup$
	$\{P(S(x),S(b))\mid x \in V_I, y \in V_{IV}, \forall b \in V_I\} \bigcup$
	$\{P(S(a),S(b))\mid x \in V_{IV}, y \in V_{IV}, \forall a \in V_I, \forall b \in V_I\}$
$Q(x,z)$	$\{Q(S(x),L(z))\mid x \in V_I, z \in TL\} \bigcup$
$Q \in V_{DP}$	$\{Q(S(a),L(z))\mid x \in V_{IV}, z \in TL, \forall a \in V_I\} \bigcup$
	$\{Q(S(x),L(c))\mid x \in V_I, z \in V_{DV}, \forall c \in TL\} \bigcup$
	$\{Q(S(a),L(c))\mid x \in V_{IV}, z \in V_{DV}, \forall a \in V_I, \forall c \in TL\}$

In fact, the *base* of a grounded program $p_{\mathcal{H}(p)}$ is $B_{\mathcal{H}(p)} = \bigcup_{A \in V_A} AI(A)$, that is to say $B_{\mathcal{H}(p)}$ is just the range of AI. According to ASP, for a set X, we have $\neg X = \{\neg l \mid l \in X\}$ where we define $\neg \neg a$ as a, and X is *consistent* if

$X \cap \neg X = \emptyset$. As a result, we have $PL = B_{\mathcal{H}(p)} \cup \neg B_{\mathcal{H}(p)}$, and $PI(p) \subseteq PL$ should be consistent.

Next, we will deal with programs and rules in an extended ontology, written in a relatively informal abstract syntax form as follows:

$$Program(p \quad Rule(r_1), \cdots, Rule(r_t)) \qquad \text{- - -(2)}$$

where $Rule(r_s)(1 \leq s \leq t)$ is of the form:

$$Rule(r_s \; Head(hl_1, \cdots, hl_l, not(hl_{l+1}), \cdots, not(hl_m))$$
$$Body(bl_1, \cdots, bl_k, not(bl_{k+1}), \cdots, not(bl_n))) \qquad \text{- - -(3)}$$

Here, $hl_i (1 \leq i \leq m)$ and $bl_j (1 \leq j \leq n)$ in $Rule(r_s)$ are programLiterals being of form "$atom$" or "$neg(atom)$". At Table 2, by the mapping LI, we handle pl which delegates either hl_i or bl_j in a rule r_s, such that for every possible assignment $S(x), L(z)$ where $x \in V_I \cup V_{IV}$, $z \in TL \cup V_{DV}$ appearing in r_s, pl is mapped to a specified ground programLiteral $LI(pl) \in PL$.

Table 2. Mapping of programLiteral pl

atom	$LI(pl)$	neg(atom)	$LI(pl)$
$C(x)$	$C(S(x))$	$neg(C(x))$	$\neg C(S(x))$
$P(x,y)$	$P(S(x), S(y))$	$neg(P(x,y))$	$\neg P(S(x), S(y))$
$Q(x,z)$	$Q(S(x), L(z))$	$neg(Q(x,z))$	$\neg Q(S(x), L(z))$

Let p be a programID assigned to a program of form(2), we have $p \in V_P, PI(p) \subseteq PL$. Let r be a ruleID assigned to a rule of form(3), we have $r \in V_R$, $RI(r) = < headlit, headnot, bodylit, bodynot >$.

For every possible assignment $S(x), L(z)$ where $x \in V_I \cup V_{IV}$, $z \in TL \cup V_{DV}$ appearing in r, the four elements in $RI(r)$ are as follows:

$$headlit = \{LI(hl_1), \cdots, LI(hl_l)\}, \qquad headnot = \{LI(hl_{l+1}), \cdots, LI(hl_m)\}$$
$$bodylit = \{LI(bl_1), \cdots, LI(bl_k)\}, \qquad bodynot = \{LI(bl_{k+1}), \cdots, LI(bl_n)\}$$

Obviously, if there is no variable (i.e., $x \in V_I$ and $z \in TL$) in Rule r, then $RI(r)$ has one and only one tuple value, else $RI(r)$ has more than one tuple values so far as the variable (i.e., $x \in V_{IV}$ or $z \in V_{DV}$) is bound with more than one values.

As we have known, all information inferred from OWL ontology are facts to the program p. Therefore it is necessary to view the information in EC and ER as ASP facts, which should be added to the program p acting as rules with $Body$ empty. The transformation is given at Table 3 and the last column is the tuple $RI(r)$ of the newly-built ASP fact r.

Since Semantic Web are huge and only partially knowable, there are good reasons for OWL not to declare explicitly a $\notin EC(C)$, $\langle a, b \rangle \notin ER(P)$ and $\langle a, c \rangle \notin ER(Q)$. Accordingly, we do not draw any facts from such unknowable information.

However, for the existing elements in EC and ER, their transformations to be ASP facts are required. Especially in the case that Class C is disjoint from Class D, we will have "$not(D(a)) \leftarrow C(a)$", as well as the symmetrical rule "$not(C(a)) \leftarrow D(a)$". Similarly, if C is the complement of D, then we will have

Table 3. Transformations from OWL EC/ER to ASP facts

If	Then r is	$RI(r)= \langle headlit, headnot, \emptyset, \emptyset \rangle$
$a \in EC(C)$, $C \in V_C$, $a \in O$	$C(a) \leftarrow .$	$headlit=\{C(a)\}$, $headnot=\emptyset$
$\langle a,b \rangle \in ER(P)$, $P \in V_{IP}$, $a \in O$, $b \in O$	$P(a,b) \leftarrow .$	$headlit=\{P(a,b)\}$, $headnot=\emptyset$
$\langle a,c \rangle \in ER(Q)$, $Q \in V_{DP}$, $a \in O$, $c \in LV$	$Q(a,c) \leftarrow .$	$headlit=\{Q(a,c)\}$, $headnot=\emptyset$
$a \in EC(C)$, $C \in V_C$, $D \in V_C$, $a \in O$		
DisjointClassses(C, D), $EC(C)\cap EC(D)=\emptyset$	$not(D(a)) \leftarrow .$	$headlit=\emptyset$, $headnot=\{D(a)\}$
C=ComplementOf(D), $EC(C)=O-EC(D)$	$neg(D(a)) \leftarrow .$	$headlit=\{\neg D(a)\}$, $headnot=\emptyset$

both "$neg(D(a)) \leftarrow C(a)$" and "$neg(C(a)) \leftarrow D(a)$". When $C(a)$ holds, these ASP rules turn to be facts "$not(D(a)) \leftarrow .$" and "$neg(D(a)) \leftarrow .$" respectively.

Now we are about to define a model employing the idea of ASP.

A set M' *satisfies* a rule r w.r.t. a set M if, for every possible assignment $S(x), L(z)$ where $x \in V_I \cup V_{IV}$, $z \in TL \cup V_{DV}$ appears in r, there is $RI(r) =< headlit, headnot, bodylit, bodynot >$ such that, whenever both $bodynot \cap M = \emptyset$ and $headnot \subseteq M$, if $bodylit \subseteq M'$ then $headlit \cap M' \neq \emptyset$.

A set M is an *answer set* of a program p if, $M \subseteq PL$ is consistent and $M = M'$ where M' is the minimal set which w.r.t M satisfies every rule $r \in V_R$ in p and every ASP fact transformed from OWL EC/ER.

An abstract extended interpretation I *satisfies* a program p if, $PI(p)$ is an answer set of p.

An abstract extended interpretation I is a *model* of an extended ontology if, I satisfies every axiom, fact, and program in the extended ontology.

An extended ontology O_1 *entails* an extended ontology O_2 if every model I of O_1 is also a model of O_2.

4.3 Interpretation of Example 1

Given an interpretation to the Example 1 in section 2.3:
$I = \langle I_0, R, L, S, PL, PI, RI, AI, LI \rangle$ with vocabulary
$V_0 = \langle V_C, V_D, V_I, V_{DP}, V_{IP}, V_{AP}, V_O, V_L \rangle$
$\quad V_C=\{ex: Bird, ex: Penguin, ex: Flying\}$, $V_D = \emptyset$, $V_I=\{ex: Guimo\}$,
$\quad\quad V_{DP} = V_{IP} = V_{AP} = \emptyset$, $V_O=\{ex: caseOntology\}$, $V_L = \emptyset$,
$\quad V_P=\{ex: caseProgram\}$, $V_R=\{ex: firstRule, ex: secondRule\}$
$\quad V_A=\{ex:Flying(ex:x), ex:Penguin(ex:x), ex:Bird(ex:x)\}$,
$\quad V_{IV}=\{ex: x\}$, $V_{DV} = \emptyset$, where
$\quad I_0 = \langle R_0, EC, ER, LV, L_0, S_0 \rangle$
$\quad\quad R_0$ is the resource of I_0,
$\quad\quad EC(ex: Penguin)=\{Guimo\}$, $EC(ex: Bird)=\{Guimo\}$, $ER = \emptyset \times \emptyset$,
$\quad\quad LV = \emptyset$, $O = EC(owl:Thing)=\{Guimo\}$, $L_0 = \emptyset \times \emptyset$,
$\quad\quad S_0 : V_I \cup V_C \cup V_D \cup V_{DP} \cup V_{IP} \cup V_{AP} \cup V_O \cup$
$\quad\quad\quad \{owl:Ontology, owl:DeprecatedClass, owl:DeprecatedProperty \} \rightarrow R$,
R is the resource of I, $L = \emptyset \times \emptyset$,
$S(ex: Guimo)=S(ex: x)=Guimo$,
$PL=\{Flying(Guimo), Penguin(Guimo), Bird(Guimo),$
$\quad \neg Flying(Guimo), \neg Penguin(Guimo), \neg Bird(Guimo)\}$,
$PI(ex:caseProgram)=\{Penguin(Guimo), Bird(Guimo), \neg Flying(Guimo)\}$.

RI	headlit	headnot	bodylit	bodynot
firstRule	¬Flying(Guimo)	∅	Penguin(Guimo)	∅
secondRule	Flying(Guimo)	∅	Bird(Guimo)	¬Flying(Guimo)
fact1	Penguin(Guimo)	∅	∅	∅
fact2	Bird(Guimo)	∅	∅	∅

Here, PI(ex: caseProgram) satisfies Rule(ex:firstRule), Rule(ex:secondRule), as well as two additional fact1 and fact2 from EC, actually PI(ex: case-Program) is an answer set of ex:caseProgram, hence I is a model of Ontology(ex:caseOntology).

5   Discussion

Since it is our preliminary work, the following are some proposals for various "work-arounds". At first, we show that local closed world information can be expressed in extended ontology. Then, we attempt to handle the iterative procedures occurring when the information in ASP answer set are viewed as new OWL assertions. However, some iterations induced from recursion may be meaningless. Thus, in section 5.3 we consider that some constraints should be presented to restrict the recursion so as to maintain a well-defined extended ontology.

5.1   LCW in Extended Ontology

As we have known, the semantics of OWL currently adopts the standard logical model of an open world assumption (OWA). Nevertheless, the opposite approach namely closed world assumption (CWA), which allows additional inferences to be drawn from the absence of information, is feasible to handle problems in incomplete information environments and then is the underlying semantic foundation of most programming languages and databases [11]. The discrepancy is in nature since, OWA assumes that a statement cannot be assumed true on the basis of a failure to prove it, while CWA assumes that a statement is true when its negation cannot be proven.

To take advantages of both OWA and CWA, local closed world (LCW) information might play an important role. That means, closed world information can be obtained on subsets of the information that are known to be complete, while still allowing other information to be treated as unknown [13].

Considering our proposal of combining OWL with ASP, there are certain ASP rules that capture LCW information in an extended ontology. Here, for every predicate pl occurred in a program p, rules "neg(pl) ← not(pl)" which are inserted into p indicate CWA in Logic Programming, while these rules are indicating LCW information in our extended ontology.

For instance, to improve the example in section3.2 we add a rule
$$r_{lcw}: \text{neg(Flying}(x)) \leftarrow \text{not(Flying}(x))"$$
If Class Cat is declared without further constraints, and there is an individual ccc of Cat, namely Cat(ccc), then from r_{lcw} we will have {Cat(ccc), ¬Flying(ccc)} involved in the answer set of p.

5.2   Iterative Procedure

For ASP answer set consists of ground formula which can be viewed as new OWL assertions, it is necessary to make use of them to update OWL ontology, even to trigger OWL inferences once more. To illuminate such situations, an OWL Class "FlyBird $\equiv$ Bird $\sqcap$ Flying" is added to our example, and we would still infer FlyBird(ddd), even if Bird(ddd) and Flying(ddd) do not occur in EC of OWL ontology but they both belong to the ASP answer set.

The following Table 4 provides the transformations from ASP answer set to new OWL assertions. Most negative programLiterals are not transformed to OWL ontology, since OWL has no axiom or fact to present negation except ComplementOf description. If $\neg C(a)$ is in ASP answer set and C=ComplementOf(D) is an OWL description, we can conclude $a \in EC(D)$ as shown at Table 4.

Table 4. Transformations from ASP answer set to new OWL assertions

If	Then
$C(a) \in PI(p)$, $C \in V_C$, $a \in O$	$a \in EC(C)$
$P(a,b) \in PI(p)$, $P \in V_{IP}$, $a \in O$, $b \in O$	$\langle a,b \rangle \in ER(P)$
$Q(a,c) \in PI(p)$, $Q \in V_{DP}$, $a \in O$, $c \in LV$	$\langle a,c \rangle \in ER(Q)$
$\neg C(a) \in PI(p)$, $C \in V_C$, $D \in V_C$, $a \in O$ C=ComplementOf(D), EC(C)=O-EC(D)	$a \in EC(D)$

Based on Table 3 and Table 4, the interleaved calls between OWL and ASP will proceed. And then, we present a theorem about its termination.

Theorem 1. *If the constants including individuals and literal values (i.e., the Herbrand universe $O \cup LV$) are finite, then the iterative inference procedures between OWL and ASP will terminate.*

Because the number of all facts is limited to $n^{|EC|} + n^{2 \times |ER|}$ where $n = |O| + |LV|$, and following every round, the facts transformed from ASP answer set to OWL assertions will be increased step by step. The iterative procedure is certain to terminate when all facts are included and no change would take place. However, if the universe is infinite, then it is less easy to determine when to end.

With regard to the finite universe, when there is no update in OWL EC/ER, the procedures are finished. If a model of an extended ontology holds, then the extended ontology is called satisfiable, indicating the OWL segment and the ASP segment are consistent. Otherwise, the extended ontology is called unsatisfiable, indicating the OWL segment and the ASP segment are inconsistent. Checking the consistency of an extended ontology O is an important reasoning task, and the failure to find an answer set $PI(p)$ of a program p in O means there exists some inconsistency between the OWL segment and the ASP segment of O.

5.3   Recursion in Extended Ontology

Once the information from ASP answer set are viewed as new OWL assertions, a new round of inferences will be triggered and iterative procedures will proceed.

Generally iterative procedures would capture more information, but some iteration induced from recursion may be meaningless. To maintain a well-defined extended ontology, recursion should be restricted with some constraints.

Though there are some constraints to handle recursion respectively in OWL and in ASP, the alternation of OWL axioms and ASP rules should be paid more attention to avoid the indirect recursion.

For example, the following is a worse case scenario.

Example 2.

OWL axiom	ASP rule	primitive facts
Lucky $\equiv \exists$ Friend.Rich	Lucky$(x) \leftarrow$ Rich(x)	Friend(a,b),Lucky(a)

At first, the ontology facts are Friend(a,b) and Lucky(a) merely. From OWL, we have Rich(b) which will be transformed to ASP rule "Rich$(b)\leftarrow$.", then from ASP we have Lucky(b) which will be transformed to "$b \in$ EC(Lucky)". According to OWL interpretation, a new individual c should be added to the ontology, and $\langle b, c \rangle \in$EP(Friend), $c \in$EC(Rich). The same scene will repeat, and Rich c is a lucky one, then Lucky c introduces its friend d, d is a rich one, then Lucky d introduces e, and it goes on. With the help of $\exists$ and the implicit recursion, the universe is unlimited and the procedures will not end up.

Another example is much more troublesome.

Example 3.

OWL axiom	ASP rule	Individual
D$\sqsubseteq$C	D$(x)\leftarrow$not C(x)	a

Firstly, no OWL information can be inferred without primitive facts, then turning to ASP, {D(a)} is an answer set of the program due to the effect of "*not*" and the absence of other facts. Transformed to OWL, it shows $a \in$EC(D), and a new bound of inferences is triggered. From the new OWL assertion and OWL subclass axiom, $a \in$EC(C) is inferred. The two ones are transformed to ASP facts: "C$(a)\leftarrow$." and "D$(a)\leftarrow$.". Now, {C(a),D(a)} is a new answer set of the program which consists of the former rule "D$(x)\leftarrow$not C(x)" and two additional ASP facts. Furthermore, this answer set can not change OWL facts any more. The final model of this ontology has been obtained.

But intuitively, the rule tells if we do not know $x \in$C, then $x \in$D is true, meanwhile $x \in$C holds due to D being a subclass of C. In short, from unknowing $x \in$C we infer $x \in$C. It is a conflict but the ontology is still satisfied with the model above. And that is the indirect recursion of C and D in Example 3 which results in the failure of satisfiability checking.

6   Related Works

In Semantic Web, using rules to add more expressive power is currently an active area of research. However, some important influences on this subject came from combining logic programs and description logics(DL), since DL is the logical foundation of OWL. Consequently, related work can be roughly divided into hybrid approaches which use DL to specify structural constraints in the logic program rules and approaches which reduce DL inference to logic programming[20].

Description Logic Programs has been introduced in [3] as a notable work about the latter approach. Inference in a subset of DL $\mathcal{SHOIQ}$ can be reduced to inference in a subset of Horn programs, and vice versa. In particular one can, to some extent, build rules on top of ontology as well as build ontology on top of rules. Another representative is Concept Logic Programming in [19], which is an extension of ASP to support inverted predicates and infinite domains, features that are present in most DLs. Especially, this extension is decidable for rules forming a tree structure, and inference in DL $\mathcal{SHIF}$ extended by transitive role closures can be simulated in it. Some other works also play an important role, such as [9] and [8]. The former one reduces inference in DL $\mathcal{ALCQI}$ to query answering from the answer sets of declarative logic programs, while the latter one deals with a combination of defeasible reasoning with description logics.

Hybrid approaches are derived from the early works which focus on using description logics as an input for the logical programs [20]. In detail, combining plain datalog with $\mathcal{ALC}$ is discussed in [5], combining Horn rules with $\mathcal{ALCNR}$ is discussed in [1], and combining disjunctive datalog with $\mathcal{ALC}$ based on a generalized answer set semantics is discussed in [18]. Recently, towards the integration of rules and ontology in Semantic Web, a proposal is worthy noting which is a combination of ASP with DL $\mathcal{SHIF}(\mathbf{D})$ and $\mathcal{SHOIN}(\mathbf{D})$ in [20]. There, not only Herbrand models for description logic programs (dl-programs) are defined, but also fixpoint characterizations are given for the (unique) minimal Herbrand model semantics of dl-programs. More closely to Semantic Web is ORL (OWL Rules Language) in [10], which is a Horn clause rules extension to OWL, extending OWL in a syntactically and semantically coherent manner.

Less closely related work includes the original work on dealing default information in DLs in [6], where Reiter's default logic is adapted to terminological knowledge bases. On the side, local closed world(LCW) assumption is proposed for Semantic Web referring to [4] and [13]. In the former one, a new default semantics to RDF type inheritance primitives is given, however it merely focuses on a non-standard meaning for daml: subClassOf. In the latter one, a limited form of LCW is expressed using DAML+OIL's existing features with a new property "lcw:hasLcw", which states that it has complete information on some subset of information.

In addition, reasoning supports are necessary for logic language implementation. And with regard to practical reasoners, there are DL-style systems such as FaCT[4] or RACER[5], answer set engines such as SMODELS[6] or DLV[7], and classical rule-based Prolog[8]. It is worthy noting that, the Rule Markup Initiative[9] has taken steps towards defining a shared Rule Markup Language (RuleML), permitting both forward (bottom-up) and backward (top-down) rules in XML for deduction, rewriting, and further inferential-transformational tasks. In particular, there are many systems of the participants involved in the RuleML Initiative.

---

[4] http://www.cs.man.ac.uk/ horrocks/FaCT/
[5] http://www.sts.tu-harburg.de/ r.f.moeller/racer/
[6] http://www.tcs.hut.fi/Software/smodels/
[7] http://www.dbai.tuwien.ac.at/proj/dlv/
[8] http://www.visual-prolog.com/
[9] http://www.ruleml.org/

7 Conclusion

In this paper we have presented an extension to OWL with general rules, namely extended ontology. We provide its abstract syntax and focus on dealing with its semantics on the basis of both OWL direct model-theoretic semantics and ASP answer set semantics.

With ASP rules as "neg(pl)←not(pl)", local closed world information can be obtained in an extended ontology and help to handle exceptions more efficiently. To capture more information inferred from both OWL and ASP, two transformations are provided, one is from OWL to ASP, and the other is vice versa. Furthermore, the iterative procedures of inference are permitted with some constraints, and the absence of a model indicates the inconsistency between the OWL segment and the ASP segment of an extended ontology.

Considering suggestions for OWL Rules in [2], our proposal is a simple kind of combination for ASP rules to refer to class or property predicates that are defined in a collection of OWL ontology axioms. Here is our primitive work, and we are about to realize a prototype implementation to support non-monotonicity (such as negation as failure, local closed world assumption etc.) in a procedural attachment, employing the description logic engine RACER and the answer set engine DLV. Moreover, our future research topics about developments of theoretical foundations and practical algorithms are in progress.

References

1. Alon Levy , Marie-Christine Rousset: Combining Horn Rules and Description Logics in CARIN Artificial Intelligence 104(1-2):165-209, 1998.
2. Benjamin Grosof: slightly revised "long" version of warning label section for OWL Rules draft. Available at
   http://www.daml.org/listarchive/joint-committee/1491.html
3. Benjamin Grosof, Ian Horrocks, Raphael Volz, Stefan Decker: Description Logic Programs: Combining Logic Programs with Description Logics. Proc. of WWW 2003, Budapest, Hungary, May 2003.
4. Elisa Bertino, Alessandro Provetti, Franco Salvetti: Answer Set Programming for the Semantic Web. IJCAI 2003.
5. Francesco M. Donini, Maurizio Lenzerini, Daniele Nardi, An- drea Schaerf: $\mathcal{AL}$-log: integrating datalog and description logics. Journal of Intelligent Information Systems, 10:227-252, 1998.
6. Franz Baader, Bernhard Hollunder: Embedding Defaults into Terminological Knowledge Representation Formalisms. J. Autom. Reasoning 14(1): 149-180, 1995.
7. Gerd Wagner: The Semantic Web Needs Two Kinds of Negation. PPSWR 2003: 33-50
8. Grigoris Antoniou, Gerd Wagner: Rules and Defeasible Reasoning on the Semantic Web RuleML 2003, LNCS 2876, pp. 111-120, 2003.
9. Guray Alsac, Chitta Baral: Reasoning in description logics using declarative logic programming. Abstract, ASU Technical Report 2001-2002.
10. Ian Horrocks, Peter F. Patel-Schneider: A Proposal for an OWL Rules Language. In Proc. of the Thirteenth International World Wide Web Conference (WWW 2004), pages 723-731. ACM, 2004.

11. Ian Horrocks, Peter F. Patel-Schneider, Frank van Harmelen: From SHIQ and RDF to OWL: The Making of a Web Ontology Language. Journal of Web Semantics. 2003.

12. Ian Horrocks, Peter F. Patel-Schneider, Harold Boley, Said Tabet, Benjamin Grosof, Mike Dean: SWRL: A Semantic Web Rule Language Combining OWL and RuleML. Available at http://www.daml.org/2004/04/swrl/

13. Jeff Heflin, Hector Munoz-Avila: LCW-Based Agent Planning for the Semantic Web. AAAI 2002 Workshop WS-02-11. AAAI Press, Menlo Park, CA, 1998. pp. 63-70.

14. Michael Gelfond, Nicola Leone: Logic programming and knowledge representation-the A-Prolog perspective. Artificial Intelligence 138(2002) 3-38.

15. Michael Gelfond, Vladimir Lifschitz: The Stable Model Semantics For Logic Programming. Proceedings of the Fifth International Conference on Logic Programming, 1988, pp.1070-1080.

16. Patrick Hayes, Brian McBride: RDF Semantics . W3C Recommendation 10 February 2004. Available at http://www.w3.org/TR/2004/REC-rdf-mt-20040210/

17. Peter F. Patel-Schneider, Patrick Hayes, Ian Horrocks: OWL Web Ontology Language Semantics and Abstract Syntax. W3C Recommendation 10 February 2004. Available at http://www.w3.org/TR/2004 /REC-owl-semantics-20040210/

18. Riccardo Rosati: Towards expressive KR systems integrating datalog and description logics: Preliminary report. In Proc. 1999 Int. Workshop on Description Logics(DL-1999), 160-164.

19. Stijn Heymans, Dirk Vermeir: Integrating Semantic Web Reasoning and Answer Set Programming. Answer Set Programming 2003.

20. Thomas Eiter, Thomas Lukasiewicz, Roman Schindlauer, Hans Tompits: Combining Answer Set Programming with Description Logics for the Semantic Web. KR 2004: 141-151

21. Victor W. Marek, Miroslaw Truszczynski: Stable Models and an Alternative Logic Programming Paradigm. The Logic Programming Paradigm: A 25-Year Perspective, Springer, Berlin, 1999, pp.375-398.

22. Vladimir Lifschitz: Answer Set Programming and Plan Generation.   Artificial Intelligence 138(2002) 39-54.

Combining Description Logic and Defeasible Logic for the Semantic Web

Kewen Wang[1], David Billington[1], Jeff Blee[1], and Grigoris Antoniou[2]

[1] Griffith University, Australia
{k.wang,d.billington}@griffith.edu.au
jeff.blee@student.griffith.edu.au
[2] University of Crete, Greece
ga@csd.uoc.gr

Abstract. The importance of integrating rules and ontologies for the Semantic Web has been well addressed by many researchers. Defeasible Logic is a simple but efficient nonmonotonic language which can handle both defeasibility and priority. In this paper we propose a novel approach to combining Defeasible Logic with Description Logics by introducing the Description Defeasible Logic (DDL). DDL is similar to Defeasible Logic but it also contains queries to the Description Logic knowledge base. DDL allows nonmonotonic reasoning to be built on top of ontologies, and to a certain degree, allows ontologies to be built on top of nonmonotonic reasoning. We give some basic properties of DDL, one of which shows that DDL is a tractable language provided that the underlying Description Logic is tractable.

1 Introduction

The Semantic Web aims to extend the current Web standards and technology so that the semantics of the Web content is machine processable. It is expected to have a dramatic impact on search engines, information integration, and automated reasoning from Web resources. In the development of the Semantic Web, related standards and technologies are divided into different layers. The layers that are higher than XML are considered to be "real" Semantic Web layers, including the metadata layer based on RDF, the ontology layer, and the logic and proof layers. Due to the invention of some Web markup languages like DAML+OIL [5] and OWL [7], it is widely believed that the ontology layer is sufficiently mature. The core of DAML+OIL and OWL are all based on expressive Description Logics [3].

The next step in the development of the Semantic Web is to realize the logic layer. This layer will be built on top of the ontology layer and provide sophisticated representation and reasoning abilities. Given that most current reasoning systems are based on rules, it is a key task to combine rules with an ontology. The RuleML initiative (http://www.ruleml.org) is considered to be a first attempt in this direction. Theoretically, the problem of integrating the ontology layer with the logic layer is reduced to combine rule-based systems with Description Logics. Recently, a number of attempts at combining Description Logic with logic programs have been made, for example, [8, 9,11].

G. Antoniou and H. Boley (Eds.): RuleML 2004, LNCS 3323, pp. 170–181, 2004.

On the other hand, Defeasible Logic [16] is a rule-based reasoning system that can resolve conflicts between rules using priority information. In contrast to most other nonmonotonic reasoning systems, an important feature of this logic is its linear complexity [14]. Moreover, this logic has very efficient implementations, for instance, a recent implementation, Deimos [15], is capable of dealing with 10,000s of defeasible rules. Antoniou and Wagner [2] advocate the expansion of RDF/RDFS by employing Defeasible Logic. In this paper, we propose a novel approach to combining any Description Logic with Defeasible Logic, which allows rules to be built on top of ontologies. We introduce Description Defeasible Logic (DDL), which consists of a knowledge base L represented as a theory in Description Logic and a finite set of rules called *ddl-rules*. A ddl-rule is a generalization of a Defeasible Logic rule which allows queries to L (*dl-literals*) as well as ordinary literals in the rule body. The notion of dl-literals is inspired by the approach in [9] and extends their *dl-atoms*. We also develop a proof theory for DDL, which is similar to the proof theory of Defeasible Logic. Unlike most approaches to combining Description Logics with nonmonotonic reasoning systems, our DDL is tractable provided that the corresponding Description Logic is tractable. i.e. The rest of the paper is arranged as follows. Section 2 briefly introduces Description Logics and Defeasible Logic. Section 3 motivates our approach by an example from the domain of selecting reviewers from some candidates. While Section 4 specifies the syntax of DDL, section 5 defines a procedural semantics for DDL. Section 6 gives some basic properties of DDL. Section 7 compares related work and concludes the paper.

2   Preliminaries

In this section we will introduce Defeasible Logic and Description Logic and its relation to Web markup languages.

2.1   Description Logic and Web Markup Languages

Although the Web is a great success, it is basically a collection of human-readable pages that cannot be automatically processed by computer programs. The Semantic Web is to provide tools for explicit markup of Web content and to help create a repository of computer-readable information. RDF is a language that can represent explicit metadata and separate content of Web pages from their structure. However, as noted by the W3C Web Ontology Working Group (http://www.w3.org/2001/sw/WebOnt/) , RDF/RDFS is too limited to describe some application domains which require the representation of ontologies on the Web and thus, a more expressive ontology modeling language was needed. This led to a number of ontology languages for the Web including the well-known DAML+OIL [5] and OWL [7]. In general, if a language is more expressive, then it is less efficient. To suit different applications, the OWL language provides three species for users to get a better balance between expressive power and reasoning efficiency: OWL Full, OWL DL and OWL Lite.

The cores of these Semantic Web languages are Description Logics, and in fact, the designs of OWL and its predecessor DAML+OIL were strongly influenced by Description Logics, including their formal semantics and language constructors. In these Semantic Web languages, an ontology is represented as a knowledge base in a Description Logic.

Description Logics are a family of concept-based knowledge representation languages [3]. They are fragments of first order logic and are designed to be expressively powerful and have an efficient reasoning mechanism. In particular, the Description Logics $\mathcal{SHIF}(D)$ and $\mathcal{SHOIN}(D)$ correspond to the two ontology languages OWL Lite and OWL DL, respectively.

The framework defined in the next section for combining Description Logic and Defeasible Logic is suitable for any Description Logic. Without loss of generality, we assume the Description Logic used in this paper is a basic description language $\mathcal{AL}$ (see [3] for more details).

A DL-knowledge base L has two components: a TBox and an ABox.

The TBox specifies the vocabulary of an application domain, which is actually a collection of concepts (sets of individuals) and roles (binary relations between individuals). So the TBox can be used to assign names to complex descriptions. For example, we may have a concept named $area$ which specifies a set of areas in computer science. Suppose we have another concept $expert$ which is a set of names of experts in computer science. We can have a role $expertIn$ which relates $expert$ to $area$. For instance, $expertIn(John, \text{``Semantic Web''})$ means "John is an expert in the Semantic Web".

The ABox contains assertions about named individuals.

A DL-knowledge base can also reason about the knowledge stored in the TBox and ABox, although its reasoning ability is a bit too limited for some practical applications. For example, the system can determine whether a description is consistent or whether one description subsumes another description.

The knowledge in both the TBox and ABox are represented as formulas of the first order language but they are restricted to special forms so that efficient reasoning is guaranteed. The formulas in $\mathcal{AL}$ are called *concept descriptions*. Elementary descriptions consists of both *atomic concepts* and *atomic roles*. Complex concepts are built inductively as follows (in the rest of this subsection, A is an atomic concept, C and D are concept descriptions, R is a role): A (atomic concept); $\top$ (universal concept); $\bot$ (bottom concept); $\neg A$ (atomic negation); $C \sqcap D$ (intersection); $C \sqcup D$ (union); $\forall R.C$ (value restriction) and $\exists R.C$ (existential quantification); $\geq nR$ (at-least restriction); $\leq nR$ (at-most restriction).

To define a formal semantics of concept descriptions, we need the notion of *interpretation*. An interpretation $\mathcal{I}$ of $\mathcal{AL}$ is a pair $(\Delta, \cdot^{\mathcal{I}})$ where Δ is a non-empty set called the *domain* and $\cdot^{\mathcal{I}}$ is an interpretation function which associates each atomic concept A with a subset $A^{\mathcal{I}}$ of Δ and each atomic role R with a binary relation $R^{\mathcal{I}} \subseteq \Delta \times \Delta$. The function $\cdot^{\mathcal{I}}$ can be naturally extended to complex descriptions:

- $\top^{\mathcal{I}} = \Delta$
- $\bot^{\mathcal{I}} = \emptyset$
- $(\neg A)^{\mathcal{I}} = \Delta - A^{\mathcal{I}}$
- $(C \sqcap D)^{\mathcal{I}} = C^{\mathcal{I}} \cap D^{\mathcal{I}}$
- $(C \sqcup D)^{\mathcal{I}} = C^{\mathcal{I}} \cup D^{\mathcal{I}}$
- $(\forall R.C)^{\mathcal{I}} = \{a \in \Delta \ : \ \forall b.(a,b) \in R^{\mathcal{I}} \text{ implies } b \in C^{\mathcal{I}}\}$
- $(\exists R.C)^{\mathcal{I}} = \{a \in \Delta \ : \ \exists b.(a,b) \in R^{\mathcal{I}} \text{ and } b \in C^{\mathcal{I}}\}$
- $(\geq nR)^{\mathcal{I}} = \{a \in \Delta \ : \ |\{b \ : \ (a,b) \in R^{\mathcal{I}}\}| \geq n\}$
- $(\leq nR)^{\mathcal{I}} = \{a \in \Delta \ : \ |\{b \ : \ (a,b) \in R^{\mathcal{I}}\}| \leq n\}$.

A *terminology axiom* is of the form $C \sqsubseteq D$ or $C \equiv D$ where C and D are concepts (roles). An interpretation $\mathcal{I}$ satisfies $C \sqsubseteq D$ iff $C^{\mathcal{I}} \subseteq D^{\mathcal{I}}$; it satisfies $C \equiv D$ iff $C^{\mathcal{I}} = D^{\mathcal{I}}$.

2.2 Defeasible Logic

Few nonmonotonic systems have linear complexity but Defeasible Logic is an exception as shown by Maher [14]. In fact most (skeptical) nonmonotonic reasoning systems are not even tractable. For example, the skeptical semantics of logic programs defined by the (preferred) answer sets is co-NP-hard and the skeptical reasoning systems defined by default extensions, autoepistemic extensions and circumscription are all Π_2^p-hard [4,6]. Although the well-founded semantics of non-disjunctive logic programs is a skeptical reasoning system with polynomial time complexity (viz $O(n^2)$), it cannot handle priority information between rules. Thus, the low complexity of Defeasible Logic is an attractive feature as a tool for knowledge representation and reasoning.

A defeasible theory is a finite set of rules together with a priority relation between rules. A priority relation is a binary relation on the set of rules. In this paper we use ">" to denote the priority relation. If r_1 and r_2 are two rules such that $r_1 > r_2$, then we say r_1 has higher priority than r_2. Intuitively, if both r_1 and r_2 are applicable, then the application of r_1 may override the application of r_2 when there is a conflict between these two rules. Rules are divided into three classes: strict rules, defeasible rules and defeaters. *Strict rules* represent certain knowledge that cannot be defeated, while *defeasible rules* represent knowledge that can be overridden by other rules. Defeaters are designed not to draw conclusions but to block some conclusions. By producing contrary evidence, they can defeat some defeasible rules.

3 An Example: Reviewer Selection

In [9], Eiter et al illustrated their approach by an example "Reviewer Selection". However, the formulation there has some ambiguities although the application domain is an interesting one. In this section we will reformulate the Reviewer Selection example and give some intuitive ideas of our approach.

Example 1. Suppose that we are assigning reviewers to papers submitted to a conference on the Web. A knowledge base L contains information about keywords, areas, experts etc on computer science and artificial intelligence. L is represented as a Description Logic theory in which "keywords", "areas" and "expert" are concepts while "inArea" and "expertIn" are roles (there may be some other concepts and roles):

$inArea(K, A)$ means that the keyword K is in the area A;

$expertIn(R, A)$ means that the referee R is an expert in the area A.

Assume that the concept "keywords" in L contains the following keywords "semantic web", "nonmonotonic reasoning", "preference", ... but not "defeasible logic". The roles "inArea" and "expertIn" contain the following knowledge:

(1) $inArea($*"nonmonotonic reasoning"*, *"Knowledge Representation"*$)$;

   $inArea($*"preference"*, *"Knowledge Representation"*$)$;

   $inArea($*"semantic web"*, *"Semantic Web"*$)$;

(2) $expertIn($*"John"*, *"Knowledge Representation"*$)$;

expertIn(*"Jenny"*, *"Semantic Web"*);
expertIn(*"Ted"*, *"Semantic Web"*).

The knowledge base L may be located on a remote server and the conference organizers are not allowed to update while they can query L.

As a specific conference, we also have certain information about papers submitted to the conference: each paper has an identity number as well as a couple of keywords. This kind of information is not included in L in general. We have the following information about paper #1 and #2:

(3) *paper*(#1);
    kw(#1, *"semantic web"*);
    kw(#1, *"nonmonotonic reasoning"*);
(4) *paper*(#2);
    kw(#2, *"semantic web"*);
    kw(#2, *"defeasible reasoning"*)
    paper(#n) means that the paper with identity number n has been submitted to the conference;
    kw(#n, K) means that K is one of the keywords of the paper with identity number n.

Rule (5) states the condition under which an expert may be assigned a paper:
(5) $\{DL[inArea](K, A), DL[expertIn](R, A), kw(P, K)\} \Rightarrow assign(R, P)$;

Intuitively, if a keyword K is in the area A and a person R is an expert in A and a paper P has a keyword K, then the paper P can be assigned to the expert R for review. Notice that we use $DL[expert](R, A)$ to denote that this is a query to the knowledge base L.

In this case, we can only derive *assign*(*"Jenny"*, #2) and *assign*(*"Ted"*, #2) but not *assign*(*"John"*, #2). If Ted is inactive in research (as we will assume later), then there is a risk that paper #2 can be assigned to only Jenny who may know nothing about nonmonotonic reasoning. Under the assumption that we cannot directly update the remote knowledge base L, an obvious way of dealing with this problem is to maintain a local knowledge base L' by updating L. However, the cost of maintaining a lot of local ontologies is expensive and impossible for many applications

To solve this problem, Eiter et al [9] proposed the notion of a dl-atom so that the keyword "defeasible logic" can be virtually (or, locally) inserted into the concept *keywords* of L. According to their convention, rule (5) can be extended to the rule:
(5)′ $\{DL[keywords \oplus \exists P kw(P, K); inArea](K, A), DL[expertIn](R, A), kw(P, K)\}$
      $\Rightarrow assign(R, P)$.

However, even if we know that the keyword "defeasible logic" is *close* to "nonmonotonic reasoning" and can be temporarily added to the concept *keywords*, we are still unable to determine that #2 is in the area of "Knowledge Representation" according to Eiter et al's approach.

In the next section, we will introduce the notion of dl-literals, which generalizes the notion of dl-atoms, and propose a novel approach to combining Description Logic with Defeasible Logic. In our approach, (5)′ is replaced by the rule
(5)″ $\{DL[\mathcal{K}(K); \mathcal{C}; inArea](K, A), expertIn(R, A), kw(P, K), \neg DL[keywords](K)\}$
      $\Rightarrow assign(R, P)$.
where $\mathcal{K}(K) = keywords \oplus \exists.Pkw(P, K)$ and
      $\mathcal{C} = close(inArea, "defeasible reasoning", "nonmonotonic reasoning")$.

Informally, $close(inArea,$ *"defeasible reasoning"*, *"nonmonotonic reasoning"*) means these two keywords are close with respect to the role $inArea$. That is,
"If $inArea($*"nonmonotonic reasoning"*$, A)$, then $inArea($*"defeasible reasoning"*$, A)$.

So, the dl-literal in the above rule means that, if K is a keyword in a paper that has not been included in the concept "keywords" and we virtually add K to L, then the query $inArea(K, A)$ can be answered using the information that "defeasible logic" is close to "nonmonotonic reasoning".

Under our DDL, we are able to derive $assign($*"John"*$, \#2)$ (see Section 5 for details).

Suppose we have another rule about assigning a referee:

(6) $\neg DL[active](R) \Rightarrow \neg assign(R, P)$;

Rule (6) explicitly asserts that if an expert is currently not an active researcher, then they cannot be assigned a paper.

If we know that Ted is not active in conducting research, then we will get two conflict conclusions: $assign($*"Ted"*$, \#1)$ and $\neg assign($*"Ted"*$, \#1)$. Notice that (6) has higher priority over (5) and we would expect to derive only $\neg assign($*"Ted"*$, \#1)$. Eiter et al's approach is unable to resolve this kind of conflict either. Under our new logic DDL, the above conflict can be easily resolved since Defeasible Logic, the underlying logic of our Description Defeasible Logic (DDL) can handle priority information between rules.

In summary, the Description Defeasible Logic (DDL) we will introduce in the next section can solve the two problems discussed in the above example:

- By employing a special predicate "close", we are able to virtually change the definition of a concept in the knowledge base and reason about it. For instance, we can derive $inArea(\#2,$ *"Knowledge Representation"*$)$ (and thus $assign($*"John"*$, \#2)$) is derivable under our new logic.
- By employing the priority relation between rules, conflicts caused by defeasible rules can be efficiently resolved. For instance, $\neg assign($*"Ted"*$, \#1)$ is derivable but $assign($*"Ted"*$, \#1)$ is not.

4   Syntax of DDL

We assume that the reader is familiar with the notation and basic notions of first order logic, such as predicates, atoms and literals.

A *DDL-theory* $\mathcal{D}$ consists of a knowledge base L in the Description Logic and a theory T in Defeasible Logic which may contain queries to L. Formally, such a query is called a *dl-literal*. A *dl-query* $Q(\mathbf{t})$ is an arbitrary formula in the description logic. For example, either a concept $C(t)$ or its negation $\neg C(t)$ can be a query; a role $R(t_1, t_2)$ or $\neg R(t_1, t_2)$ can also be a query. A *dl-literal* is a formula l of the form

$$DL[S_1 \circ_1 L_1, \ldots, S_m \circ_m L_m; close(R_1, c_1, c_1'), \ldots, close(R_n, c_n, c_n'); Q](c).$$

where each S_i is a concept or a role, each L_i is an ordinary formula of the form $\exists x P(x, y)$ or $\exists y P(x, y)$ where P is an ordinary predicate, each $\circ_i$ is an operator belonging to $\{\oplus, \ominus\}$, each c_i is a constant in $\mathcal{D}$, each c_i' is a constant in L, and $m, n \geq 0$. Notice that our dl-literal is different from the dl-atom in [9] in that we allow a more general form. For the above dl-literal l, we say Q is its query, and denote it by Q_l.

$S_i \oplus L_i$ means that an individual is added to the concept S_i if it satisfies the condition L_i.

$S_i \ominus L_i$ means that an individual is deleted from the concept S_i if it does not satisfy the condition L_i.

Informally, the above dl-literal l represents the knowledge that $Q(\mathbf{t})$ is queried against the virtual update of L obtained by inserting/deleting some items of the concepts $S_1, \ldots, S_m$ and incorporating the observations $close(R_1, t_1, t'_1), \ldots, close(R_n, t_n, t'_n)$ (see Example 1).

A *generalized literal* is either an ordinary literal or a dl-literal. If l is a generalized literal, $\tilde{l}$ denotes the complementary literal (if l is an atom p then $\tilde{l}$ is $\neg p$; and if l is $\neg p$, then $\tilde{l}$ is p).

A *rule* r consists of its *antecedent* (or *body*) $A(r)$ which is a finite set of generalized literals, an arrow, and its *consequent* (or *head*) $C(r)$ which is an ordinary literal.

We say an interpretation I is a model of a ground rule r iff "$I \models A(r)$ implies $I \models C(r)$".

As in Defeasible Logic, DDL has three types of rules: strict rules, defeasible rules and defeaters. However, their meanings are a bit different from the corresponding rules in Defeasible Logic. A big difference of the semantics for DDL from Defeasible Logic is that *DDL is able to distinguish the credibility of different resources as well as the defeasibility of conclusions represented by rule types*. In Example 1, we put more credibility on a keyword in the ontology (e.g. "nonmonotonic reasoning") than a keyword in a paper (e.g. "defeasible logic").

Facts are indisputable observations from outside of the knowledge base. For example, "semantic web" is a keyword of the paper #1. This can be formally written as $kw(\#1, \text{"semantic web"})$.

Strict rules are rules in the classical sense: whenever the premises are indisputable (e.g. facts, any knowledge stored in the knowledge base) then so is the conclusion. The arrow for strict rules is $\rightarrow$. For example, "An expert is a person" is a strict rule written as: $expert(R) \rightarrow person(R)$.

Defeasible rules are rules that can be defeated by contrary evidence. The arrow for defeasible rules is $\Rightarrow$. For example, "If somebody is an expert in a topic, then, normally, they are eligible as a referee for papers on this topic". However, there may be some exceptions, for instance, the expert may be too busy to review the paper. This rule is formally expressed as: $expert(R) \Rightarrow eligible\text{-}referee(R)$.

Defeaters are rules that cannot be used to draw any conclusions. Their only use is to prevent some conclusions. In other words, they are used to defeat some defeasible rules by producing evidence to the contrary. The arrow for defeaters is $\rightsquigarrow$. An example is "If an expert is over-loaded, then they might not be able to review papers for the conference". Formally: $over\text{-}loaded(R) \rightsquigarrow \neg referee(R)$. It has been proved in [1] that defeaters can be simulated by means of strict rules and defeasible rules. Thus defeaters can be eliminated from Defeasible Logic.

The *superiority relation* $>$ is used to define priorities among rules, that is, where one rule may override the conclusion of another rule. If $r_1 > r_2$, then r_1 is superior to r_2. If both r_1 and r_2 are applicable, then the application of r_1 blocks the application of r_2 when there is a conflict between them. The superiority relation is required to be acyclic in this paper.

Given a set R of rules, we denote the set of all strict rules in R by R_s, the set of strict and defeasible rules in R by R_{sd}, the set of defeasible rules in R by R_d, and the set of defeaters in R by R_{dft}. $R[l]$ denotes the set of rules in R with consequent l.

Definition 1. *(Syntax of DDL) A description defeasible logic theory (or DDL theory) $\mathcal{D}$ is a quadruple $(L, F, R, >)$ where L is a theory of Description Logic, F is a finite set of facts, R is a finite set of rules, and $>$ is a superiority relation on R.*

Example 2. (continuation of Example 1) The DDL $\mathcal{D}$ in Example 1 can be formalized as follows.

The Description Logic knowledge base L contains three concepts and two roles:
(L1) $keywords(\text{"semantic web"})$, $keywords(\text{"nonmonotonic reasoning"})$;
(L2) $area(\text{"Semantic Web"})$, $area(\text{"Knowledge Representation"})$;
(L3) $expert(\text{"John"})$, $expert(\text{"Jenny"})$, $expert(\text{"Ted"})$;
(L4) $expertIn(\text{"John"}, \text{"Knowledge Representation"})$;
    $expertIn(\text{"Jenny"}, \text{"Semantic Web"})$;
    $expertIn(\text{"Ted"}, \text{"Semantic Web"})$.
(L5) $inArea(\text{"nonmonotonic reasoning"}, \text{"Knowledge Representation"})$;
    $inArea(\text{"semantic web"}, \text{"Semantic Web"})$;

The set of facts and rules:
(T0) $paper(\#1)$, $kw(\#1, \text{"semantic web"})$, $kw(\#1, \text{"nonmonotonic reasoning"})$;
    $paper(\#2)$, $kw(\#2, \text{"semantic web"})$, $kw(\#2, \text{"defeasible reasoning"})$
(T1) $\{DL[inArea](K, A), DL[expertIn](R, A), kw(P, K)\} \Rightarrow assign(R, P)$
(T2) $\{DL[\mathcal{K}(K); \mathcal{C}; inArea](K, A), expertIn(R, A), kw(P, K), \neg DL[keywords](K)\}$
    $\Rightarrow assign(R, P)$
where $\mathcal{K}(K) = keywords \oplus \exists.Pkw(P, K)$ and
    $\mathcal{C} = close(inArea, \text{"defeasible reasoning"}, \text{"nonmonotonic reasoning"})$.
(T3) $\neg active(R) \Rightarrow \neg assign(R, P)$.
(T4) $inArea(R, A) \to goodAt(R, A)$.
    Priority relation: $(T3) > (T1)$ and $(T3) > (T2)$.

5   Procedural Semantics of DDL

We first define the semantics of dl-literals. Let $\mathcal{D} = (L, T)$ be a DDL theory.

If l is a dl-literal of the form in Section 4, we say l is derivable from L wrt $\mathcal{D}$ iff

$$L \cup \bigcup_{i=1}^{\boxed{a}^u} A_i \cup \bigcup_{j=1}^{\boxed{a}^u} B_j \models Q(c)$$

where
    $A_i = \{S_i(c') \ : \ L_i(c'), c' \text{ is a constant in } \mathcal{D}\}$ for $\circ = \oplus$,
    $A_i = \{\neg S_i(c') \ : \ \neg L_i(c'), c' \text{ is a constant in } \mathcal{D}\}$ for $\circ = \ominus$,
    $B_j = \{R_j(c_j, c') \ : \ R_j(c'_j, c') \text{ for any constant } c'\}$
    $\cup \{R_1(c', c_j) \ : \ R_1(c', c'_j) \text{ for any constant } c'\}$.
The notion of *conclusion* in Defeasible Logic can be extended to DDL in the following way. A *conclusion* of a DDL theory $\mathcal{D}$ is a tagged literal which has one of the following four forms:

$+\Delta l$ which is intended to mean that l is definitely provable in $\mathcal{D}$ (using only facts, strict rules and queries from the knowledge base).

$-\Delta l$ which is intended to mean that we have proved that l is not definitely provable in $\mathcal{D}$.

$+\partial l$ which is intended to mean that l is defeasibly provable in $\mathcal{D}$.

$-\partial l$ which is intended to mean that we have proved that l is not defeasibly provable in $\mathcal{D}$.

Provability is based on the concept of a *derivation* (or *proof*) in $\mathcal{D} = (L, F, R, >)$. A derivation is a finite sequence $P = (P(1), \ldots P(n))$ of tagged literals satisfying four conditions (which correspond to inference rules for each of the four kinds of conclusion).

$+\Delta$:If $P(i+1) = +\Delta l$ then either

$\quad l$ is an ordinary literal and $l \in F$ or

$\quad l$ is a dl-literal and its query Q_l can be derived from L:

$$L \models Q_l \text{ or}$$
$$\exists r \in R_s[l] \; \forall a \in A(r) : +\Delta a \in P(1..i)$$

$-\Delta$: If $P(i+1) = -\Delta l$ then one of the following two conditions holds:

(1) l is a dl-literal and $L \not\models Q_l$ or

(2) l is an ordinary literal such that $l \notin F$ and $\forall r \in R_s[l] \; \exists a \in A(r) :$
$\quad -\Delta a \in P(1..i)$

$+\partial$: If $P(i+1) = +\partial l$ then either

(1) $+\Delta q \in P(1..i)$ or

(2) l is a dl-literal such that $L \models l$ or

(3) $\exists r \in R_{sd}[l]$ such that

$\quad$ (3.1) $\forall a \in A(r) : +\partial a \in P(1..i)$ and

$\quad$ (3.2) $-\Delta \tilde{l} \in P(1..i)$ and

$\quad$ (3.3) $\forall s \in R[\tilde{l}]$, either

$\quad\quad$ (3.3.1) $\exists a \in A(s) : -\partial a \in P(1..i)$ or

$\quad\quad$ (3.3.2) $\exists t \in R_{sd}[l]$ such that

$\quad\quad\quad \forall a \in A(t) : +\partial a \in P(1..i)$ and $t > s$

$-\partial$: If $P(i+1) = -\partial l$ then

(1) either l is a dl-literal with $L \not\models l$ or

(2) the following conditions are satisfied

$\quad$ (2.1) $-\Delta l \in P(1..i)$ and

$\quad$ (2.2)(2.2.1) $\forall r \in R_{sd}[l] \; \exists a \in A(r) : -\partial a \in P(1..i)$ or

$\quad\quad$ (2.2.2) $+\Delta \tilde{l} \in P(1..i)$ or

$\quad\quad$ (2.2.3) $\exists s \in R[\tilde{l}]$ such that

$\quad\quad\quad$ (2.2.3.1) $\forall a \in A(s) : +\partial a \in P(1..i)$ and

$\quad\quad\quad$ (2.2.3.2) $\forall t \in R_{sd}[l]$ either

$\quad\quad\quad\quad \exists a \in A(t) : -\partial a \in P(1..i)$ or $t \not> s$

If some tagged literal α can be derived from DDL theory $\mathcal{D}$, then it is denoted $\mathcal{D} \vdash \alpha$.

Example 3. (continuation of Example 1) Consider the DDL theory $\mathcal{D}$ in Example 2. Then the following tagged literals are derivable from $\mathcal{D}$ as well as others:

$\quad \mathcal{D} \vdash +\Delta DL[keywords]($ *"semantic web"* $)$,

$\quad \mathcal{D} \vdash +\Delta goodAt($ *"Jenny"*, *"Semantic Web"* $)$,

$\mathcal{D} \vdash +\partial DL[inArea]("Jenny", "Knowledge Representation"),$

$\mathcal{D} \vdash +\partial assign(John, \#2),$

$\mathcal{D} \vdash -\Delta DL[\mathcal{K}_0; \mathcal{C}; inArea]("defeasible reasoning", "Knowledge Representation"),$

$\mathcal{D} \vdash -\partial DL[\mathcal{C}; inArea]("defeasible reasoning", "Knowledge Representation").$

Here $\mathcal{K}_0 = keywords \oplus \exists.Pkw(P, K)$ and

$\mathcal{C} = close(inArea, "defeasible reasoning", "nonmonotonic reasoning").$

6   Properties of DDL

In this section, we study some basic properties of DDL. First, we notice that DDL generalizes Defeasible logic.

Proposition 1. *If a DDL $\mathcal{D}$ does not contain any dl-literal, then it is equivalent to the corresponding Defeasible Logic theory.*

Thus, DDL can be considered as an extension of Defeasible Logic. Some properties of Defeasible Logic can also be generalized to DDL.

Like Defeasible logic, it can be seen from the previous section that, for every generalized literal l, we have four types of conclusions: $\mathcal{D} \vdash +\Delta l$, $\mathcal{D} \vdash -\Delta l$, $\mathcal{D} \vdash +\partial l$, $\mathcal{D} \vdash -\partial l$.

In general, the tag Δ is stronger than ∂ in the following sense.

Proposition 2. *Let $\mathcal{D}$ be a DDL theory and l be a generalized literal in $\mathcal{D}$. Then we have the following relations among the above four types of conclusions:*

1. *If $\mathcal{D} \vdash +\Delta l$, then $\mathcal{D} \vdash +\partial l$.*
2. *If $\mathcal{D} \vdash -\partial l$, then $\mathcal{D} \vdash -\Delta l$.*

The next result shows that DDL is coherent with respect to both Δ and ∂.

Proposition 3. *Let $\mathcal{D}$ be a DDL theory. Then*

1. *There is no generalized literal l such that both $\mathcal{D} \vdash +\Delta l$ and $\mathcal{D} \vdash -\Delta l$ are true.*
2. *There is no generalized literal l such that both $\mathcal{D} \vdash +\partial l$ and $\mathcal{D} \vdash -\partial l$ are true.*

Due to the linear complexity of Defeasible Logic, DDL is tractable if the corresponding Description Logic is tractable. In general, we have the following result.

Proposition 4. *Description Defeasible Logic (DDL) has the same complexity as its underlying Description Logic.*

As we have mentioned before, most combinations of different nonmonotonic logics result in intractable (even undecidable) logics. This important result provides a unique feature for our DDL, which is highly needed for a web markup language.

7 Related Work and Final Discussion

There has been a lot of work on combining different logics (or knowledge bases) with Description Logics. The aims of those approaches are largely to resolve conflicts and inconsistencies so that information from different knowledge bases can be shared. The representative works in this area include [8,13,17]. In these approaches roles are allowed to appear in rule bodies as constraints. There are also some proposals which reduce one logic to another more efficient logic. The rationale of this approach is to employ a more efficient system for reasoning in other systems. For example, some work has been done to reduce Description Logic to logic programming [11,12,18,19].

The works that are closest to our work are by Eiter et al [9], Antoniou and Wagner [2] and Governatori [10]. Eiter et al proposed an approach to combining logic programming with Description Logics. They introduced a class of logic programs called dl-programs and defined two kinds of answer set semantics for those logic programs. In their approach, while logic programs can be built on top of Description Logics, Description Logics can also be built on top of logic programs in a very limited sense (see Example 1). To obtain an efficient language, Antoniou and Wagner proposed that Defeasible Logic be built on top of the RDF/RDFS based metadata layer rather than on the OWL based ontology layer. More recently, Governatori addressed the issue of extending Description Logic by allowing defeasible rules (his logic is called Defeasible Descirption Logic). Thus, the Description Logic knowledge base L in our approach can be naturally extended to any knowledge base in the Defeasible Description Logic. Obviously, the aim of his approach is different from ours but these two approaches can be benefited from each other.

In this paper, we combined Description Logic (OWL based ontology layer) with Defeasible Logic and introduced Description Defeasible Logic (DDL). DDL allows Defeasible Logic to be built on top of the ontology level, and the ontology layer to be built on top of Defeasible Logic in a more flexible way than Eiter et al's approach. DDL can efficiently handle priority information between rules. The semantics of DDL can not only distinguish defeasible knowledge from indisputable knowledge as does Defeasible Logic, but also can reasoning about the credibility of knowledges from different sources. In Example 1, $inArea($ "*defeasible reasoning*", $KR)$ is given less credibility than $inArea($ "*nonmonotonic reasoning*", $KR)$ where KR means "Knowledge Representation". As we have noted before, most approaches to combining logic programs with Description Logics are not tractable. However, DDL is tractable provided that the Description Logic is tractable (fortunately, a lot of Description Logics are tractable). Needless to say, a number of issues remain to be explored. An interesting topic is to investigate theoretic foundations of DDL and its relation to some other logic systems. In particular, it is possible to define a model-theoretic semantics for DDL. Another important issue is to explore the combination of DDL with OWL in the same way as SWRL (http://www.daml.org/2003/11/swrl/) We also plan to apply DDL to specifying business rules.

References

1. G. Antoniou, D. Billington, G. Governatori, and M. J. Maher. Representation results for defeasible logic. *ACM Transactions on Computationl Logic*, 2(2):255–287, 2001.

2. G. Antoniou and G. Wagner. A rule-based approach to the semantic web (preliminary report). In *Proceedings of the 2nd Workshop on Rules and Rule Markup Languages for the Semantic Web (RuleML2003)*, pages 111–120, 2003.

3. F. Baader, D. Calvanese, D.McGuinness, D. Nardi, and P. Patel-Schneider. *The Description Logic Handbook*. Cambridge University Press, 2002.

4. M. Cadoli and M. Schaerf. A survey on complexity results for non-monotonic logics. *Journal of Logic Programming*, 17, 1993.

5. D. Connolly, F. van Harmelen, I. Horrocks, D. L. McGuinness, P. F. Patel-Schneider, and L. A. Stein. Daml+oil (march 2001) reference description. http://www.w3.org/tr2001/note-daml+oil-reference-20011218, W3C Note, 18 December 2001.

6. E. Dantsin, T. Eiter, G. Gottlob, and A. Voronkov. Complexity and expressive power of logic programming. *ACM Computing Survey*, 33(3):374–425, 2001.

7. M. Dean, D. Connolly, F. van Harmelen, J. Hendler, I. Horrocks, D. McGuinness, P. Patel-Schneider, and L. Stein. Owl web ontology language reference. http://www.w3.org/tr2003/wd-owl-ref-20030331, W3C Working Draft, 31 March 2003.

8. F. Donini, M. Lenzerini, D. Nardi, and A. Schaerf. AL-log: Integrating datalog and description logics. *Journal of Intelligent Information Systems*, 10(3):227–252, 1998.

9. T. Eiter, T. Lukasiewicz, R. Schindlauer, and H. Tompits. Combining answer set programming with description logics for the semantic web. In *Proceedings of the 9th International Conference on Principles of Knowledge Representation and Reasoning*, pages 141–151, 2004.

10. G. Governatori. Defeasible description logic. In *Proceedings of RuleML'2004 (to appear)*. Springer-Verlag, 2004.

11. B. Grosof, I. Horrocks, R. Volz, and S. Decker. Description logic programs: Combining logic programs with description logics. In *Proceedings of the 12th International World Wide Web Conference*, pages 48–57, 2003.

12. S. Heymans and D. Vermeir. Integrating semantic web reasoning and answer set programming. In *Proceedings of ASP'03*, pages 194–208, 2003.

13. A. Levy and M. Rousset. Combining horn logic rules and description logics in carin. *Artificial Intelligence*, 104(1-2):165–209, 1998.

14. M. J. Maher. Propositional defeasible logic has linear complexity. *Theory and Practice of Logic Programming*, 1(6):691–711, 2001.

15. M. J. Maher, A. Rock, G. Antoniou, D. Billington, and T. Miller. Efficient defeasible reasoning systems. In *Proceedings of the IEEE Conference on Tools with Artificial Intelligence*, pages 384–392, 2000.

16. D. Nute. Defeasible logic. In D. M. Gabbay, C. J. Hogger, and J. A. Robinson, editors, *Handbook of Logic in Artificial Intelligence and Logic Programming Vol.3*, pages 353–395. Oxford University Press, 1994.

17. R. Rosati. Towards expressive kr systems integrating datalog and description logics: Preliminary report. In *Proceedings of DL'99*, pages 160–164, 1999.

18. T. Swift. Deduction in ontologies via asp. In *Proceeding of LPNMR-7*. Springer-Verlag, 2004.

19. K. van Belleghem, M. Denecker, and D. de Schreye. A strong correspondence between description logics and open logic programming. In *Proceedings of the International Conference on Logic Programming(ICLP'97)*, pages 346–360, 1997.

Rewrite Rules as Service Integrators

Jing-Ying Chen[1]

Computer and Information Science Department,
National Chiao Tung Unviersity
Hsinchu, Taiwan, R.O.C.
jyc@cis.nctu.edu.tw

Abstract. Web Services is transforming the information sharing Web into a heterogeneous, distributed resource integration platform, aiming at enabling a global service market in which individuals and organizations can offer their competitive services to potential clients across the Web. To succeed, if not just survive, in such an emerging Web Services market, companies need effective strategies and methods to help them design reusable Web services and build Web services-based applications rapidly. In this paper, we present a dynamic service customization and composition framework for Web services. In particular, we propose a rule-based service integration language with concepts borrowed from rewriting systems. We show how the language can be used to model complex collaboration patterns among services, and compare our framework with other service integration approaches.

1 Introduction

Web Services [1] are emerging as a new interoperability platform that promises to enable flexible integration of software applications distributed across the Web. One of the fundamental differences between the Web and Web Services is the dramatic paradigm shift from information sharing, to the integration of distributed, heterogeneous computing resources. Such an integration platform can enable a global service market in which individuals or organizations can offer their competitive software services to potential clients across the Web.

For companies to best leverage their development resources targeting the Web Services platform, two important aspects need to be considered. First, for service providers, Web services should be designed such that together they achieve high reusability. Since Web services are independently developed and maintained, and presumably not custom made for specific customers, disciplined software engineering practices are needed to make sure that the services designed are individually useful, mutually supportive for each other, yet can be flexibly combined with services developed by other providers. Secondly, for service users, the question of how to tailor independently developed Web services for their own problems and to coordinate these services in a robust, timely manner needs to be answered.

---

[1] This work is partially supported by National Science Council and MediaTek, Inc.

G. Antoniou and H. Boley (Eds.): RuleML 2004, LNCS 3323, pp. 182–187, 2004.

It is therefore clear that effective strategies and concrete mechanisms for Web services customization and coordination will play an important role in the emerging Web Services era. Our goal is to develop a fully dynamic service customization framework for Web services-based application development. In this paper, we first outline the model and architecture of our framework, and then describe a rule-based language for heterogeneous service integration. We use a simple data mining system as an example to demonstrate how the language can be used to model complex inter-service collaboration, and compare our work with other service integration approaches.

2 A Service Composition Framework

We view Web services, or services for short, as standalone, network addressable software components with XML-based access interfaces. Each service functions by processing requests from clients and responding with answers; during the process it may interact with its *context* for assistance. This leads to the concept of service *polymorphism* which we refer to as *the ability of a service to behave differently under different contexts*. Therefore, service customization corresponds to the construction of a suitable context around a service to alter its behavior. Similarly, service collaboration can also be modeled using polymorphism, in the sense that two services can collaborate with each other through the context they share.

Accordingly, service composition corresponds to the construction of a proper context in which a group of services can work cohesively towards a designated goal. We use *manager* to refer to the part of software artifacts created specifically for service composition, although in practice the composition logic may be centralized in one place or distributed among multiple services, expressed explicitly or implicitly.

Based on the service model above, we recognize a special class of services, called *service containers*. A service container hosts other non-container services and maintains their contexts. Although the actual context implementation may involve complex intra- or inter-container protocols, such details are invisible to non-container services.

The overall service composition framework consists of multiple interconnecting service containers. For illustration purpose, consider the simplified data mining system in Fig. 1 containing three service containers. In particular, the *User* container is running inside user's process so that the GUI-enabled services `FileTreeView` and `FileContentView` can interact with the user directly. The `DataMiner` service, on the other hand, serves as an integrator that coordinates other services and interprets user's actions. Table 1 outlines the responsibility and polymorphism of each service.

To compose the data mining system dynamically, the user communicates with service containers individually. For example, the following XML message to the *ToolProvider* container creates a `ClusteringService` instance at location `my-Tool/cluster`, with the context set to the `FileSystemService` instance in the *DataProvider* container:

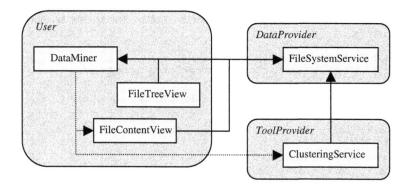

Fig. 1. A simple data mining system containing three distributed service containers

```
<create path="myTool/cluster">
        class="com.tool.ClusteringService">
    <cntx name="fileserv" path="myData" host="data.com"/>
    <config dest="myData/results"/>
</create>
```

To further customize individual services, additional configuration information can be passed through <config> elements. For example, the ClusteringService tool above requires a target location for it to generate analysis results.

Table 1. Summary of participating services in the data mining system

Service	Context	Description
FileSystemService	-	File system service
ClusteringService	FileSystemService	Clustering algorithms
FileTreeView	FileSystemService DataMiner	Displaying file system in tree structure.
FileContentview	FileSystemService	Displaying file content based on file type.
DataMiner	ClusteringService FileContentView	Coordinating services and providing data mining facilities to the end user.

3   Rule-Based Service Composition

To transform independently developed services into a cohesive system that satisfies user's needs, flexible gluing mechanisms are needed to cope with diverse, versatile behaviors of services. In our framework, a rule-based language is designed for such purpose. The example below illustrates how DataMiner translates a double-clicking event generated from FileTreeView, into a request to Clustering-Service for computation. This example also indicates that DataMiner is created from scratch by the user dynamically, compared to other preexisting services being used.

```
<create path="dataMiner">
  <cntx name="cluster" path="myTool/cluster"
        host="tool.com"/>
  <cntx name="content" path="dataMiner/content"/>
  <rules>
    <rule>
      <if>
        <event action="doubleClick">
          <file path="@path" type="Matrix"/>
        </event>
        <rw:call cntx="cluster">
          <perform tool="kMeans" path="@path"/>
        </rw:call>
      </if>
      <ok/>
    </rule>
    <rule>
      <if>
        <event action="click">
          <rw:var name="clickedFile"/>
        </event>
        <rw:call cntx="content">
          <show> <rw:var name="clickedFile"/> </show>
        </rw:call>
      </if>
      <ok/>
    </rule>
  </rules>
</create>
```

The interpretation of the rewrite rules is outlined below. Upon receiving an XML message, a rule-based service examines its own rewrite rules one by one until it successfully transforms the input into a valid message[2]. A rule has the following form:

```
<rule>
  <if> Pattern
       Condition*
  </if>
  Template
</rule>
```

When applying a rewrite rule to an input message, the input is matched structurally against *Pattern*, which is just an ordinary XML element possibly containing some "variables" (e.g. the @path attribute and <rw:var> elements in the example above). Note that "@" and the rw namespace are used to distinguish meta-constructs from ordinary ones. If *Pattern* and the input match, a binding is produced mapping

---

[2] We use null messages to indicate failed patterning matching or service invocation.

variables to corresponding attributes or elements, respectively. The binding can be combined with *Template* to build an output message for return.

A rewrite rule may also contain multiple *Condition*s each serving as an additional guard. *Condition* can be a "directive" such as an `<rw:call>` element which initiates a call to another service, using its own child element as the template to build the input message. In addition to `<rw:call>`, other directives are possible. For example, `<rw:this>` calls current service recursively, while `<rw:callback>` calls back the service that invoked current service. More interestingly, `<rw:delegate>` performs like `<rw:call>` excepts that if later the callee calls back, the request is relayed to the caller of current service. Fig. 2 depicts the differences among these directives. It should be noted that these directives can be combined to form a highly sophisticated distributed system. In practice, however, advanced features such as `<rw:callback>` and `<rw:delegate>` should always be used with care and discipline.

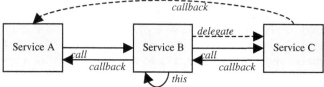

Fig. 2. An illustration of the call, callback, this, and delegate directives

In addition to the directives above, *Condition* can also have the form similar to variable assignment in common programming languages, i.e. `<eq>` *Pattern Directive* `</eq>`, which is useful for temporary data storage and complex structure building. Intuitively, *Directive* is evaluated using the binding prior to the evaluation, and the result matched with *Pattern*, resulting in a valid binding if everything goes well.

4 Related Work

Traditionally, service integration models have been an important topic addressed by concurrent programming languages and coordination models research [2], [3]. Examples include Linda [4] and Actors [5]. Accordingly, many composition frameworks for Web services are also based on existing coordination models. For example, TSSuite [6] adopts the shared tuple space concept from Linda. In comparison, our framework adheres to a message-passing style and focuses on establishing communication channels among services.

Web services choreography is currently an active area receiving extensive research interests [7]. Standards published or currently under development include BPEL4WS [8], ebXML, and so on. [9] gives a systematic comparison among some of these standards. One of the objectives targeted by these choreography standards is to support interorganization workflows for coordinating distributed, autonomous Web services toward specific goals. Therefore, they emphasize on the specification of roles and responsibilities of participating partners from a global perspective. In contrast, we are more interested in supporting bottom-up, component-based Web services development. In fact, the framework described so far constitutes the core of an integrated bioinformatics environment we are developing. Such an explorative scientific computing domain demands a more flexible composition framework to cope with highly heterogeneous, rapidly evolving computing resources distributed across the Web.

5   Conclusions

We have proposed a flexible, dynamic composition framework for Web services development and described a rule-based language for service integration. We achieved the goal by exploiting the pattern matching mechanism of rewriting systems [10] for XML processing. In addition, we borrowed and adapted the procedural semantics of rewriting systems in the design of the language so that the rule-based services can interact with other RPC-style services straightforwardly. More importantly, the expressiveness of rewriting systems allows us to realize a system capable of modeling complex inter-service collaboration with inexpensive development cost, yet amenable for further optimization.

References

1.   Web Services Activity, W3C. http://www.w3.org/2002/ws/
2.   Ciancarini, P.: Coordination Models and Languages as Software Integrators. ACM Computing Survey, Vol. 28, No. 2. (1996) 300-302
3.   Gelernter, D., Carriero, N. Coordination Languages and Their Significance. Communication of the ACM, Vol. 35, No. 2. (1992) 97-107
4.   Gelernter, D.: Generative Communication in Linda. ACM Transaction on Programming Languages and Systems, Vol. 7, No. 1. (1985) 80-112
5.   Agha, G., Frolund, S., Kim, W.Y., Panwar, R., Patterson, A., Sturman, D.: Abstraction and Modularity Mechanisms for Concurrent Programming. IEEE Parallel & Distributed Technology: Vol. 1, No. 2 (1993) 3-14
6.   Fontoura, M., Lehman, T., Nelson, D., Truong, T.: TSpaces Services Suite: Automating the Development and Management of Web Services. World Wide Web Conference (2003) http://www2003.org/
7.   Web Services Choreography Working Group, W3C. http://www.w3.org/2002/ws/chor/
8.   Khalaf, R., Mukhi, N., Weerawarana, S.: Service–Oriented Composition in BPEL4WS. World Wide Web Conference (2003), http://www2003.org/
9.   Bernauer, M., Kappel, G., KRAMLER, G., Retschitzegger, W.: Specification of Interorganizational Workflows - A Comparison of Approaches. Proceedings of the 7th World Multiconference on Systemics, Cybernetics and Informatics (2003) 30-36
10. Dershowitz, N., Jouannaud, J.-P.: Rewrite Systems. In Formal Models and Semantics, volume B of Handbook of Theoretical Computer Science, chapter 6, pages 243-320. Elsevier, Amsterdam, 1990.

SweetProlog: A System to Integrate Ontologies and Rules

Loredana Laera[1], Valentina Tamma[1], Trevor Bench-Capon[1], and
Giovanni Semeraro[2]

[1] Department of Computer Science, University of Liverpool, L69 3BX, Liverpool, UK
{lori, valli, tbc}@csc.liv.ac.uk
[2] Dipartimento di Informatica, Universita' di Bari, Via Orabona 4,70125, Bari, Italy
semeraro@di.uniba.it

Abstract. This paper describes the design and implementation of
SweetProlog, a system for translating Web rules into Prolog. It enables
the integration of ontologies and rules on the Semantic Web. This is
achieved via a translation of OWL ontologies described in Description
Logics and rules expressed in OWLRuleML into a set of facts and rules
described in Prolog. Finally, the resulting logic program is interrogated
by a Prolog engine to deduce new knowledge.

1 Introduction

Rules play an important role in the Semantic Web, as envisioned by Tim-Berners
Lee [BLHL01]. The realization of the rule layer will allow further means to
deduce knowledge and combine information. This layer should be built on top
of ontology languages, such as OWL, and will offer enhanced representation
and reasoning capabilities. The effort to define rule languages and to enable
interoperability between major commercial rule systems has been undertaken
by the RuleML Initiative[1]. The RuleML Initiative aims to develop a canonical
Web language for rules called RuleML [BTW01], which permits both forward
(bottom-up) and backward (top-down) rules in XML for deduction, rewriting,
and further inferential-transformational tasks.

But there is a crucial problem to solve, how is it possible to enable an OWL
ontology to reason over its instances using such rules? One possible solution is
to use a Logic Programming Language, such as Prolog, which offers efficient
automatic reasoning to accomplish this.

This paper therefore investigates how rules may be used to enhance the content
of a ontology and allow the dynamic inclusion of derived facts that are not
captured by the ontological taxonomy alone.

---

[1] see http://www.dfki.de/ruleml

G. Antoniou and H. Boley (Eds.): RuleML 2004, LNCS 3323, pp. 188–193, 2004.

2   Representation of Rules in OWLRuleML

As a first step we focus attention on how to define the rules and how to link the rules to description logics in OWL [DSHHHMPS03]. For this reason we used RuleML as a *lingua franca* to exchange rules between different rule systems and rule components in application software. The rules are therefore specified in OWLRuleML, which is an OWL ontology of the CLP (Courteous Logic Programs) RuleML rule syntax.

Using Description Logics of OWL to specify a meta ontology for RuleML rules, has some advantages:

- arbitrary OWL classes (e.g., descriptions) can be used as predicates in rules;
- rules and ontology axioms can be freely mixed;
- ontology and rules can be parsed in the same way;

OWLRuleML is a language appropriate for specifying derivation rules. It offers, among the others, the following features:

- Support for URI reference;
- Position dependent elements in RuleML;
- Preserved semantics of all constraints in the RuleML;
- Support for strong negation and weak negation;
- Support for prioritised conflict handling via Courteous Logic Programs;

Another advantage of representing rules in OWLRuleML concerns non-monotonic reasoning [Ant02]. OWL is incapable of representing non-monotonicity as is First Order Logic. By using OWLRuleML we can represent non-monotonicity via Courteous Logic Programs, a subset of RuleML. We believe that the non monotonic rules will play an important role in he area of the Semantic Web, where the available information is often incomplete. The next subsection will briefly introduce Courteous Logic Programs.

2.1   CLP

Courteous Logic Programs (CLP) [Gro97] extend expressively Ordinary Logic Programs (OLP), and are tractably compilable to OLP by a Courteous Compiler [Gro99]. CLP provide a method to resolve conflicts between rules using partially prioritized information to guarantee a consistent and unique set of conclusions (answer-set). Partially ordered prioritization among rules is optionally specified via a reserved predicate, called *overrides*. Each rule has an optional label, which has the form of a logical term. The atom *OVERRIDES (label1, label2)* specifies that a rule with *label1* has higher priority than a rule with *label2*. A pairwise exclusion integrity constraint (*mutex*) specifies the scope of conflict, stating that inconsistency for a particular pair of literals can be inferred, given another particular condition. As we mentioned above, CLP can be compiled as ordinary logic programs that are semantically equivalent. More precisely, we use a courteous compiler of IBM CommonRules to transform CLP into Prolog.

3   OWLRuleML Rules on Top of OWL Ontologies

The next step is to find a possible way to integrate rules with OWL in logic programming environments such as Prolog. We follow the approach proposed in [Gro03], which is to *build rules on top of ontologies*. This enables rules to have access to the Description Logic ontological definitions of the vocabulary primitives used by the rules. In this way OWLRuleML rules can reference OWL ontologies. The names of predicates in the OWLRuleML rules are URI's that link to classes and properties in an OWL ontology. The OWL ontology that is referenced forms a background theory for the rulebase. In this approach, the unary and binary predicates represent, respectively, OWL classes and OWL properties. Likewise, assertions about instances of class and properties are viewed as facts.

To enable such integration it was necessary to define a intermediate knowledge representation contained within the intersection of Description Logics and Prolog. This intersection, called Description Logic Programs (DLP) [GHVD03], enables ontological definitions to be supplemented by rules. DLP provide a significant degree of expressiveness, substantially greater than the RDFS fragment of Description Logics. DLP also capture a substantial fragment of OWL, including the whole of the OWL fragment of RDFS, simple frame axioms and more expressive property axioms.

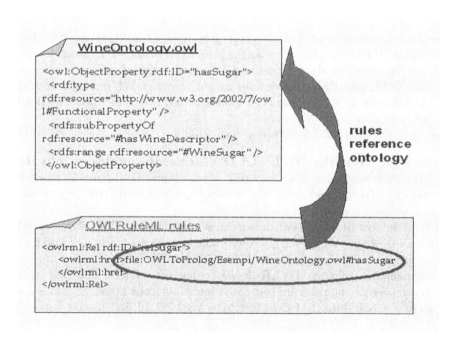

Fig. 1. Rules on top of Ontologies

4   Representation of OWL into PROLOG

The subset of OWL implemented in Prolog includes:

- RDF Schema features of OWL Lite, which provide the following primitives: *rdfs:subClassOf*, *rdfs:subPropertyOf*, *rdfs:domain* and *rdfs:range* (T-box axioms);
- Transitivity of *rdfs:subclass* and *rdfs:subProperties* relationships;
- Equality of classes, properties and individuals of OWL: *owl:equivalentClass*, *owl:equivalentProperty*, *owl:sameIndividualAs* and *owl:sameAs*;
- All property characteristics;
- Cardinality constraints with minimum cardinality 0 and maximum cardinality 1. This is equivalent to defining a property as functional;
- Range restrictions on properties: *owl:allValuesFrom* and *owl:hasValue*;
- Conjunction of classes;
- Construction of classes by enumeration;

5   Implementation

SweetProlog, which stands for *Semantic WEb Enabling Technologies for Prolog*, is a system for the interoperability of rules between RuleML and Prolog. The idea of SweetProlog follows the approach of another existent project SweetJess [GGF03], which it is a system for interoperability of rules between RuleML and Jess.

SweetProlog is implemented in Java and makes use of three languages: Prolog as a rule engine, OWL as a ontology language and OWLRuleML as a rule language that reasons over the data model of OWL, and a set of inference rules that translate OWL into Prolog. It enables reasoning over OWL ontologies by rules via a translation of OWL subsets into simple Prolog predicates which a JIProlog engine[2] can understand and process.

SweetProlog consists of five principal functions:

1. **Translation of the OWL and OWLRuleML ontologies into RDF triples:** SweetProlog reads an OWL ontology and OWLRuleML rules, and extracts RDF triples[3] out of the ontologies, where each RDF triple consists of a subject, a predicate, and a object.
2. **Translation of the OWL assertions into Prolog:** The extracted RDF triples that represent OWL concepts and instances are translated into Prolog predicates via the mapping defined in Section 4.
3. **Translation of the OWLRuleML rules into CLP:** The RDF triples that represent the rules are translated into Courteous Logic Programs rules, more precisely into IBM CommonRules V3.0 "SCLPfile" format [4].

---

[2] http://www.ugosweb.com/jiprolog/index.shtml
[3] http://www-db.stanford.edu/ melnik/rdf/api.html
[4] http://alphaworks.ibm.com/tech/commonrules.

4. **Transformation of CLP Rules into Prolog:** The rules are transformed by a Courteous Compiler into Prolog rules.
5. **Interrogation of the output logic programs:** Finally, the translated predicates are then fed into the working memory of a JIProlog engine and it is able to infer new knowledge.

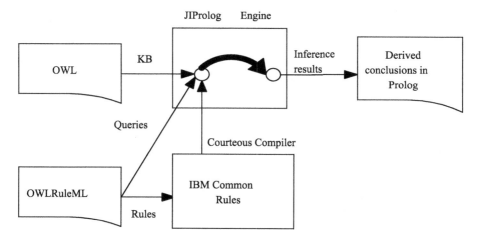

Fig. 2. Architecture of SweetProlog

Example

We consider a wine ontology, which is constituted of 91 concepts and 14 properties and is designed to find suitable wines for particular dishes. For brevity and ease of human-readability, we define our example rules in a Prolog-like syntax:

- pastaWithSpicyRedSouce(X) :- hasColour (X, Red), hasFlavor(X,Moderate), hasSugar(X,Dry), hasBody(X, Medium).
- pastaWithCreamSouce(X) :- hasColour(X,White), hasFlavor(X,Strong), hasSugar(X, Dry), hasBody(X, Full).

SweetProlog is able to derive the following new facts:

pastaWithRedSouce(file:OWLToProlog/Esempi/WineOntology.owl#SaucelitoCanyonZinfarel1998).
pastaWithRedSouce(file:OWLToProlog/Esempi/WineOntology.owl#WhitehallLaneCabernetFranc).
pastaWithRedSouce(file:OWLToProlog/Esempi/WineOntology.owl#MariettaPetiteSyrah).
pastaWithRedSouce(file:OWLToProlog/Esempi/WineOntology.owl#MariettaCabernetSauvignon).
pastaWithRedSouce(file:OWLToProlog/Esempi/WineOntology.owl#PageMillVineryCabernetSauvignon).
pastaWithRedSouce(file:OWLToProlog/Esempi/WineOntology.owl#SaucelitoCanyonZinfarel).
pastaWithRedSouce(file:OWLToProlog/Esempi/WineOntology.owl#MariettaZinfadel).
pastaWithRedSouce(file:OWLToProlog/Esempi/WineOntology.owl#MountadamPinotNoir). pastaW-
ithRedSouce(file:OWLToProlog/Esempi/WineOntology.owl#GaryFarrellMerlot).
pastaWithRedSouce(file:OWLToProlog/Esempi/WineOntology.owl#ChiantiClassico).
pastaWithRedSouce(file:OWLToProlog/Esempi/WineOntology.owl#SaucelitoCanyonZinfarel1998).
pastaWithCreamSouce(file:OWLToProlog/Esempi/WineOntology.owl#MountadamChardonnay).

6   Conclusions

We have presented an approach for adding a rule layer on top of the ontology layer of the Semantic Web. This approach develops Grosof and Horrocks' idea of specifying RuleML rules *on top of* OWL ontologies, suggesting a mapping of a Description Logic subset (OWL) into Logic Programs (Prolog). This intersection of DL with LP (Description Logic Programs) covers RDF Schema and a significant fragment of OWL.

The prototype realized, called SweetProlog, provides semantic and inferential interoperation between ontologies and rules. An immediate result of this project is that it possible to reason over the instances of an ontology within rule definitions that use vocabulary from these ontologies using a Prolog engine, thus through backward chaining. This is an initial step to layer rules on top of ontological languages, as proposed by the vision of the Semantic Web.

References

[Ant02] G. Antoniou. A nonmonotonic rule system using ontologies. In *Proceedings of the International Workshop on Rule Markup Languages for Business Rules on the Semantic Web*, 2002.

[BLHL01] T. Berners-Lee, J. Hendler, and O. Lassila. The semantic web. *Scientific American*, 2001. http://www.sciam.com/2001/0501issue/0501berners.

[BTW01] H. Boley, S. Tabet, and G. Wagner. Design rationale of RuleML: A markup language for semantic web rules. In *International Semantic Web Working Symposium (SWWS)*, 2001.

[CM87] W.F. Clocksin and C.S. Mellish. Programing in Prolog. Springer-Verlag, Berlin, 1987.

[DSHHHMPS03] M. Dean, G. Schreiber, F. van Harmelen, J. Hendler, I. Horrocks, D. McGuinness, P. Patel-Schneider, and L. Stein. OWL Web Ontology Language Reference. http://www.w3.org/TR/2003/WD-owl-ref-20030331/.

[GGF03] Benjamin N. Grosof, Mahesh D. Gandhe, and Timothy W. Finin. SweetJess: Inferencing in situated courteous ruleml via translation to and from jess rules. Working paper, May 2, 2003. http://ebusiness.mit.edu/bgrosof/.

[GHVD03] Benjamin N. Grosof, Ian Horrocks, Raphael Volz, and Stefan Decker. Description logic programs: Combining logic programs with description logic. In *Proc. of the Twelfth International World Wide Web Conference (WWW 2003)*, pages 48–57. ACM, 2003.

[Gro97] B. Grosof. Courteous logic programs: Prioritized conflict handling for rules. Technical report, IBM Research Report RC 20836, Dec. 30 1997, revised from May 8 1997.

[Gro99] B. Grosof. A courteous compiler from generalized courteous logic programs to ordinary logic programs (Preliminary Report). Technical report, IBM T.J. Watson Research Center, http://www.research.ibm.com/people/g/grosof/papers.html,July 1999.

[Gro03] Benjamin N. Grosof. SweetDeal: Representing Agent Contracts with Exceptions using XML Rules, Ontologies, and Process Descriptions. In *Proceedings of the twelfth international conference on World Wide Web*, Budapest, Hungary, 2003.

SWRLp: An XML-Based SWRL Presentation Syntax

Christopher J. Matheus

Versatile Information Systems, Inc.
Framingham, Massachusetts U.S.A.
cmatheus@vistology.com
http://www.vistology.com

Abstract. This paper introduces an XML presentation syntax, SWRLp, that facilitates the reading and editing of SWRL rules. A description of the language design and motivation is presented along with a simple example of the improvement afforded in rule readability by the use of SWRLp. XSLT transformation scripts for translating to and from SWRLp and SWRL, RuleML, pseudo-Prolog and Jess are also described.

1   Introduction

Although RuleML has been around for a number of years and is enjoying a growing popularity as a standard XML-based rule representation language it continues to evolve. One branch in this evolution is SWRL, the Semantic Web Rule Language recently introduced as a way to integrate rules with OWL DL ontologies. Whereas RuleML is designed to be flexible and all encompassing, SWRL was purposely constrained so as to retain many of the attractive computational characteristics of OWL DL. One of these characteristics is the restriction to unary- and binary-termed user-defined predicates. While this constraint does not limit the logical statements that can be represented by SWRL it does add significantly to the complexity and readability of rules. In addition, aspects of the SWRL XML Concrete Syntax (SWRLx), such as the manner in which properties are specified within attributes, exacerbate the problem of reading and editing SWRL rules. While one might argue that SWRL rules are intended for machine consumption rather than human processing it is the case that until more powerful graphical editors are available for SWRL most SWRL rules sets will be written and maintained using text editors. This paper proposes an XML presentation syntax for SWRL intended to ease human reading and editing of SWRL rules. It begins with the presentation of a simple rule and demonstrates the increasing complexity encountered as one moves from pseudo-Prolog syntax to RuleML syntax to SWRLx syntax. The next section introduces the proposed presentation syntax, SWRLp and discusses the set of conventions that are needed to permit its simplified structure. In concluding, several XSLT scripts are described that were written to translate between the presentation syntax and SWRLx, RuleML, Jess and pseudo-Prolog syntax.

G. Antoniou and H. Boley (Eds.): RuleML 2004, LNCS 3323, pp. 194–199, 2004.

2   Representations of a Simple Rule

Assume we have a set of rules defining knowledge pertinent to the domain of supply logistics. Included among these will be rules that capture the basic notion of what it means for a consumer to be "in supply of" a given resource at a given point in time. Let us define the predicate representing this notion to be `inSupplyOfAt(_,_,_)` with the three ordered arguments representing the `consumer`, the `resource` and the `time`. Assume we wish to state that a consumer is in supply of a resource at a particular time if it has sufficient reserves of that resource to meet its expected consumption per interval of time. One way to capture this knowledge is with the following pseudo-Prolog rule:

```
inSupplyOfAt(Consumer,Resource,Time) :-
    reserve(Consumer,Resource,Time,Reserve)
    consumption(Consumer,Resource,Consumption)
    greaterThanOrEqual(Reserve,Consumption).
```

The first line of the pseudo-code represents the head of the rule (i.e., the consequence) and the subsequent lines capture the rule's body (i.e., the antecedent). The `reserve` predicate binds the quantity of a particular `resource` held in by the `consumer` at the specified `time`. The `consumption` predicate binds the quantity of consumption of the resource by the consumer for a unit interval of time. The `greaterThanOrEqual` predicate returns true if the amount in `reserve` is greater than or equal to the amount of `consumption`. This pseudo-Prolog representation of our sample rule can be easily translated into the following RuleML representation:

```
<imp> <_head> <atom>
  <_opr><rel>inSupplyOfAt</rel></_opr>
  <var>?consumer</var>
  <var>?resource</var>
  <var>?time</var></atom> </_head>
 <_body> <and> <atom>
   <_opr><rel>reserve</rel></_opr>
   <var>?consumer</var>
   <var>?resource</var>
   <var>?time</var> </atom>
  <atom>
   <_opr><rel>consumption</rel></_opr>
   <var>?consumer</_var>
   <var>?resource</_var>
   <var>?consumption</_var> </atom>
  <atom>
   <_opr><rel>greaterThanOrEqual</rel></__opr>
   <var>?reserve</var>
   <_var>?consumption</var> </_atom>
 </_and></_body> </_imp>
```

The `imp` tag contains the specification of a single rule comprised of a `head` and a `body` that are in turn made up of **atom**s consisting (in this case) of relational operands (`<_opr><rel>`) with variables (`<var>`) as arguments. Clearly, this representation is more verbose and not as easy to take in at a glance as is the pseudo-Prolog code. Though more cumbersome, the basic logical structure of the rule remains intact and apart from the verbose syntax the rule is readily comprehensible. While it would be somewhat tedious to write and maintain this rule with a text processor, it is not a terribly onerous task for someone well versed in XML and RuleML.

To represent this same rule in SWRLx requires some additional transformations, both syntactic and structural. First, the three-termed predicates in the rule must be converted into binary predicates as SWRL's conformance to OWL prohibits the use of user defined higher-order predicates. It is always possible to convert rules with higher-order predicates into rules with only binary predicates through the introduction of reified variables that carry along the additional terms as property values (described below). Unfortunately this process changes the basic structure of the rule and adds considerably to its length and complexity, as evidenced in the rule's SWRLx representation shown below. Second, the SWRLx syntax distinguishes between predicates representing OWL class individuals representing object properties and those representing datatype properties. This requirement means that different XML elements must be used depending upon the nature of the particular predicate being used (i.e., `<swrlx:classAtom>` for class individuals, `<swrlx:individual PropertyAtom>` for object properties and `<swrlx:datavaluePropertyValue>` for datatype properties). Having this additional semantic information embedded in the element's name might prove useful to the reader unfamiliar with the ontologies used in the rules but it also forces the reader to spend additional cognitive effort in parsing the rules. Third, SWRLx intermixes elements from the ruleml, swrlx, swrlb and owlx namespace. One consequence of this that namespace prefixes must be used on all element names. In RuleML there is only a single namespace, which means namespace prefixes can be omitted from element names rendering them a bit more readable and concise.

Collectively, these requirements of SWRLx render the relatively simple original rule into the following complex and much more difficult to read representation:

```
<ruleml:imp> <ruleml:_head>
    <swrlx:classAtom>
       <owlx:Class owlx:name="InSupplyOfAt"/>
       <ruleml:var>?reifiedRelation</ruleml:var>
    </swrlx:classAtom>
    <swrlx:individualPropertyAtom swrlx:property="consumer">
       <ruleml:var>?reifiedRelation</ruleml:var>
       <ruleml:var>?consumer</ruleml:var>
    </swrlx:individualPropertyAtom>
    <swrlx:individualPropertyAtom swrlx:property="resource">
       <ruleml:var>?reifiedRelation</ruleml:var>
       <ruleml:var>?resource</ruleml:var>
    </swrlx:individualPropertyAtom>
    <swrlx:datavaluedPropertyAtom swrlx:property="dateTime">
      <ruleml:var>?reifiedRelation</ruleml:var>
      <ruleml:var>?time</ruleml:var>
    </swrlx:datavaluedPropertyAtom> </ruleml:_head>
  <ruleml:_body>
    <swrlx:individualPropertyAtom swrlx:property="reserve">
       <ruleml:var>?consumer</ruleml:var>
       <ruleml:var>?reserve</ruleml:var>
    </swrlx:individualPropertyAtom>
    <swrlx:individualPropertyAtom swrlx:property="resource">
       <ruleml:var>?reserve</ruleml:var>
       <ruleml:var>?resource</ruleml:var>
    </swrlx:individualPropertyAtom>
```

```
<swrlx:datavaluedPropertyAtom swrlx:property="dateTime">
  <ruleml:var>?reserve</ruleml:var>
  <ruleml:var>?time</ruleml:var>
</swrlx:datavaluedPropertyAtom>
<swrlx:individualPropertyAtom swrlx:property="quantity">
  <ruleml:var>?reserve</ruleml:var>
  <ruleml:var>?quantity</ruleml:var>
</swrlx:individualPropertyAtom>
<swrlx:datavaluedPropertyAtom swrlx:property="amount">
  <ruleml:var>?quantity</ruleml:var>
  <ruleml:var>?amount</ruleml:var>
</swrlx:datavaluedPropertyAtom>
<swrlx:individualPropertyAtom swrlx:property="consumption">
  <ruleml:var>?consumer</ruleml:var>
  <ruleml:var>?consumption</ruleml:var>
</swrlx:individualPropertyAtom>
<swrlx:individualPropertyAtom swrlx:property="consumptionType">
  <ruleml:var>?consumption</ruleml:var>
  <ruleml:var>?resource</ruleml:var>
</swrlx:individualPropertyAtom>
<swrlx:datavaluedPropertyAtom swrlx:property="consumptionRate">
  <ruleml:var>?consumption</ruleml:var>
  <ruleml:var>?rate</ruleml:var>
</swrlx:datavaluedPropertyAtom>
<swrlx:builtinAtom swrlx:builtin="&swrlb;greaterThanOrEqual">
  <ruleml:var>?amount</ruleml:var>
  <ruleml:var>?rate</ruleml:var>
  <ruleml:var/>
</swrlx:builtinAtom>
</ruleml:_body> </ruleml:imp>
```

Whereas we have a single predicate in the head of the pseudo-Prolog and RuleML rules, the SWRLx rule head has four predicates. Similarly, the pseudo-Prolog and RuleML rule bodies contained just three predicates each while the SWRLx rule body consists of nine. This expansion is the result of having to convert the three-term predicates in the original rule into sets of binary predicates. To see how this took place consider the predicate in the head of the rule. To capture the three terms a new class was created in the ontology (not shown) called InSupplyOfAt and three properties were associated with it, each corresponding to one of the terms consumer, resource and time. An instance of this class is created in the head in the first predicate and the three properties are then associated with variables that become bound when the predicates in the body are satisfied. Note also that this same reified-object technique is employed in the body although in this case the objects are not create but are expected to be found in the working memory of the inference engine.

Counting the number of lines required for the SWRLx rule we find an expansion factor of around 15 times relative to the pseudo-Prolog code and approximately two times over the RuleML code. Add to this the additional cognitive processing required to parse the various predicate types and namespace elements and it is undeniably the case that the SWRLx rule is significantly more difficult to construct and maintain. The author's first hand experience with writing this rule is what led to the development of SWRLp.

3   SWRLp

The best way to introduce SWRLp is with consideration of the code that captures the sample supply logistics rule:

```
<rule><head>
  <InSupplyOfAt          indv="?reifiedRelation"                      />
  <consumer              subj="?reifiedRelation" objt="?consumer"/>
  <resource              subj="?reifiedRelation" objt="?resource"/>
  <dateTime              subj="?reifiedRelation" data="?time"/> </head>
 <body>
  <reserve               subj="?consumer"        objt="?reserve"/>
  <resource              subj="?reserve"         objt="?resource"/>
  <dateTime              subj="?reserve"         data="?time"/>
  <quantity              subj="?reserve"         objt="?quantity"/>
  <amount                subj="?quantity"        data="?amount"/>
  <consumption           subj="?consumer"        objt="?consumption"/>
  <consumptionType       subj="?consumption"     objt="?resource"/>
  <consumptionRate       subj="?consumption"     data="?rate"/>
  <greaterThanOrEqual arg1="?amount"             arg2="?rate"/>
 </body> </rule>
```

Like SWLRx, SWRLp is XML-based but all of the pertinent information about the predicates and terms has been moved into element names and attribute values – note that except for the rule, head and body tags, all elements are empty. The advantage this affords is that it flattens the structure of the code and permits each predicate to fit on a single line making it significant easier to parse and permitting a grasp of the overall structure in a single glance. This format very closely approximates the code that would result if pseudo-Prolog syntax were used to represent the binary-predicate-restricted version of the rule (i.e., what the pseudo-Prolog rules would look like if higher-order predicates were transformed into binary predicates). This in fact was the intent: to make the rules as concise and readable as the pseudo-Prolog syntax to the extent permissible under the language constraints of XML.

Aside from the desire to make the rules highly readable it was also critical that they capture all information required to be able to generate the corresponding SWRLx code. The major technique used to achieve this was the use of different attribute names to distinguish the various types of SWRLx predicates. If an element has subj (subject) and objt (object) attributes it represents a swrlx:individualPropertyAtom; if it has subj and data attributes it is a swrlx:datavaluePropertyAtom; if it has an indv attribute it is a swrlx:ClassAtom.; if it has one or more attributes beginning with "arg" it is a swrlx:builtinAtom. Another simplifying technique assumes the convention that all variables begin with a question mark. With this assumption it is possible to encode all terms as non-structured values thereby permitting them to be used as attribute values.

To illustrate how these techniques are employed let us walk through their applicaption to the first predicate. The element's name is "InSupplyOfAt" and it has a single indv attribute. Because of this indv attribute we know it is a swrlx:ClassAtom definition and since the value of the indv attribute begins with a question mark we know it is a variable. These pieces of information are sufficient to be able to generate the following SWRLx coded needed to represent the predicate:

```
<swrlx:classAtom>
  <owlx:Class owlx:name="InSupplyOfAt"/>
  <ruleml:var>?reifiedRelation</ruleml:var>
</swrlx:classAtom>
```

4   XSLT Translations

SWRLp by itself would not be very useful if it were not possible to translate it into forms that can be directly used by other tools, reasoning systems or humans. A number of XSLT scripts have been written to perform these translations as illustrated in Figure 1.

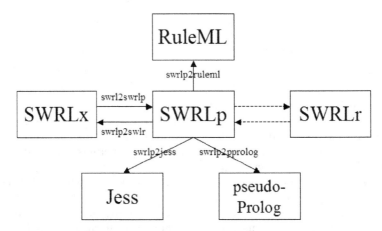

Fig. 1. Translations between rule representation syntaxes. Solid arrows represent translations implemented as XSLT scripts; dotted lines represent possible future scripts.

The two primary scripts (swrl2swrlp and swrlp2swrl) translate between SWRLx and SWRLp. Two additional scripts were developed to generate pseudo-Prolog and RuleML code from SWRLp more for completeness than any other reason. Since we use Jess as an engine for running our rules the swrlp2jess script for generating Jess rules from SWRLp was developed out of necessity. Note that while we could developed a script to go from SWRLx directly into Jess the script for going from SWRLp to Jess is actually quite a bit simpler to write. If and when SWRLr (SWRL RDF Concrete Syntax) becomes widely used it will be possible to write scripts to convert between it and SWRLp.

XET as a Rule Language for Consistency Maintenance in UML

Nimit Pattanasri[1], Vilas Wuwongse[1], and Kiyoshi Akama[2]

[1] Computer Science & Information Management Program,
Asian Institute of Technology, Pathumthani 12120, Thailand
{a028250,vw}@cs.ait.ac.th
[2] Hokkaido University, Kita 11, Nishi 5, Kita-ku, Sapporo, 060-0811, Japan
akama@cims.hokudai.ac.jp

Abstract. Although XET is a powerful rule language, a mechanism to provide an automatic update on an XML document according to monitored events cannot be realized easily under the common use of XET. Proposed in the paper is a simple XML-expression transformation by XET enabling applications to perform update actions on an XML document when an event is detected. As a case study, it will be shown that XET is capable of maintaining consistency between UML diagrams. The capabilities include inconsistency detection according to user changes and automatic resolution process.

1 XET

XML Equivalent Transformation (XET) [2] is a new paradigm of programming languages, which is based on an efficient computing paradigm namely *Equivalent Transformation* (ET) [1] and XML serving as the standard for data representation. An XET program consists of a set of XET rules, each of which is used to specify a transformation of a given problem into a simpler one while preserving the semantics of the problem. Basic concepts are explained first in order to understand XET. An *XML expression* is an XML element that can carry variables to represent implicit information and to enhance XML elements' expressive power, e.g., an E-variable (Evar) can represent a sequence of XML expressions, and an S-variable (Svar) can represent a string. An *XML clause* is of the form: $H \leftarrow B_1, ..., B_n$ where n≥0, and H and B_i are XML expressions. A logical reading of the form is: H is true if $B_1, ..., B_n$ are all true. In general, a given problem is formulated in terms of an XML clause which will be transformed step by step into a simpler one by XET rules. For simplicity, a limited class of XET rules is shown: *Head*, {*Condition*} $\Longrightarrow$ {*Execution*}, *Body*. which has the meaning:

```
A target XML expression (in the body of a clause) that is matched by
Head (an XML expression) will be transformed to Body (a sequence of
XML expressions) if Condition (a sequence of XML expressions) is
satisfied. After transformation, Execution (a sequence of XML
expressions) will be executed if it exists.
```

G. Antoniou and H. Boley (Eds.): RuleML 2004, LNCS 3323, pp. 200–204, 2004.

The contributions of this paper are twofold. First, a simple XML-expression transformation by XET is proposed. This serves as an important mechanism for a variety of applications that update XML documents when events are detected. Second, in order to demonstrate its usefulness, a new application to the consistency problem in UML is also presented. Section 2 presents a simple XML-expression transformation by XET, Section 3 demonstrates an application to consistency maintenance in UML, Section 4 discusses related work, and Section 5 proposes future work.

2   A Simple XML-Expression Transformation by XET

In Fig. 1 (a), a query clause $P_1 \leftarrow P_1$ (representing a problem) is first formulated and transformed step by step according to predefined XET rules until an answer is reached. In general, P_1 contains implicit information (variables) which will be specialized step by step during the execution of XET until a unit clause is obtained, i.e., the body of a clause disappears, and all variables are finally specialized. In short, P_1 is specialized until it becomes P_1', which is an answer. This is considered *general problem transformation* by XET.

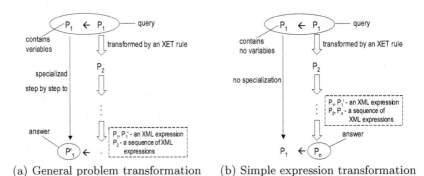

(a) General problem transformation   (b) Simple expression transformation

Fig. 1. Problem transformation by XET

By the general transformation, an answer is derived from the head of a clause only when a unit clause is obtained. Consider Fig. 1 (b), which is a special case of the general transformation where an answer can be directly obtained from the body of a non-unit clause. Given a query clause $P_1 \leftarrow P_1$, it will be transformed repeatedly by XET rules until no rule is applicable. In this case, P_n cannot be further transformed. As a result, a non-unit clause $P_1 \leftarrow P_n$ whose body is an answer is obtained. This is considered *simple XML-expression transformation* by XET. In this way, XET rules will be more comprehensible in the sense that they reflect explicitly results of computation (transformation).

Before the rule specification is proposed, an important term is introduced in order to represent a change in an XML document. An *explicit change* is an XML

element containing a special attribute, named *delta*, providing change information. It is used to represent a change in an XML document explicitly. Possible
values of the attribute are *added*, *deleted*, and *modified*. Events and actions on
an XML document, namely *adding*, *deleting*, or *modifying* XML elements, are
represented by explicit changes.

The rule specification which supports a mechanism to provide actions on an
XML document (when an event is detected) is:

$$Head\,,\ \{Condition\}\ ==>\ Body.$$

Head is an XML expression representing a pattern of an XML document before
applying with actions. *Condition* is a sequence of XML expressions specifying
conditions (e.g. inconsistency conditions) for rule execution. *Body* is an XML
expression representing a pattern of an XML document after applying with actions. Monitored events are specified in either *Head* or *Condition*, and actions
are specified in *Body*. Compared to ECA rules in active databases [4], the proposed rule is more general in the sense that an event part or a condition part
can be omitted in the rule. In other words, an ECA rule is just a special case of
the proposed rule.

3   An Application to Consistency Maintenance in UML

Typically, most CASE tools can detect and resolve (syntactical) inconsistency
in UML diagrams. Nevertheless, such a process is hard-code and not customizable. This sometimes impedes users who need more freedom in design. Therefore,
a static (or batch) consistency check that is customizable is proposed. Due to
space limitation, the approach to consistency maintenance in UML is described
through a concrete example. Assume in the following that user changes are correct. Given UML diagrams ver.1 in Fig. 2 that are consistent, one realizes that
an operation *b02* is not used any longer. Therefore, it can be deleted without an
effect to the sequence diagram being recognized. At the same time, due to an
additional requirement, a message *b03* is added to the sequence diagram without defining the corresponding operation in class *B*. As a result, inconsistency
arises in the modified diagrams (ver.2), i.e., the messages *b02* and *b03* have no
corresponding operations in class *B*. After maintained by the XET approach,
the diagrams ver.2' are obtained as the result. Figure 3 shows consistency rules
and transformation of the modified diagrams (ver.1 + user changes). Rule A is
stated that a message will be deleted if such a message corresponds to a deleted
operation. Rule B is stated that a new operation will be added to a class if there
is no corresponding operation for an added message. The diagrams ver.1 containing user changes, i.e. the deleted operation *b02* and the added message *b03*,
are represented by an XML document, which can be obtained from calculating
differences between two versions of the diagrams.

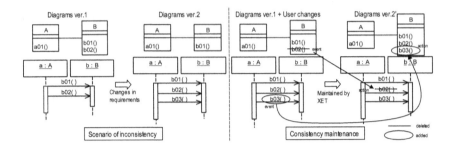

Fig. 2. Resolving inconsistency by the XET approach

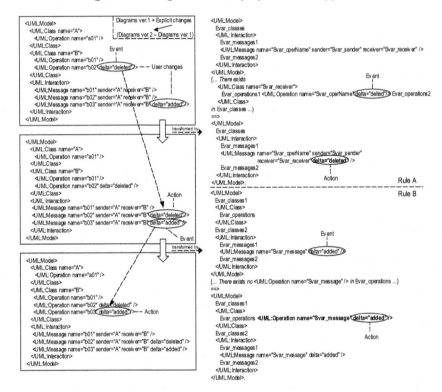

Fig. 3. Consistency rules and their execution (transformation)

4   Related Work

xlinkit [7] is a rule language based on the first order logic for expressing constraints between documents. It uses XPath to select (UML) elements to be examined, and then generates a set of links providing consistency information. Proposed in [3] is a UML model-based approach to impact analysis that can be applied before any implementation of changes. In this case, OCL is used to select impacted UML elements according to (user) changes in UML diagrams. The present work is similar to these works in the sense that it is a static (or batch) checking approach. Nevertheless, both XPath and OCL are just the query languages; they are not capable of providing repair actions on UML diagrams (XML document). In addition to the issue of rule languages, (user) changes in UML diagrams can also be notified directly by a CASE tool as real-time event changes, which allow dynamic consistency check [5,8]. However, those approaches must know the implementation inside and rely on a specific CASE tool, which can be considered CASE tool dependent.

5   Future Work

A prototype system will be implemented. Two versions of UML diagrams are the input of the system. Diagrams containing explicit changes are produced by DeltaXML [6]. After that, such diagrams are sent to the XET system, and will be transformed according to a set of predefined XET rules. Finally, the system produces (a set of) consistent diagrams as the result. In addition to the system implementation, composite events as well as complex actions will also be studied.

References

1. Akama, K., Shimitsu, T., Miyamoto, E. Solving Problems by Equivalent Transformation of Declarative Programs. J. Japanese Society of Artificial Intelligence, Vol.13 No. 6, pp. 944–952 (1998)
2. Anutariya, C., Wuwongse, V., and Wattanapailin, V. An Equivalent-Transformation-Based XML Rule Language. Proc. International Workshop on Rule Markup Languages for Business Rules in the Semantic Web (2002)
3. Briand, L. C., Labiche, Y., O'Sullivan, L. Impact Analysis and Change Management of UML Models. Proc. of the Int. Conference on Software Maintenance (2003)
4. Lewis, P.M., Bernstein, A., and Kifer, M. Databases and Transaction Processing: An Application-Oriented Approach. Addison Wesley. (2001)
5. Liu, W., Easterbrook, S., and Mylopoulos, J. Rule Based detection of Inconsistency in UML Models. Workshop on Consistency Problems in UML-based Software Development, 106-123. (2002)
6. Monsell EDM Ltd, Malvern, UK. DeltaXML.
7. Nentwich, C., Emmerich, W., and Finkelstein, A. Ellmer, E. Flexible Consistency Checking. ACM Transactions on Software Engineering and Methodology (TOSEM), 12(1) (2003) 28–63
8. Wagner R., Giese H., Nickel, U. A. A Plug-In for Flexible and Incremental Consistency Management. Workshop on Consistency Problems in UML-based Software Development II, 78-85. (2003)

A System for Automated Agent Negotiation with Defeasible Logic-Based Strategies – Preliminary Report

Thomas Skylogiannis[1], Grigoris Antoniou[2], and Nick Bassiliades[3]

[1] Department of Computer Science, University of Crete
P.O. Box 2208, GR-71409 Herakleion Greece
dogjohn@csd.uoc.gr
[2] Institute of Computer Science, FO.R.T.H
P.O. Box 1385, GR 71110, Herakleion Greece
antoniou@ics.forth.gr
[3] Department of Informatics, Aristotle University of Thessaloniki
GR-54124. Thessaloniki, Greece
nbassili@csd.auth.gr

Abstract. This paper reports on a system for automated agent negotiation. The negotiation strategies are expressed in defeasible logic, and are applied using the implemented reasoning system DR-DEVICE. The overall system architecture is described, and a particular 1-1 negotiation scenario is presented in detail.

1 Introduction

In the last few years, there has been a great interest in electronic commerce potential. As the number of transactions carried out through the Internet increases, the interest for partial or full automation of these transactions, increases as well [1], [2]. This automation is achieved by the use of software agents. A basic stage of e-commerce procedure that can be automated is the negotiation step.

The focus of our work is on the automated negotiation aspect of e-commerce. As stated in [18], *Automated Negotiation* is the process by which two or more agents communicate and try to come to a mutually acceptable agreement on some matter. The basic dimensions of automated negotiation are negotiation protocols and negotiation strategies. *Negotiation Protocol* is a set of rules which govern the interaction and a *negotiation strategy* is a decision making model, which participants employ in order to achieve their goal, in line with the negotiation protocol.

The use of defeasible logic as a formal framework to model protocols and strategies for automated negotiation, seems to be a promising solution. In [9] defeasible logic is used for the modelling of a simple bargaining strategy and the English auction protocol. Also, a brokering scenario is examined and the strategy of a buyer who seeks to buy a yacht via a broker is presented. Lastly, a bargaining scenario with multiple parties is examined. Our work builds upon the work of [9]. However, we go a step further as we implement a system for automated negotiation based on agent technology.

G. Antoniou and H. Boley (Eds.): RuleML 2004, LNCS 3323, pp. 205–213, 2004.

The paper is organized as follows. Section 2 provides a short discussion of defeasible logics. Section 3 provides some details of the technologies used for implementation, while sections 4-6 illustrate the functionality and use of the system based on a concrete case.

2   On Defeasible Logic

Defeasible reasoning is a simple rule-based approach to reasoning with incomplete and inconsistent information. It can represent facts, rules, and priorities among rules. This reasoning family comprises defeasible logics [14,16] and Courteous Logic Programs [15]. This approach has the following characteristics: a) They are rule-based, without disjunction b) Classical negation is used in the heads and bodies of rules, but negation-as-failure is not necessarily used in the object language (it can easily be simulated, if necessary [17]) c) Rules may support conflicting conclusions d) The logics are skeptical in the sense that conflicting rules do not fire. Thus consistency is preserved e) Priorities on rules may be used to resolve some conflicts among rules f) Finally, the logics take a pragmatic view and have low computational complexity.

The above properties, make this family a good candidate to be used on the Semantic Web, as well as to be used in applications where timely response is essential. Automated agent negotiations, e.g. as part of e-Commerce scenarios, is such an application. Generally speaking, defeasible logics have two kinds of rules: *strict rules* which behave like standard, classical rules (once their premises are satisfied they fire) and *defeasible rules*, which may not fire even when their premises are satisfied, because they are blocked by other rules. More complex logics have a further kind of rules, so-called defeaters.

At this point we must justify the choice of defeasible logic among various schemes for representing strategies and protocols. Firstly is *formal*, that is, its semantics and syntax are properly defined. This means that both humans and computers can interpret them the same way. Another characteristic of defeasible logic is that it is *conceptual* meaning that offers a good level of abstraction. So anyone can focus only on protocol or strategy design, being indifferent to the implementation. Defeasible logic is also *comprehensible* and *expressive* as well. The latter is very important because enables us to describe a wide range of protocols and strategies. Lastly, if there is a defeasible logic inference engine available it is also *executable*.

3   Implementation Details

In this section, we discuss some basic terms with regard to agent technology and multi-agent systems and subsequently, we describe the architecture of our agent which is a defeasible logic-based intelligent agent.

Agent Technology

As we have already stated, a tool is needed for the automation of the negotiation process. It has been proved that agent-based technology constantly evolves, offering a promising technology for this purpose [1], [2]. The last few years, a terminology relevant to agent technology has started to be used. In [3], the following terms regarding agent technology are being recognized: *Agent Architectures, Agent System Architectures, Agent Frameworks* and finally *Agent Infrastructures.* Agent Architectures describe agents as separate entities, consisting of three basic modules named perception, reasoning and action module. Agent System Architectures define the interaction of agents under constraints. Agent Frameworks are sets of tools and integrated environments, for the development of agents and multi-agent systems (see [4] for a survey). Finally Agent Infrastructures, provide means for agent communication and common understandings of various concepts. Their basic components are *ontologies, interaction protocols, communication languages* and *communication infrastructures.* Ontologies are formal specifications which describe concepts, their properties and relations in a particular domain of interest. Agent Communication Languages (ACLs) provide agents with means of exchanging information and knowledge [5]. Interaction Protocols are the rules which enable agents to reason over the effects of their communications [6]. Finally, Communication Infrastructures provide communication channels among agents.

Implemented Agent Architecture

The *Agent Framework* we used was Jade [7], [8]. Jade is an open-source middleware for the development of distributed multi-agent applications based on the peer-to-peer communication architecture. Jade is java-based and compliant with the FIPA specification. It provides libraries for agent communication and interaction, based on FIPA standards. Jade provided us with the *Agent Infrastructure* we desired. In our case, there is no *Agent System Architecture* as we only have implemented a demonstrator and not a complete multi-agent system.

The *Agent Architecture* we implemented was primarily based on the architecture proposed by Dumas et al.[9]. Particularly, an agent consists of four components: a) A memory which contains past decisions and interactions (Knowledge Base), b) A communication module which handles incoming and outcoming messages (Jade platform), c) A reasoning module (DR-Device Inference Engine) d) A control module for the coordination of the above components (script in Java).

For the reasoning module of the agent we used DR-Device [12]. DR-Device is a defeasible reasoning system. Its user interface is compatible with RuleML, the main standardization effort for rules on the semantic web and is based on a CLIPS-based implementation of deductive rules.

The architecture of the negotiating agent is depicted in Fig.1. When the agent is notified of an external event, such as an incoming message (step 1), the control module initially retrieves a fact template from the local storage unit (step 2) and consequently, the negotiation parameters from the memory (step 3). The template is an empty placeholder in line with DR-Device system syntax. When the template is filled with the negotiation parameters, is then regarded as "the facts". The control module updates the knowledge base with the new facts (step 4) and then activates DR-Device (step 5). DR-Device in turn retrieves from the knowledge base the facts, along with the strategy (step 6) and starts the inferencing process. After the inferencing has been completed, the knowledge base is updated with the results (step 7). The control module queries the knowledge base for the result (step 8) and after a short processing; an appropriate message is posted to the communication module.

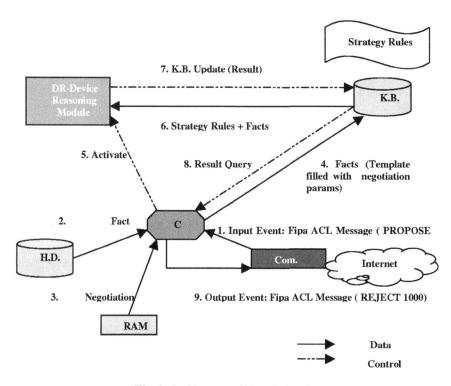

Fig. 1. Architecture of Negotiating Agent

4   The Negotiation Protocol: An Example

We implemented a negotiation protocol proposed in [10]. This protocol is a finite state machine that must be hard-coded to all agents, participating into the negotiation. The protocol is depicted in Fig. 2. S0 to S6 represent the states of a negotiation and E is the final state in which there is an agreement, or a failure of agreement between the participants. Send and Recv predicates represent the interactions which cause state transitions. We make the convention that the agent, which plays the role of the buyer starts the negotiation by posting a CFP message. So, while the protocol can be used as it is by a buyer, it needs a small modification for a seller. Particularly instead of the transition S0→ S1, there should be a transition S0→ S2 with label "Recv CFP".

5   The Negotiation Strategy: An Example

The strategy of a potential buyer or seller during a negotiation scenario is very critical for the outcome of the encounter. Every strategy is always designed in line with a particular protocol. We based the strategies we used, on the work of Tsang et al. [11]. They define the simple constrained bargaining game between one buyer and one seller. For more information about the strategy and its assumptions refer to [11]. For the buyer, participating into the negotiation, we used a modified version strategy of Tsang's et al. strategy and we expressed it in defeasible logic. For the seller, we used a strategy, hard coded in java to demonstrate that agents with diferrent architecture, can interact without any problems. Seller's strategy is quite similar with that of buyer, except for the general bidding strategy. Seller decreases his offer by a fixed amount and buyer increases it in a linear fashion. Buyer's strategy characteristics are summarized in Table 1.

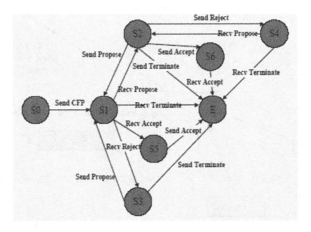

Fig. 2. A 1-1 Negotiation Protocol

Table 1. Buyer's Strategy Characteristics

Strategy Name	First Bid Algorithm	Offer-Acceptance Criterion	Last Day BiDDING	General Bid Algorithm
Simple Buyer	Utility/DTB	Counteroffer +Minimum Profit< Utility	Utility -MP	Bid half way between previous bid price and utility

For our example we expressed the strategy in a general defeasible logic format (Fig.3.), but for the implementation we used DR-Device syntax [12]. The predicates we used are the following:

- Step(s): The step of the negotiation. When a buyer or seller sends a message and then receives another one the step is increased by one
- Counteroffer(c): The offer which a buyer or seller receives from the opponent
- Min_profit(mp): The minimum profit the buyer seeks after buying the product
- Utility(u): The utility of the buyer if he buys the product

- Ttb(ttb): The time (negotiation steps) the buyer has at his disposal in order to buy the product
- State(st): The current state of the negotiation according to the protocol.
- First_bid(fb): The initial bid of the buyer
- Previous_bid(prb): The previous bid of the buyer

R1: State(st), Counteroffer(c), Min_profit(mp),Utility(u), st=2, c+mp ≤ u/2 ⇒ ACCEPT_PROPOSAL

R2: State(st), Counteroffer(c), Min_profit(mp),Utility(u), st=2, c+mp > u ⇒ ~ACCEPT_PROPOSAL

R3: State(st), st=5 ⇒ ACCEPT_PROPOSAL

R4: Step(s), Counteroffer(c), Min_profit(mp),Utility(u), First_Bid(fb), State(st), s=0 ,st=2, u/2 < c+mp ≤ u, bid=fb   ⇒PROPOSE(bid)

R5: Step(s), Ttb(ttb), State(st), Counteroffer(c), Min_profit(mp),Utility(u), First_Bid(fb), Previous_bid(prb), 0<s<ttb-1, st=2, u/2 < c+mp ≤ u, prb=0, bid=fb ⇒PROPOSE(bid)

R6: Step(s), Ttb(ttb), State(st), Counteroffer(c), Min_profit(mp),Utility(u), Previous_bid(prb), 0<s<ttb-1,st=2, u/2 < c+mp ≤ u, prb!=0, bid=(u-prb)/2+prb ⇒PRELIM_PROPOSE(bid)

R7: Step(s), Ttb(ttb), State(st), Previous_bid(prb), Utility(u), 0<s<ttb, st=3, bid=(u-prb)/2+prb⇒PRELIM_PROPOSE(bid)

R8: Min_profit(mp),Utility(u), PRELIM_PROPOSE(bid) ⇒ PROPOSE(bid)

R9: Min_profit(mp),Utility(u), PRELIM_PROPOSE(bid), bid>u-mp ⇒ ~PROPOSE(bid)

R10: Min_profit(mp),Utility(u), PRELIM_PROPOSE(bid), bid>u-mp, new_bid=utility-min_profit ⇒ PROPOSE(new_bid)

R11: Step(s), Ttb(ttb), State(st), Min_profit(mp),Utility(u), s=ttb-1, st=2, bid=utility-min_profit ⇒PROPOSE(bid)

R12: Step(s), Ttb(ttb), State(st), Min_profit(mp),Utility(u), s=ttb-1, st=3 , bid=utility-min_profit ⇒PROPOSE(bid)

R9>R8

Fig. 3. Buyer's Strategy in Defeasible Logic

Rules R1, R2, and R3 define the conditions for the acceptance or rejection of a proposal. More specific Rule R1 states that if the current state of the negotiation is S2 (agent has received a "propose" message) and if opponent's offer plus the minimum profit is less or equal to half the utility, the counteroffer is accepted in all cases. R2 describes the case in which opponent's offer plus the minimum profit is greater than his utility and the counteroffer is rejected. Finally R3 defines that if the current state of the negotiation is S5 (agent has received an "accept" message) he also sends an "accept" message. Rules R4 through rule R9 define different bidding scenarios according to the step of the negotiation. There are three levels for the bidding policy. Bidding of first step, bidding of last step and finally general bidding policy.   R4 states that if the negotiation is at state S2 and at the first step, the utility divided by the ttb is offered. Rules R5, R6, R7, R8, R9, R10, R11, R12 are the rules for the general bidding policy. According to R5 if the current state of the negotiation is S2 (Agent has received a "propose" message) *but* it has not made one, it offers the utility divided by the ttb.R6 defines that if the current state of the negotiation is S2 (agent has received a "propose" message) *and* it has made an offer in the previous step, it increases linearly its offer, which derives from the type:

$$bid = \frac{utility - previous\_bid}{2} + previous\_bid$$

R7 describes that if the current state of the negotiation is S3 (agent has received a "reject" message) it also offers the above bid. R8 defines that if R7 or R6 is true then the computed amount for the bid is to be offered. However, R9 checks if the bid to be offered is lower than the utility minus the minimum profit and if it is not, R10 is fired. Rules R9 and R10 are an additional check that ensures that the offered amount of money for the product, is not against the benefit of the buyer. Finally, rules R11 and R12 define that if the negotiation is about to terminate according to the value of ttb variable, agent offers the utility minus the minimum profit. At this point, we must say that the control and the termination condition of the negotiation process is handled by the control module and there is no rule for that purpose.

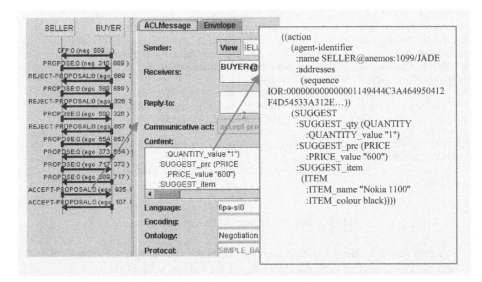

Fig. 4. An ACL Message and its Content

6 Negotiation Trace

ACL messages are built up of three layers of languages [13]. a) Elements of the world are defined in an ontology. b) An agent's intention to describe or alter the world is expressed by a communicative act or speech-act such as INFORM and c) statements about the world are expressed by means of a Content Language. In order for agents to be able to reason about the effects of their communication ,ACL messages should be inserted into proper Agent Interaction Protocol which describe allowed sequences of actions among agents.

The trace of figure 4 was taken with the help of sniffer agent, provided by Jade platform. At this time the negotiation had terminated. At the left-hand side one can see all the interactions among the buyer and the seller agent, represented by the blue arrows. We analyze the interaction which is indicated by the arrow 12 directed from the seller to buyer.The ACL which corresponds tointeraction 12, is indicated by arrow no.1. The *communicative act* (or speech-act) of this ACL message is "accept-proposal". The *ontology,* which both buyer and seller share is called "Negotiation" and the used *interaction* protocol is called "Simple-Bargaining". The used content language was FIPA SL0 and the the content of the message is indicated by arow no.2. The negotiation is about a black NOKIA1100 mobile phone, which finally seller accepts to sell to buyer for 600 money units.

7 Conclusions and Future Work

Planned future work includes: a) Designing graphical user interfaces which will enable user to enter the negotiation parameters, load the file with the strategy, adjust the speed of the negotiation process and finally graphically monitor the negotiation process b) Examining DR-Device-based representation of negotiation strategies vs. pure java hard-coded strategies. c)Implementing a semantic brokering system which will eventually integrate with the negotiation system.

References

1.   Pattie Maes, Robert H.Guttman and Alexandros G. Moukas (1999). "Agents That Buy and Sell". *Communications of the ACM Vol. 4 March 1999.*
2.   Minghua He, Nicholas R. Jennings, and Ho-Fung Leung (2003). "On Agent-Mediated Electronic Commerce". *IEEE transactions on knowledge and data engineering Vol. 15, No 4 July/August 2003.*
3.   Roberto A. Flores-Mendez (1999). "Towards a Standardization of Multi-Agent System Frameworks". *ACM Crossroads – Intelligent Agents. Summer 1999*
4.   Agent Construction Tools. http://www.agentbuilder.com/AgentTools/index.html
5.   Yannis Labrou, Tim Finin, Yun Peng (1999). "Agent Communication Languages: The current Landscape". *IEEE Intelligent Systems March/April 1999.*
6.   FIPA Interaction Protocols Specification. http://www.fipa.org/repository/ips.php3
7.   JADE Project. http://jade.cselt.it/
8.   F.Bellifemine, G Caire, A.Poggi, G. Rimassa (2003). " JADE A White Paper".*Telecom Italia EXP magazine Vol 3, No 3 September 2003*
9.   Marlon Dumas, Guido Governatori, Arthur H.M ter Hofstede, Phillipa Oaks (2002). "A Formal Approach to Negotiating Agents Development". *Elsevier Science – Electronic Commerce Research and Applications Vol.1,Issue 2 Summer 2002 pp. 193-207*
10.   Stanley Y. W. Su, Chunbo Huang and Joachim Hammer (2000). "A Replicable Web-based Negotiation Server for E-Commerce". *In proceedings of the 33rd Hawaii International Conference on System Sciences.*
11.   Edward Tsang and Tim Gosling (2002). "Simple Constrained Bargaining Game". *In proceedings of the Distributed Constrained Satisfaction Workshop-First International Joint Conference on Autonomous Agents and Multi-Agent Systems (AAMAS) Bologna Italy 2002*
12.   N. Bassiliades, G. Antoniou, I. Vlahavas (2004) "A Defeasible Logic Reasoner for the Semantic Web", *Workshop on Rules and Rule Markup Languages for the Semantic Web (RuleML 2004)*, G. Antoniou, H. Boley (Ed.), Springer-Verlag, Hiroshima, Japan, 8 Nov. 2004
13.   Chris van Aart, Ruurd Pels, Giovanni Caire, Federico Bergenti (2002). "Creating and Using Ontologies in Agent Communication". *Telecom Italia EXP magazine Vol 2, No 3 September 2002.*

14. D. Nute (1994). "Defeasible logic". *In Handbook of logic in artificial intelligence and logic programming (vol. 3): nonmonotonic reasoning and uncertain reasoning.* Oxford University Press

15. B. N. Grosof (1997). "Prioritized conflict handing for logic programs". *In Proc. of the 1997 International Symposium on Logic Programming*, 197-211

16. G. Antoniou, D. Billington, G. Governatori and M.J. Maher (2001). "Representation results for defeasible logic". *ACM Transactions on Computational Logic 2, 2 (2001): 255 - 287*

17. G. Antoniou, M. J. Maher and D. Billington (2000). "Defeasible Logic versus Logic Programming without Negation as Failure". *Journal of Logic Programming* 41,1

18. N.R.Jennings, S.Parsons, C.Sierra, P.Faratin (2000). "Automated Negotiation". *In proceedings of 5th Int. Conf. on the Practical Application of Intelligent Agents and Multi-Agent Systems (PAAM-2000)*

Author Index